THE POPULATION
DILEMMA

The American Assembly, *Columbia University*

THE POPULATION

DILEMMA

(Second Edition)

Prentice-Hall, Inc., *Englewood Cliffs, N.J.*

PRENTICE-HALL OF AUSTRALIA, PTY. LTD. (*Sydney*)
PRENTICE-HALL OF CANADA, LTD. (*Toronto*)
PRENTICE-HALL OF JAPAN, INC. (*Tokyo*)
PRENTICE-HALL OF INDIA PRIVATE LIMITED (*New Delhi*)
PRENTICE-HALL INTERNATIONAL, INC. (*London*)

Preface to the Second Edition

The first edition of this volume, which appeared in 1963, was designed by its editor, Philip M. Hauser, University of Chicago, as background reading for the Twenty-third American Assembly, which met at Arden House, Harriman, New York, to consider the implications for national and international policy of rapid population growth. The book was also used as advance reading for subsequent Assemblies held across the nation under the sponsorship of The World Affairs Council of Northern California, The George Washington University, Occidental College, the University of Nebraska, Tulane University, the University of Oregon, the University of Missouri, the Associated Colleges of the Midwest, the World Affairs Council of Boston, Rice University, Utah State University, the University of Minnesota, the Phelps-Stokes Fund, Chautauqua Institution, and Alma College.

In addition, two international meetings were held: The Pan-American Assembly at Cali, Colombia, 1965, with Universidad del Valle, and The Central American Assembly, 1968, with the University of Costa Rica in San José.

However, the volume found a much wider readership, in the general public, in colleges and universities, and government circles. Indeed, over a five-year period the circulation grew beyond anything predicted for it, and the book went through thirteen printings in English and into several foreign editions. In 1968 in order to keep current with the continuing demand, editor Hauser and The American Assembly decided to revise the chapters in the light of the latest knowledge and perspectives on population problems. Herewith then the second edition, under the supervision of Dr. Hauser and with most of the original authors.

The first edition of *The Population Dilemma* and the Assembly conference program were supported by grants from the Ford Foundation, The Population Council and the Laurel Foundation. The edition at hand was financed through the generosity of The Population Council. Neither the Council nor The American Assembly is responsible for the views herein, which are the authors' own.

Clifford C. Nelson
President
The American Assembly

Table of Contents

4   *Ansley J. Coale*
     Population and Economic Development   59

5   *Philip M. Hauser*
     The Population of the United States,
     Retrospect and Prospect   85

6   *Joseph L. Fisher and Neal Potter*
     Natural Resource Adequacy for the United
     States and the World   106

nomic Aspects of Rapid Population Growth,
178; *Relation Between the Control of Fertility
and Other Developmental Processes,* 179; *The
Trend Toward a Secular Consensus on the Central Issue of Population Policy,* 181; *Domestic
Population Policy,* 186; Concerning the Total
Population Trend, 186; Immigration, 190; *Demographic Aspects of Domestic Social Problems,*
191; Aspects of the Distribution of Our National
Population, 192; The Social Structure of Metropolitan Aggregations, 193; The Diverse Effects
of Rapid Mass Migration, 195; Differential Reproduction Within the Demographic Pool, 200.

Philip M. Hauser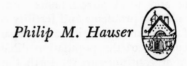

1

Introduction and Overview

Our ever-shrinking, more complex and interdependent world is increasingly confronted with global problems. Among those recognized and dealt with historically are epidemics and contagious diseases; narcotic and white slave traffic; postal, telegraphic and radio communication; weather forecasting; and international air transport. New global problems have emerged in the post-war world such as atomic fallout and the exploration and use of outer space. Another global problem of long making is becoming ever more acute and threatens to assume crisis proportions in the coming generation. It is the problem posed by accelerating population growth.

Certainly more attention is being devoted to population problems today, nationally and internationally, than at any time since Malthus. On the world scene a number of governments as a matter of policy are striving to dampen rates of population increase by means of fertility control. On the domestic scene in the United States there is also

PHILIP M. HAUSER *is professor of sociology and director of the Population Research Center at the University of Chicago. He has combined an academic career with various public assignments in the United States government and the international agencies, having served in such posts as acting director and deputy director of the United States Bureau of the Census, United States representative to the Population Commission of the United Nations, U.N. statistical advisor to Burma and Thailand, and general rapporteur of UN/ UNESCO Seminars on Urbanization in Asia and in Latin America. He is a past president of the Population Association of America, of the American Sociological Association, and of the American Statistical Association.*

ample evidence of the mounting interest in population growth and its consequences. There has been significant action taken by the federal, state and local governments and widespread public discussion of population problems and fertility control.

This volume was originally prepared as an aid to American Assembly discussions of the population dilemma. In this updated and revised form it continues to set forth the key population facts, the major problems being generated by accelerating growth, the basic policy issues, and the more important policy and action alternatives. The materials presented are designed to provide the reader with a sound basis for participating in the decisions on population matters that this democratic nation must make in the coming years.

The history of, and prospect for, world population growth, together with its key economic and political implications, are presented in chapter 2. Despite the deficiencies in historical data, the fact that a remarkable acceleration in the rate of world population growth has occurred, especially in the past three centuries, is indisputable. Also indisputable is the explanation of this demographic revolution—man's increasing mastery over nature in effecting remarkable declines in mortality. Even though the major gains in longevity for most of the modern era, and especially before World War II, were restricted to a relatively small proportion of the world's peoples—those enjoying "Western civilization"—the explosive increase of Western populations together with the slower increase of the rest of the world's population produced amazing acceleration in total world growth. Since the Second World War, the death rates in the non-western world have decreased sharply without the corresponding increases in productivity that occurred when western death rates declined over a longer period.

Given the new post-World War II situation, what is the prospect? In the long run the answer is quite clear. Given a finite globe, in the long run space is the limiting factor to population growth. In the long run any rate of population growth, let alone the present excessive rate of 2 per cent per annum, which doubles world population every 35 years, would produce saturation. In the long run man will have no reasonable alternative to achieving a zero rate of growth.

Greater interest, however, attaches to the prospects for the short run as, for example, to the end of this century. World population of 3.5 billion in 1968 could double by the century's end. The significance of such an increase can be grasped when this prospect is restated as follows: It took all of the time man has been on this planet to achieve the population of 3.5 billion reached in 1968; but a population equal to this number will be added in the mere 32 years between 1968 and 2000.

Population growth during the remainder of this century will vary greatly between the economically advanced nations and the developing nations. Between 1968 and 2000, the developing nations could considerably more than double, rising from 2.4 billion to 5.4 billion—an increment which would match total world population, 3 billion, in 1960. In contrast, the advanced nations are likely to increase at about half the rate of the developing nations, 60 per cent, and reach a level of some 1.6 billion in 2000 from the total of a little over 1 billion in 1968.

In the short run, the prospect is that population growth will obstruct the efforts of the developing nations to achieve higher levels of living. In consequence, the world is likely to experience increased social unrest, political instability, and threats to peace during the remainder of this century. Failure of the developing nations to obtain their economic aspirations has operated to intensify the cold war between the capitalist and communist blocs and intensify competition between the blocs for winning the allegiance of the uncommitted nations. The continuation, let alone the possible increase, in the gap between levels of living in the developed and developing nations together with the schism between Mainland China and the Soviet Union could lead to a new axis of world political cleavage—conflict between the "have" and "have-not" rather than between the capitalist and socialist blocs. Hence, before the end of the century, continued failure on the part of have-not nations substantially to increase their incomes-per-capita could lead to a North-South rather than the present East-West confrontation. In any case, the prospect for appreciable increases in levels of living in the developing nations and, therefore, for world order, for at least the remainder of this century, appears to be a dismal one.

In the short run the crucial effect of excessive population growth is to be found in the developing nations of the world—in Asia, Latin America, and Africa. In chapter 3, Dr. Irene B. Taeuber subjects these areas to more intensive analysis. Using the "medium" rather than the "high" projections of the United Nations employed in chapter 2, Dr. Taeuber points out that a half billion persons were added to the population of these nations in the single decade from 1960 to 1970. Moreover, she reports that even without "Mainland East Asia," mainly Mainland China, the less developed countries could total 3.6 billion by 2000. This would constitute a doubling of the population of these areas even with allowance for anticipated great, and as yet unrealized, reductions in the birth rate on which the "medium" estimates are based. Population growth in "Mainland East Asia," mainly Communist China, could add another billion to 1½ billion to the population of the developing countries by 2000.

Dr. Taeuber presents specific historical cases of "the demographic transition" including the United States and Japan as examples of what has happened, but concludes neither nation can be used as a guide to the future of the developing countries. She examines also the transitions underway in areas of the Western Pacific and indicates various respects in which they, also, cannot be taken as models of what is likely to happen in the other developing nations. She concludes, wisely, that the future is truly unpredictable, but that some hope lies in the fact that "that which is not predictable from past trends may occur." She notes that "the decade of the seventies is critical not alone for demographic transition to lower birth rates but for human survival."

Of special significance for assaying the future of the developing countries is Dr. Taeuber's consideration of their age-structures and their implications for the future labor force, marriage and family formation, education, and production and distribution. Finally, her description of the nature of traditional societies in relation to population and social and economic change and the specific questions she raises about future prospects set the stage well for the continuing consideration of chronic and acute problems of the less-developed countries.

The way in which population growth and its demographic accompaniments tend to obstruct efforts to raise levels of living is comprehensively treated by Dr. Ansley Coale. He clearly traces the impact of population factors on per capita income and on productive employment of the labor force. He shows how a decline in the birth rate operates to increase per capita income, in the short run, by dampening the rate of population increase and reducing the burden of child dependency without major effect on the size of the labor force; and, in the longer run, by reduction in the growth rate of the labor force and lower population density. Reduced birth rates could increase income per consumer by over 40 per cent in thirty years, by 86 per cent in fifty years and more than 100 per cent in sixty years. "After one hundred and fifty years the low fertility population," concludes Coale, "would have an income per consumer six times as high as the faster growing population with unchanged fertility."

Dr. Coale, in summary, concludes that "the underdeveloped areas in the world for the next fifty years or so have a choice at best between very rapid growth and moderately rapid growth in population." The result of the first of these choices is contained, in general, in the projections given in chapter 2 and of the second, in chapter 3. Dr. Coale's models indicate the great economic gains that could accrue to any developing country that succeeds in effecting an immediate reduction in fertility; and, also, demonstrates the great cost of awaiting fertility declines in the future—as urbanization, industrialization and modernization may, perhaps, bring them about. Moreover, he documents with alarming numbers "the overwhelming multiplication of density that continued rapid growth implies." Dr. Coale, in his chapter, has managed to present the most succinct and yet comprehensive consideration that has yet appeared of population changes in relation to economic growth.

The chapters by Dr. Taeuber and Dr. Coale, within the framework of the world picture set forth in chapter 2, clarify the crucial implications of contemporary rates of population increase for the underdeveloped areas and for the world as a whole. In doing this they also make it evident that the United States has a huge stake in both developments. For the citizenry of the United States there is no way to evade either the long-run implications of accelerating world population growth or the short-run consequences of events in the underdeveloped areas.

Many Americans erroneously believe that although population problems beset other nations they do not seriously afflict the United States. The materials in chapter 5 indicate that such a belief is ill-founded for it fails to come to grips with the many domestic population problems of the nation. Moreover, it also fails to give adequate consideration to the implications for this nation of world population problems.

The United States is perhaps the world's most dramatic example both of the population explosion and of the population implosion— urbanization and metropolitanization. Between 1790 and 1960, the population increased from less than 4 million to 180 million and urban population from 5 per cent of the total to 70 per cent. In 1968, the population of the United States exceeded 200 million, and it may well exceed 300 million by the end of the century. Moreover, the evidence indicates that urban and metropolitan concentration has continued.

The recent decline in the birth rate of the nation dating from 1957– 58 has led some persons to believe that the era of excessive national growth has come to a halt. Yet the data clearly show that we stand at the threshold of a second baby boom because the post-World War II babies are now reaching reproductive age. This second baby boom would have begun a year or two ago were it not for the reversal of the downward trend in age at marriage and age at first birth. There are three considerations that bolster the prediction that a new baby boom is soon to begin. First, there is taking place a 35 per cent increase, between 1967 and 1975, in the women who do most of the childbearing—those 20 to 29 years of age. Second, national surveys report that women in this age group expect to give birth to an average of 3.0 children, as did their predecessors. Third, there has been a pronounced increase in the number of marriages since 1959 and the marriage rate since 1963. Even with relatively low fertility at each age, the increase in women 20 to 29 is bound to reverse the downward trend in number of births and in the crude birth rate. All in all, it is quite reasonable to anticipate a population of some 300 million by 2000—an increase of about 100 million persons in 32 years!

The United States has already paid a high price, in human as well as monetary terms, for its explosive postwar growth and the anticipated growth will continue to exact a high price. The problems which have been generated or exacerbated by rapid growth include physical, personal, social, economic and governmental problems, examples of which are given in chapter 5.

Among the more significant implications of accelerating population growth is that concerning its effect on the relation between population and resources—or the "man-land" ratio. The salient facts about resources in the United States and in the world are summarized in chapter 6 by Dr. Joseph L. Fisher and Neal Potter. Their answer to the question "Are resources becoming scarcer?" should, on the one hand, quiet the cries of alarmists who foresee early mass starvation and the imminent exhaustion of critical materials. On the other hand, they give reason for further reflection to the optimists who are convinced that man's ingenuity can resolve all the problems which may be precipitated by the increasing pressure of population on land and other resources.

In their consideration of the future of food production and consumption in relation to population growth, they take into account the recent breakthroughs in wheat and rice production which may be introducing the developing nations to the "agricultural revolution." Yet, despite the gratifying increases in food production in Mexico, Venezuela, India, Pakistan, the Philippines and some other Asian nations, the problem of adequately meeting the developing nations' need for food remains far from resolved. There is a great gap between increased actual and potential production and increased levels of consumption for the populations of the poor nations. Problems of capital investment in agriculture, land tenure and distribution, as well as the resistance of traditional societies to change, still loom large. In respect to the food picture Fisher and Potter conclude that "the past thirty years have shown a moderate improvement but there is still a long way to go, and progress is largely lacking where is it needed the most."

Fisher and Potter provide the basic data for a realistic appraisal of the political significance of accelerating population growth. The world political problem posed is not one arising from any immediate threat of mass starvation or lowered living levels. It is, rather, that arising from the inability of the mass populations in the less-developed areas to achieve significant increases in their levels of living consistent with their aspirations as generated by the "revolution of rising expectations." It is the continued frustration and poverty of the mass populations of the underdeveloped nations, to which rapid population growth contributes, that portends continued political instability and unrest. In the bipolar world rent by the Cold War, explosive population growth may thus become a major factor in determining whether the mass populations of the underdeveloped nations, still neutral or uncommitted, swing to the free or communist way of life.

In chapter 7, Drs. Notestein, Kirk and Segal consider the problem of population control. They present the background of developments in both the economically advanced regions and the developing regions which have generated "the problem" and the "necessity of population control."

Attention is then devoted to the means of fertility control. Emphasis is placed on "the modern era of contraception" based on the availability of effective oral contraceptives and the intra-uterine contraceptive devices. Explanation is given of the mechanisms involved in modern contraception which, although written by a bio-medical expert (Dr. Segal), is intelligible to the perceptive layman. The prospects for further advances in modern contraception are presented in treating problems relating to the inhibition of ovulation, the tubal transport of ova, the corpus luteum function, the suppression of sperm production, the fertilizing capacity of spermatozoa and human seminal fluid.

The problem of population control is concluded with reflections on the "practical prospects" of fertility limitation. Note is taken of the more favorable attitudes toward birth control which have evolved in the United Nations and other international agencies, among the communist nations, among Catholic populations if not the Church, and in the governments and peoples of many of the developing nations.

Notestein, Kirk and Segal present a balanced, albeit an optimistic picture about the prospects for fertility control. They acknowledge that family planning programs are not likely to achieve a zero rate of population growth in the near future nor, in the main, during the remainder of this century. They stress the importance, however, of the possible declines from 3 to 2 per cent or from 2 to 1 per cent rates of growth—necessary steps in the direction of achieving a zero rate of growth.

The relatively optimistic outlook of Notestein, Kirk and Segal is not necessarily in conflict with the obviously more pessimistic outlook of Hauser in chapter 2. The former are focusing on the prospects of family planning programs initiating fertility declines—their immediate objective. The latter is considering the prospects for effecting reductions in population growth rates during the remainder of this century of sufficient magnitude to ameliorate the difficult economic and political problems which afflict the developing nations. Even if family planning programs achieve birth rate declines in the developing nations, a development yet to be documented for the more populous developing nations, continued declines in mortality for some time are not likely to permit declines in fertility to produce corresponding decreases in rates of population growth. In consequence, the economic and political outlook for the remainder of the century may remain dark even if appreciable declines in fertility are achieved. But successes in decreasing birth rates will certainly pave the way for future declines in population growth rates and greatly enhance future prospects for economic advances and a more favorable picture.

Dr. Frank Lorimer concludes this volume in his consideration of issues of population policy. Recognizing that "questions of policy relative to population trends are, in large part, regional and specific . . . ," Lorimer nevertheless appropriately holds that "the development of American policies . . . must . . . be framed in a world context." Objective analysis is beset with obstacles of cultural and personal preconceptions—including the Neo-Malthusian and Marxist postures and the positions of diverse religious groups. Nonetheless, it is necessary to face the issues and take the appropriate policy decisions.

Dr. Lorimer presents a summary of theological and religious oppositions to fertility control, and points up the ethical and social questions "that demand more serious consideration than they have usually received." Lorimer also considers the demographic aspects of social and economic development as a springboard for discussing policy issues.

He stresses that "control of population," on the one hand, and "advances in economic productivity, health and education" on the other, are not *"alternative* solutions" but "are essentially *complementary* and, in fact, mutually dependent."

Lorimer traces the "trend toward a secular consensus on the central issue of population policy" attributable to two basic forces: first, the actual acceleration in world population growth; and second, the rapid advances in the social and biological sciences and the dissemination of their findings. The result has been a quickening of the pace of national and international efforts to control fertility and diminishing opposition to such control in practice if not in dogma. This trend has, in a sense, been climaxed in the resolution on Population Growth and Economic Development unanimously adopted on December 17, 1966 by the General Assembly of the United Nations. The resolution recognized "the sovereignty of nations in formulating and promoting their own population policies, with due regard to the principle that the size of the family should be the free choice of each individual family." It also offered technical aid on population matters to nations which requested it.

In respect of domestic population issues Dr. Lorimer feels that "the most central issues in the immediate future are . . . not those concerning our national population as a whole but rather the social implications of its distribution, diverse reproductive trends, and internal migration." Immigration policy has been modified since the first edition of this volume in 1963 by legislation initiated by President Kennedy and passed by the Congress in 1965, which became effective on July 1, 1968. The new policy, advocated in the first edition of this volume, eliminates the racial and ethnic discrimination of the past and restricts total immigration. Although it has generated some new problems which may call for some further legal modifications, the present immigration policy of this nation is likely to remain fixed for some time. This implies that, in the period ahead, inequalities among nations in levels of living, reflecting imbalance between population and utilized resources, must be dealt with through capital transfers, terms of trade, and economic measures rather than free international migration.

Dr. Lorimer, after discussing the social domestic problems generated by internal migration of both whites and blacks, directs attention to the types of policies and measures that could help to resolve the problems. He discusses the need for "truly effective Federal programs for increasing employment opportunities, assuring higher incomes, improving conditions of living and equalizing the level and quality of education in the component areas of the nation and among the ethnic elements of its 'demographic pool'. . . ."

To deal with the problems raised by differential birth rates, with the highest fertility manifest among the poor and uneducated, Lorimer states the need for "more vigorous and well designed programs for the diffusion of information concerning methods of controlling contraception and the provision of contraceptive facilities and services to all people in all parts of the country."

Differential mortality remains an indicator of inequality in economic and social conditions and points to the need for what may be termed social and economic, as distinguished from bio-medical, epidemiology. Racial and regional differences in mortality, especially the racial, persist in the United States and call for aggressive social policy and action for their elimination.

Finally, Dr. Lorimer raises a question about legalization of abortion and calls attention to the resolution of the American Public Health Association which in January, 1968, gave endorsement to the movement underway to repeal restrictive laws "so that pregnant women may have abortions performed by qualified practitioners of medicine and osteopathy." In closing his chapter, Dr. Lorimer indicates that "we have raised more questions than we have answered. This is our intent. Let the discussion proceed." With this closing remark he may well have spoken for all the authors who have contributed to this volume.

We are forced to live with and in some manner to deal with the population problems that we have inherited from the past. For example, under the pressures generated by our postwar resurgence in population growth, we have expanded our school plant. But despite our efforts, we have experienced depreciation in the quality of our education. As our postwar babies reached labor force age during the sixties, we paid a high price in striving to provide jobs or support of some kind for the tidal wave of new workers. We seem to deal with the consequences of accelerated population growth only as they become acute problems that cannot be evaded. It is easier to ignore the tasks that aim at preventing the population problems of the future. In consequence, we are expending huge resources for treating the deleterious consequences of past rapid population growth while, in the main, we continue to do little or nothing about the excessive growth which will produce even more acute problems in the future. For example, as a nation we are just beginning to implement the recently adopted policy of assisting the underprivileged who desire such assistance to control their fertility—both within the United States itself and abroad.

In this situation lies the dilemma which gives this volume its title— the choice of unsatisfactory alternatives. It is to be found in the necessity to choose between continued indifference to the implications for the future of present population growth and the acceptance of the consequences of such indifference. To formulate appropriate population policy and take necessary action requires changes in established attitudes and behavior which meet with resistance—more from some quarters than from others. But to take the easy way out at the present time is to compound the difficulties of the future. To avoid the ounce of prevention in the present will, in the future, require many pounds of cure.

It is undoubtedly a fact that the vast majority of the people of the world, including a large proportion of the people in the United States, do not yet recognize this dilemma. It is the major purpose of this volume to call attention to it, to clarify the issues involved, and to press the point that to continue to ignore the population problem is, in effect, to choose one of the horns of the dilemma—the more costly and dangerous one.

Philip M. Hauser

2*

World Population Growth

Human inhabitants of this planet exceeded 3.5 billion at the close of the year 1968. Three centuries ago world population approximated .5 billion, a century ago 1.3 billion, and a half century ago 1.8 billion. By the end of this century the population on this earth could easily reach 7.0 billion. In a half century from now (2018) it could almost triple to approximate 10 billion; and in a century from now (2068) world population could exceed 20 billion. These numbers explain the increasing awareness on the part of the world's peoples, nations and international organizations of the "population explosion."

The population explosion and its concomitants have transformed man's attitudes, values, institutions and, in general, his way of life. Moreover, they have generated unprecedented problems, chronic and acute; local, national and international; personal, social, economic and political. Most of the problems that afflict the contemporary world may be better understood when viewed in relation to the tremendous acceleration in the rate of population growth and in its accompanying concentration of people into huge urban and metropolitan clumpings.

Retrospect—World Population

The first complete census of mankind has yet to be taken but, despite this, it is possible to reconstruct the history of world population growth. Man, or a close relative, has inhabited this planet for from

* In this chapter previous writings of the author have been drawn upon, especially materials prepared for the Foreign Policy Association of America.

2 to 2½ million years. By the Neolithic Period, some 10,000 years ago, world population reached a level of about ten million persons. By the beginning of the Christian era the earth's inhabitants had reached a total of, perhaps, 250 to 300 million. At the beginning of the modern era, at about mid-seventeenth century, world population numbered some 500 millions. It therefore took all the millennia before 1650 that man has been on this globe to reach a total of half a billion persons. But to add a second half billion took only two centuries (before 1850); a third half billion less than half a century (before 1900); a fourth half billion little more than a quarter of a century (shortly after 1925); a fifth half billion less than a quarter of a century (by 1950). The sixth half billion added to world population required only ten years (by 1960), and the seventh addition of half a billion took only eight years (by 1968).

These numbers demonstrate dramatically why the accelerated rate of population growth has been called the "population explosion." Further justification for the use of such language is found in an examination of the growth rates involved. From a growth rate of perhaps 2 per cent per millennium during the Paleolithic Period, the old Stone Age spanning some 600,000 years, the rate accelerated to about 2 per cent per annum at the present time—a thousandfold increase. Although 2 per cent per annum is with present interest rates a ridiculously low return on investment, it can readily be demonstrated that it is a fantastically high rate of population growth. At 2 per cent per annum a dozen persons could have produced a population of 3 billion, world population in 1960, in 976 years; yet, it is known that man abounded in prolific numbers some 25,000 years ago. Similarly, a dozen people increasing at this rate since the beginning of the Christian era could have had over 300 million living descendants for every person now alive.

Causes of the Population Explosion

The remarkable acceleration in the rate of world population growth is explained by "the theory of the demographic transition." Although continued research has resulted in various refinements and qualifications of this theory, its basic tenet remains unshaken, namely, that explosive growth has resulted from the increased gap between fertility and mortality, mainly by reason of reductions in mortality. Man, the only culture-building animal on the globe, has in the development of his cultures achieved increasing control over mortality well before achieving comparable control over fertility.

Five major factors have contributed to mortality declines: first, increased productivity has increased levels of living; second, the emergence of stable government over increasingly greater territory has tended to eliminate internecine warfare and make possible better distribution of goods and services from areas of surplus to areas of deficit; third, environmental sanitation has drastically reduced the incidence of major causes of death attributable to polluted food and water; fourth, improved personal hygiene has greatly reduced the ravages of many diseases; and fifth, the development of modern medicine and public health programs has directly contributed both to disease prevention and control. In addition, nature herself has contributed to the reduction of some mortality through the disappearance of some agents of morbidity and mortality of which scarlet fever is a good example. The agents of this disease, one of the earlier scourges of childhood, failed to survive in nature's ever ongoing competitive struggle for existence.

The exact contribution of each of these factors to mortality reduction is not known. But, in general, it is probably not too far off to hold that increased levels of living and stable government lowered mortality in Western experience by perhaps a third; that the combination of environmental sanitation and personal hygiene contributed an equal reduction in deaths; and that modern medicine has been responsible for the remaining one-third decrease in mortality. The contribution of medicine, in fact, has come largely during this century. As recently as 1900, a patient in a hospital had about as much chance of dying from a disease he contracted in the hospital as from the disease which brought him there.

In Europe at the beginning of the modern era—the mid-seventeenth century—the death rate approximated 40, that is 40 deaths per 1000 persons per year. At the present time death rates in Western nations are generally below ten. Thus, if the rough approximations of reductions in mortality by factor are assumed correct, each of the combinations of developments set forth above reduced the death rate by about ten points. The net effect of mortality reduction is dramatically demonstrable in the increased survivorship of infants born. Among males in the Netherlands, for example, in 1840 one-fourth of all infants born were dead by 2.5 years after birth, one-half by 37.5 years, and three-fourths by 62.5 years. In contrast, a century later in 1940 one-fourth of male infants born were not dead until 62.5 years after the year of birth, one-half not until 72.5 years, and three-fourths not until 82.5 years.

Most of the reduction in mortality in the Western world has been effected since mid-nineteenth century. In fact, reductions in death rates during the past century have probably been greater than in the preceding 2000 years. In the Western world no comparable gains can be anticipated in the years which lie ahead unless dramatic new developments in medicine, including organ transplants and the like, should make it possible greatly to decrease death rates at the older ages—over 60. For up to this time the great gains in mortality reduction have been achieved among infants, children and, in general, the younger ages.

In the United States, for example, expectation of life at birth has increased about 20 years from 1900 to 1968, about 10 years at age 10, and almost 8 years at age 20. But expectation of life over the same period has increased only some 3 years at age 45, and a little over 1 year at age 65. Thus, even if there were no deaths under age 55, life expectation at birth, with death rates in 1959–61 at the older ages, would be increased by only 6.5 years (from 69.9 years to 76.4 years). Similarly, even if deaths at 55 years and over in the United States were decreased by 50 per cent, expectation of life at birth would go up by only 5.7 years (to 75.6).

While mortality was declining in the Western world, and spectacularly since mid-nineteenth century, fertility, on the whole, remained at relatively high levels until about the last quarter of the nineteenth century. In France, the United States and Ireland, fertility decreased before then, probably beginning in the later part of the eighteenth century in France, early in the nineteenth century in the United States and the mid-nineteenth century in Ireland. Birth rates did not decrease appreciably in the remainder of Northern and Western Europe until the last quarter of the nineteenth century; and the pattern of decline did not spread to Southern and Eastern Europe until after the turn of the century. Once the fertility decline began in a country it continued without interruption and the rate of decline increased the later it began. Despite the decreases in the birth rate, however, large population increases continued because death rates continued to decline rapidly. The population explosion was therefore the result primarily of the increasing gap between fertility and mortality, the increase in natural increase. The "demographic transition" was effected by a decline in mortality followed, with considerable lag, by the decline in fertility.

The population explosion first occurred in Western civilization. Prior to World War II death control was mainly restricted to the economically advanced nations, the peoples of European stock. Of the non-European stocks only Japan had managed greatly to decrease death rates. The two-thirds of the world's peoples in Asia, Latin America and Africa were, in the main, not partly to the great decreases in mortality, although by reason of contact with the economically advanced nations some gains had been achieved. On the whole, however, the populations of Asia, Latin America and Africa had death rates prior to World War II at levels about that experienced in Europe during the Middle Ages. Since World War II, however, this situation has dramatically changed. The death rate in the developing areas has declined much more rapidly since World War II than it ever did among the Western nations. A combination of factors including the advent of the United Nations and the Specialized Agencies with programs emphasizing economic development and the dissemination of modern public health techniques and modern medicine have opened up to the mass of the world's peoples the achievement of the twentieth century death rates. The reason for a more rapid decline of mortality occurred in the developing nations than in the economically advanced nations is easily explained. The same ship that anchors in the harbor of Colombo, Ceylon, can carry in her hold virtually all of the means by which mortality declines were effected in the Western World during the three centuries of the modern era. The ship can carry, in one delivery, fertilizer and tractors for increased productivity; chlorine, insecticides, and tooth brushes for improved environmental sanitation and personal hygiene; and the methods of modern medicine including chemotherapy.

The more rapid decline of mortality in the developing nations has generated population growth rates well above those experienced by the Western nations. During the population explosion in the West rarely did nations increase, by reason of natural increase (the excess of births over deaths, excluding migration) at rates above 1 to $1\frac{1}{2}$ per cent. But the developing nations are now increasing at rates reaching 3 to $3\frac{1}{2}$ per cent, rates which double population every 18 to 23 years. The contrast in the growth rates of the economically advanced and the developing nations is great enough to refer to the demographic transition among the former as the "first population explosion" and to the latter as the "second population explosion." The special problems of the developing areas are treated separately in chapter 3, by Dr. Irene B. Taeuber.

Among the non-Western nations of appreciable size, only in Japan has the birth rate declined. The developing nations in Asia, Latin America, and Africa, with their twentieth century death rates and medieval birth rates, are not only perpetuating but they are actually accelerating the world population explosion.

By reason of the above developments, in the first three centuries of the modern era while world population quintupled, the continental regions showed great variation in growth rates. During these three centuries, the population of Africa only doubled, that of Asia increased about four to five-fold, and the population of Europe increased six-fold. The population of Latin America and of North America increased much more rapidly by reason of immigration, the former 23–fold and the latter 166–fold. The areas of European settlement in the Western Hemisphere and in Oceania increased 8– to 9–fold, so that the population of Europe and European settlement combined increased 7–fold.

Examples of Growth

By reason largely of the decline in mortality the population of the nations in the vanguard of industrialization and modernization increased tremendously. For example, the United Kingdom, the first area to become industrialized and modernized, with a population of about 16 million in 1800, had, despite emigration, more than doubled by 1880, when it exceeded 35 million. By 1961, despite declining fertility and continued emigration, it had reached a level of almost 53 million. Growth in the United States was even more spectacular because of heavy immigration in addition to high natural increase. Thus, the United States with a population of less than 4 million in 1790 had increased to over 50 million by 1880, and to 180 million by 1960. Between 1790 and 1960, in 170 years, the population of the United States increased about 45–fold.

Similarly, most Western nations, and Japan, the only non-Western nation which experienced the population explosion prior to the twentieth century, showed great population growth during the nineteenth century. France with a population of some 27 million in 1800 had reached almost 40 million by 1910, at the eve of World War I. Germany with less than 25 million in 1800 had reached 65 million by 1910; Russia with 37 million had reached 140 million; Italy with 18 million had reached 35 million. Japan with perhaps 25 million in 1800 and 37 million in 1880, had, after her contact with the West, increased to almost 50 million by 1910, and almost 73 million by 1940 before World War II.

Although explosive population increase did not occur among the mass populations of the world in the developing regions until the twentieth century and, especially, after World War II, even modest growth rates under the initial impact of declining death rates by reason of diffusion from the West, produced enormous populations. Thus, China with a population of perhaps 400 million (uncertain estimate) by mid-nineteenth century and approximately the same population in 1900 (uncertain estimate) had achieved a mainland total of perhaps 583 million by 1953 and an estimated population of 650 million by 1960. India with a population of 236 million in 1891 increased by only 12 million in the 30 years to 1921; but, as her mortality declined, increased by 180 million in the 30 years between 1921 and 1951 to reach a total of 356 million. India had a population of 438 million by 1961, increasing by 82 million in the single decade between 1951 and 1961. Similarly Pakistan had reached 94 million by 1961, and Indonesia 93 million by the same date.

In and around 1968, seven nations had among them over two billion persons, or about three-fifths of the total population of the world. These nations were China with perhaps 728 million, India with 523 million, the U.S.S.R. with 239 million, the United Sttaes with 201 million, Pakistan with 126 million, Indonesia with 113 million, and Japan with 101 million.

Projections of World Population to 2000

Just as it has been demonstrated above that the present rate of world population growth could not possibly have been sustained for long periods in the past, it is possible to show that it cannot possibly persist for very long into the future. For example, the 2 per cent per annum increase of world population would produce a person for every square foot of land surface on the planet in about 6½ centuries; and a population whose weight would match that of the earth in about 15½ centuries. These are arithmetic ways of saying that in the long run space is the limiting factor in world population increase. In the long run any rate of growth would exhaust the space available on this globe. In the long run, therefore, mankind has no alternative to achieving a zero rate of growth.

It is the shorter run, however, that is of greater interest and concern. The United Nations, which since its inception has seriously considered world population problems, has periodically released projections of future world population by various geographic areas. Its most recent projections to the year 2000 were published in 1966. They show that if present fertility patterns were to hold along with mortality trends, the population of the world by the century's end would be some 7.5 billion. In addition to this calculation the United Nations has also prepared three "variant" projections—"high," "medium," and "low"—based on differing assumptions with respect to the decline of fertility. The low projection gives a world population of 5.4 billion; the medium, 6.1 billion; and the high, 7 billion.

Each of the variant projections of the United Nations, other than the 7.5 billion projection based on the assumption of present fertility levels assumes decreased birth rates in the developing areas. But, it must be emphasized that up to this time there is no firm evidence, despite specific efforts, that such reductions in the birth rate have yet occurred among the mass illiterate and impoverished populations of Asia, Latin America, and Africa. In consequence, the projection based on the continuation of present fertility cannot be dismissed as outside the range of possibility. Any of the other variant projections have built into them assumptions of fertility decline that at the present may include elements of wishful thinking and optimism. For purposes of this discussion the United Nations "high" variant projection will be employed, therefore, even though the United Nations accepts its "medium" variant as the most probable. It should be stressed, however, that the discussion which follows and the conclusions reached would not vary significantly if the "medium" projection were used.

On the basis of the "high" projection, the population of the world as a whole would increase from about 3.5 billion in 1968 to 7.0 billion by the year 2000. Hence, the world population would double during the remainder of this century. Of special economic and political import is the differential in the rate of the "developed" and the "developing" areas, respectively. The United Nations "high" projections indicate that the less-developed areas would have an aggregate population of about 5.4 billion persons by 2000, whereas the more developed areas would total about 1.6 billion (see Table 1).

According to these projections, then, the less-developed areas with a population of 2.4 billion in 1968 would increase by some 3.0 billion persons by the end of the century, or by over 120 per cent. In contrast, the more-developed areas would increase by only 598 million persons, or by about 60 per cent. The population increase in the less-developed areas would be five times as great as that in the more developed areas.

Table 1. World Population by Major Areas 1960 to 2000 According to the "High"
Variant Projection of the United Nations (Population in millions)

Area	1960	1968	1980	1990	2000
World Total	2,998	3,479	4,551	5,690	6,994
More Developed Areas[a]	976	1,069	1,245	1,402	1,574
Less Developed Areas[b]	2,022	2,409	3,306	4,288	5,420

a—Includes Europe, the U.S.S.R., Northern America, Japan, Temperate South America, Australia and New Zealand.

b—Includes East Asia less Japan, South Asia, Africa, Latin America less Temperate South America and Oceania less Australia and New Zealand.

Source: United Nations, *World Population Prospects as Assessed in 1963* (United Nations, New York, 1966), p. 135; 1968 figures are from *People* (Population Reference Bureau, Columbia Books, Washington, D.C., 1968), pp. 6off.

Moreover, the less developed areas, according to this projection—a quite plausible one—would increase in the last four decades of this century by a number of persons as great as the population of the entire globe in 1960.

In 1968, about two-thirds of the world population lived in the less-developed areas and only one-third in the more-developed areas. By 2000, it is possible that the population in the less developed areas will have increased to 77 per cent of the world's total, and that the population in the present more developed areas will have shrunk to 23 per cent.

Projections to 2000 of Large Nations

Population projections to the year 2000 for the seven nations that were the largest in 1960 also are available or can be derived from the United Nations estimates. These, also based on the "high" variant, indicate that Mainland China, by 2000, could have 1.4 billion persons; India 1.1 billion; the Soviet Union 403 million; the United States some 338 million; Indonesia about 300 million (estimate by writer based on United Nations data); Japan 139 million; and Pakistan 342 million. Thus, with the exception of Japan, by 2000 each of these nations would have grown enough to at least retain its present ranking. Japan would drop below Pakistan to become the seventh rather than the sixth most populous nation. These projections of the seven largest countries indicate that, although they would constitute a somewhat smaller proportion of the world population in 2000 than they did in 1960, their aggregate population by the end of the century at over 3.8 billion would exceed total world population in 1968.

Projections of World Population by 2018 and 2068

Using the United Nations "high" projections as a starting point the writer has made population projections for the world and for the developed and developing areas to the years 2018 and 2068, a half century and a century beyond the present. The purpose of these projections is not to indicate what the future population of the world will be, for it is not possible, with present knowledge, to make such a prediction. The purpose of these projections is rather to indicate what future population could be with present trends and the assumptions on which the calculations are based. The figures show the possible course of events if the trends and assumptions hold and, thus, serve more to provide a basis for understanding the implications of the trends and assumptions rather than to predict the future. What the future will actually be will, of course, depend on many unpredictable factors, including unforeseeable positive and negative developments such as space travel, on the one hand, or, on the other, catastrophic thermo-nuclear war.

The projections to the year 2018 depend, then, on the following three major assumptions:

First, that the United Nations "high" projection of 7 billion by 2000 is a reasonable starting point.

Second, that the world growth rate will decline between 2000 and 2018 by the amount projected by the United Nations for its "medium" estimates for the period 1965 to 2000. This provides the "medium" projection.

Third, that a "low" and a "high" projection for 2018 would be given by starting with the "medium" United Nations estimate for 2000 (6.1 billion) and, alternatively, starting with the United Nations figure based on the continuation of present fertility levels to 2000 (7.5 billion).

Similarly, the projections for the year 2068 are based on the assumptions that during the half century following 2018 the world growth rate implicit in the U.N. "low" variant projections to 2000 would operate. No low or high projections were made for 2068.

The assumptions described may be defended as reasonable in the light of present knowledge. That is, it does not appear to be unreasonable to hold that at least two human generations will be necessary to achieve appreciable progress in the reduction of the birth rate among the mass peasant populations of Asia, Latin America and Africa; and that the deceleration in birth rates in the half century following 2018 would continue at the rate indicated. These assumptions will undoubtedly be regarded as "pessimistic" by some but it is to be remembered that India which has had a national policy of population limitation since 1951–52 has yet to achieve a measurable decrease in her birth rate. The projections are shown in Table 2 for the world and for the more developed and developing areas.

The world by 2018 could have a population ranging from 8.5 to 10.4 billion with 9.7 billion as a medium estimate. Hence, world population could in the half century from 1968 to 2018 increase by from 5.0 to 6.9 billion with a medium increase of 6.2 billion. Under the assumptions used world population could about triple in the next half century. Even under the low projection the world's peoples could much more than double in roughly the next two generations.

By the year 2068, over the course of a century, under the assumptions employed, the world could have a population of 20.4 billion, a figure almost six times the present world total.

Needless to say, the developing areas, under the impact of the second population explosion, would increase much more rapidly than the developed nations. By 2018 the developing areas could have a medium population of 7.7 billion, an increase of over 5 billion or more than a tripling. In contrast, by 2018 the economically advanced nations would have a population of less than 2 billion, representing an increase of less than 1 billion, or about a doubling. The population increase in the developing nations could, then, be five times that in the developed nations over the course of the next half century. By 2018 the developing nations could contain almost four-fifths of the world's peoples (79.6 per cent) as compared with less than seven-tenths in 1968 (69.6 per cent).

By 2068 the developing areas could have a population of 16.9 billion representing an increase of 14.5 billion over 1968, or a sextupling during the coming century. In the half century from 2018 to 2068 the developing areas could increase by 9.2 billion, or conceivably more than a doubling over that half century despite the assumption of more rapidly declining fertility. Again, in contrast, the economically advanced areas by 2068 could have a population of 3.6 billion, increasing by only 2.6 billion during the century from 1968, even though more than tripling. In the half century between 2018 and 2068 the developed nations could increase by only 1.6 billion. Over the course of the next century, then, on the basis of the assumptions indicated, the increase in the population of the developing areas in Asia, Latin America and Africa could be more than four and one-half times the increment in the economically developed nations.

The effect of the continuing population explosion can be summarized by comparing anticipated growth with past growth since 1900. Between 1900 and 1950, world population increased by less than one billion persons. Between 1950 and 2000, the United Nations "high" projection indicates an increase of 4.5 billion persons. That is, the absolute increase in the population of the world during the second half of this century may be four- and one-half times as great as that during the first half of the century. During the second half of this century, there could be a greater increase in world population than was achieved in all the millennia of human existence up to the present time. Between 2000 and 2018, according to the writer's calculations, world population could increase by 2.7 billion, and between 2018 and 2068 by an additional 10.7 billion. Thus, during the first half of the twentieth century the world's peoples increased by an average of 20 million per year. During the second half of this century, according to the United Nations projections, it could increase by an average of 90 million per year. According to the writer's estimates world population could increase by an average of about 150 million persons per year during the first 18 years of the twenty-first century and by over 200 million persons per year during the half century from 2018 to 2068. Thus, a population the size of that of the United States at the present time could begin being added annually to the world's population after the year 2018 and for at least fifty years thereafter.

Economic and Political Implications

The role of population in determining the world's economic and political destinies during the remainder of this century may be grasped by considering simultaneously the following nine propositions:

1. We live in a world of "have" and "have-not" nations.
2. The international differences in levels of living, by reason of the "revolution of rising expectations," have become "felt" differences.
3. The have-not nations are striving to achieve higher living levels and they have made this goal, apart from independence if they have not yet achieved it, their major national aspiration.

4. There is an inverse correlation between levels of living and present or projected rates of population growth.
5. Rapid population growth is obstructing efforts to raise levels of living in the developing regions of the world.
6. Despite national and international efforts to raise levels of living, disparities between have and have-not nations are increasing rather than decreasing.
7. The accelerating rate of urbanization in the developing areas is exacerbating social unrest, political instability, and threats to world peace.
8. The bipolar world political alignment—the confrontation between "capitalist" and "communist" nations or the "East-West" cold war— is augmenting the tensions arising from frustrations in efforts to raise levels of living in the developing regions.
9. The bipolar political world is being fragmented by have and have-not differentiation within the communist bloc. Possible world political realignment is under way on a have, have-not basis rather than on a capitalist-communist basis. This would produce a "North-South" rather than "East-West" confrontation.

Let us proceed to an elaboration of each of these propositions and a consideration of their interrelationships.

HAVE AND HAVE-NOT NATIONS

In 1968 per capita income by continents ranged from $123 per year in Africa to $2,793 per year in Northern America (America north of the Rio Grande). Asia with 56 per cent of the world's population had but 14 per cent of the world's income. In contrast, Northern America together with Northern and Western Europe and Central Europe excluding the Sino-Soviet countries, with only 14 per cent of the world's population, had 56 per cent of the world's income.

Per capita income in 1968 averaged $493 for the world as a whole. The continental sub-regions with per capita income above the world average, one measure of "more developed" areas, had an average per capita income of $1,422. In contrast, the continental regions with per capita income below the world average, the "less developed" areas, had a per capita income per year of but $144.

Questions can be raised about the precision of the estimates of per capita income. Nonetheless it is clear that, by and large, there are great disparities among the nations in levels of living.

THE REVOLUTION OF RISING EXPECTATIONS

Throughout human history there have been important differences in levels of living both among and within nations. This fact, however, has gained a new significance in recent times and particularly since the end of World War II. The world has been swept by the "revolution of rising expectations." No longer are there any peoples on the face of the earth who are willing to settle for second place and who are not insisting upon independence if they have not already achieved it.

In consequence, differences between have and have-not nations have in our own time become "felt" differences, a term used some time ago by Warren S. Thompson in his discussion of population problems and world tensions.

ECONOMIC DEVELOPMENT PROGRAMS

The have-not nations of the world are striving to achieve higher living levels. They have made economic development a major national aspiration. The economic development of the underdeveloped areas has indeed become an international goal as set forth in the charter of the United Nations and as manifest in the foreign aid programs of many of the economically advanced nations, both governmental and private. It is probably correct to say that never before the present time was the achievement of higher living levels as universal a goal among all of mankind.

INVERSE RELATION BETWEEN POPULATION GROWTH AND LEVELS OF LIVING

There is an inverse correlation between present and projected rates of population growth and the level of living. For example, in all of the 11 continental sub-regions which had growth rates above the average for the world as projected from 1968 to 2000, per capita income was below the average of the world. Contrariwise, in every one of the continental regions in which per capita income was above the world average the annual population growth rate projected between 1968 and 2000 was below that of the world average.

In general, for the world as a whole, poverty is associated with relatively high rates of population increase. Among poor European nations, however, despite their poverty, relatively low population growth rates obtain. But poverty in Europe is a relative matter. It is significant that per capita product in the poor countries of Europe is about 4 to 5 times that of poor countries in Asia, and almost twice that of the poor countries in South and Middle America.

RAPID POPULATION GROWTH OBSTRUCTS ECONOMIC DEVELOPMENT

Study of the relationship between population growth and composition and economic development in recent years has disclosed that population factors operate to obstruct efforts to achieve higher levels of living. Per capita income cannot be increased unless aggregate output rises more rapidly than does population. Rapid population growth obstructs increases in per capita income in a number of ways as indicated in chapter 4 by Professor Ansley Coale.

GAP BETWEEN "HAVE" AND "HAVE-NOT" NATIONS IS INCREASING

Despite multilateral and bilateral efforts to assist the developing nations to achieve higher levels of living, such evidence as is available indicates that the disparities between have and have-not nations are increasing rather than decreasing. Have-not nations, relative to have nations, are doubly handicapped in efforts to reduce the disparity in levels of living. First, by reason of their small productive and technological base, even relatively large percentage rates of growth produce rather small absolute increments in levels of living. In contrast the increments attained by the advanced nations are relatively large, even with low rates of economic growth. For example, a ten per cent increase in 1968 income in Asia produces an absolute annual increment of about $13 per capita; in Northern America a ten per cent increase produces an increment of $279 per capita. Second, the rapid rate of population growth in the developing areas requires more rapid rates of economic growth than in the developed areas merely to maintain already existing levels of living. Northern America, for example, during the remainder of this century can maintain its present level of living by an economic growth of 1.1 per cent per annum. Asia, in contrast, to maintain even her present level of living must achieve an economic growth rate of 2.2 per cent per annum.

THE IMPACT OF URBANIZATION

The rate of world urbanization has been accelerating since 1800— or for the entire period over which it has been possible to measure world urbanization. In the nineteenth century the major impetus to world urbanization was given by the urbanization in Europe and North America. During the twentieth century, however, the major impetus to world urbanization was given by rapid urbanization in the developing regions of Asia, Latin America and Africa.

Rapid urbanization in the developing areas has a special significance in any effort to evaluate factors associated with mounting world tensions. For poverty and frustration concentrated in the urban setting have a potential for generating social unrest, political instability and threats to world peace of a much greater magnitude than poverty and frustration dispersed widely over the countryside.

BIPOLAR POLITICAL WORLD

Since the end of World War II the world has been increasingly divided into a capitalist bloc, a communist bloc, and a third neutral or uncommitted bloc. Interestingly enough approximately one-third of the world's population is to be found in each of these blocs. Never before have such gigantic antagonists as those represented by the capitalist and communist, or "Western" and "Eastern" blocs been manifest. They confront one another on ideological, economic, social, political, and, from time to time, military fronts. The East and West, respectively, have each been trying to win the allegiance of the neutral or uncommitted blocs of nations. This is manifest in the prolonged struggle for the minds and allegiance of the peoples of South and Southeast Asia. More recently, it has given rise to increasingly intense competition in Africa; and it continues to constitute a threat to Latin America's identification with the West, especially since the advent of Castro's Cuba. The weapons employed in this confrontation are varied including propaganda, economic aid, subversion, and military confrontation.

The outcome of the cold war, in large measure, may depend on the ability of the developing nations to control their rates of population growth and, thereby, to effect higher levels of living as measured by per capita income. It is almost certain that failure to advance their levels of living would leave the have-not nations of the world more open to the blandishments of the communist world. The communist bloc is in the advantageous position of appealing to anti-imperialist sentiment as it blames Western imperialism for the present poverty of the underdeveloped nations; and of being able thus far, more successfully to exploit the inequities and iniquities characterizing economic and social organization in many of the less-developed nations. Moreover, the communist appeal is apparently more alluring and appealing to many peoples than appeals yet developed by the West. The communist appeal in terms of agrarian reform, racial equality, and fuller stomachs seems on the whole to be more effective than the more abstract Western appeal for freedom and democracy.

To the extent, then, that population is a major factor in obstructing economic development, it is a factor which, in the contemporary world, is contributing to mounting social unrest, political instability

and threats to world peace which are being exacerbated by the Cold
War.

NORTH-SOUTH ALIGNMENT

Over recent years, a schism has become manifest within the communist bloc producing increased tensions. The split between the
U.S.S.R. and China may well have occurred not only from publicized
ideological differences but, also, from their disparity in economic development—from the relative "have" and "have-not" positions of the
U.S.S.R. and China, respectively.

The annual per capita income in 1968 for all the Sino-Soviet countries combined was $327. China had a per capita income estimated at
$80 per annum, whereas that in the U.S.S.R. was $928. The present
reluctance of the U.S.S.R. to use war as an instrument of policy for the
expansion of world communism, in contrast with the willingness of
China to do so, may well be attributed to some part of the "have"
position which Russia has achieved in contrast with China's relatively
desperate "have-not" situation. China with a population of perhaps
over seven hundred millions and a growth rate approximating perhaps
1.5 per cent per year may be growing increasingly conscious of the
disparities in the man-land ratios in China and in Russian Siberia.
In China, inability to control population growth, even though there
is much evidence that she is attempting such control, could well constitute a severe threat not only to her neighbors to the south, but also
to her communist neighbors to the north.

This split within the communist bloc may conceivably contribute
to increased tensions between the have and have-not nations throughout the world. It is not impossible that the U.S.S.R. will find she has
more in common with the have than with the have-not nations, especially if she is successful in her efforts to advance consumption levels.
This possibility may be enhanced and accelerated by her fear of China's
growing stock of atomic weapons.

Thus, it may be that in the coming decades world tensions may re-
volve around a "North-South" rather than "East-West" axis. The chief
threat to peace may be in the level of living disparities between have
and have-not nations rather than in differences between capitalist and
communist ideologies and systems.

It is demonstrated in chapter 4 that reduction of the birth rate in
the developing regions would contribute greatly towards increases in
levels of living. As Dr. Coale shows, lowered fertility would simultaneously dampen rates of population increase, produce an age struc-

ture more favorable for economic development, decelerate the trend towards disastrously high densities and, in a number of specific ways, operate to increase income per capita.

The standard of living cannot be raised unless aggregate output increases more rapidly than total population. This relationship is shown in the following oversimplified equation: $L = \dfrac{O}{P}$ where "L" equals levels of living, "O" equals aggregate output and "P" equals population. It is clear from this equation that an increase in aggregate output does not result in any increase in level of living if, simultaneously, there is a corresponding increase in total population. The greater the rate of population increase, then, the higher must be the rate of economic growth to effect any increase in per capita income.

Given their projected rates of population growth, the less-developed regions must achieve unprecedented increases in national income over a long period of time to match, by 2000, the levels of living in Northern and Western Europe as they were in 1968. That is, Asia and Africa must achieve a sustained annual economic growth rate of over 11 per cent (geometric), and Latin America over 7 per cent. Similarly, given their projected population increases Asia and Africa, to match the 1968 Northern American level of living by the year 2000, must achieve an economic growth rate in excess of 13 per cent per annum for the remainder of the century; and Latin America an economic growth rate in excess of 10 per cent per annum.

The magnitude of this task is evident, when it is realized that the United States throughout this century has averaged about a 3 per cent per annum rate of growth in gross national product (GNP). The growth rates in GNP required for the less-developed regions to match, by 2000, either the Northern American or European 1968 per capita income are well above the economic growth rates for so prolonged a period of time ever achieved by any economically advanced nation. In consequence, the conclusion follows that unless the rates of population growth in the underdeveloped areas diminish, they face impossible tasks through the remainder of this century, to match 1968 European levels of living, let alone the North American level. At the best, given their projected rates of population growth they can achieve only meager absolute advances in living levels.

Prospects for Fertility Control

In view of these considerations it is important to examine the prospects for fertility control, prospects which are considered in greater detail in chapter 7. Although the economically advanced areas are approaching complete population control, the developing nations of the world are not yet even in sight of it. While death rates in Asia, Latin America, and Africa are declining much more rapidly than they ever did in the economically advanced areas, birth rates, as has been indicated, are still at their traditional high levels. Some decreases in birth rates are evident in the areas which are experiencing rapid economic and social change, as in Taiwan, Hong Kong, Singapore and South Korea, but such areas are few and their populations constitute but a small fraction of the mass populations in the developing areas which constitute two-thirds of the world's total.

If one restricts oneself to the evidence it must be concluded from the experience of population control programs in developing areas that:

1. There are as yet no satisfactory methods of measuring small changes in fertility and growth rates over short periods of time in the developing areas containing the mass populations of the world.
2. There are as yet no experiments in family planning which have precisely measured the impact of an action program on fertility differentiated from other forces as embodied in secular trend. The program in Taiwan may yet achieve this.
3. There are as yet no significant examples of declines in fertility by reason of action programs in areas in which secular decline in fertility has not already occurred.
4. The examples of fertility declines to date in areas in which action programs are under way (Taiwan, Hong Kong, Singapore, South Korea, Ceylon) are not only areas in which declines in birth rate had already occurred but, also, are areas with special characteristics that preclude extension of the results to mass populations in Asia, Latin America or Africa that are still steeped in illiteracy and in poverty, and that are predominantly still "traditional societies."
5. The evidence of differential fertility in the developing regions provides, at best, a basis for wishful thinking about the potential of action programs in such areas. It is not yet known just what the forces are that produced the differential patterns and it is a great leap into the unknown to assume that action programs will therefore increase the differentials or change the behavior of the "traditionalists."

It is not at all clear yet, then, that the mass populations of the world in the developing areas can manage to control their population growth during the remainder of this century. The results of experiments to induce birth control among populations which are illiterate and poor are as yet disheartening. They do not indicate that such a nation as India can be expected greatly to reduce her birth rate in the near future. There are three reasons for this dismal outlook:

First, illiteracy and poverty in the developing nations, together with their traditional social organization and attitudes and resistance to social change, operate as tremendous barriers to the effective adoption of family planning methods.

Second, the social sciences have not achieved sufficient knowledge and knowhow to break the "cake of custom" and to evoke sufficient motivation and incentive among such populations to practice family planning.

Third, the bio-medical sciences are still so ignorant about the physiology of human reproduction that they have not yet produced methods of conception control that are acceptable enough, feasible enough, and efficacious enough to meet the problem in the developing areas.

The picture is not all dismal, however. Never before have so many nations as a matter of national policy adopted family planning programs to control population growth. Never before has so much been done as is now under way in the fields of bio-medical and social science research to obtain better knowledge to achieve fertility control. Moreover, the breakthrough in new methods represented by the oral progestins and the intra-uterine devices (the I.U.D.) holds forth promise of even greater breakthroughs. (See chapter 7.)

There has never been an example of a people who, having achieved education and a higher level of living, did not reduce their birth rate. Unfortunately, the converse of this proposition is also true. It is yet to be demonstrated that a nation steeped in illiteracy and poverty can control its birth rate. This fact constitutes the greatest challenge that has ever faced both the bio-medical and social sciences and policy makers and administrators throughout the world. For failure to meet the challenge of excessive population growth holds forth the prospect of unprecedented misery for all of mankind.

Thus, there is still a question as to whether world population control is possible. For the economically advanced areas the answer appears to be "yes," for they need to do only a little more of what they are already doing. For the developing nations, which now contain two-thirds of the world's population and by the century's end may have three-fourths, the answer is as yet "we do not know." But there is one thing we do know. We cannot afford not to exert every possible effort to help the developing nations to control their birth rates. Fortunately, this has now become the policy of the United States Government and also of the United Nations, the World Health Organization, and the other relevant specialized agencies.

Concluding Observations

The general world economic and political climate for the remainder of this century is not likely to be a happy one. During the remainder of this century it is likely in light of the available evidence that at least as many people will be added to world population as now exist on the face of this earth. That is, the increase in world population in the next 31 years will at least match the population that mankind, from the beginning of his time on this planet to the present, managed to generate simultaneously alive. Moreover, great increases are also possible during the first two-thirds of the twenty-first century. Rapid population growth is impeding efforts to increase levels of living in the developing nations of the world in Asia, Africa and Latin America.

Realism compels us to recognize that to change the world outlook substantially would require major reallocation of present world resources to a combined program of economic development and population control that is not yet in prospect. Perhaps only funds that would match and exceed present annual world military budgets, about one hundred and fifty billion dollars, could greatly alter the prospect—and that only if we could acquire the necessary knowledge to expend the funds to good effect, by no means a certainty.

Seven of the nations in the world, Mainland China, India, the U.S.S.R., the U.S.A., Indonesia, Pakistan and Japan had over 2 billion persons, or about 60 per cent of the world's population in 1968. Only the equivalent of an unlikely miracle could prevent these seven nations from having a population approximating 3.8 billion in the next 31 years—by the year 2000—a population greater than that of the entire world today! Of these nations it would seem, from present knowledge, that the United States, the U.S.S.R. and Japan are likely to continue to advance their relatively high levels of living during the last part of this century. But it remains extremely doubtful that Mainland China, India, Indonesia and Pakistan, nations with a possible population of 3 billion by the year 2000, can achieve their national aspirations of realizing materially greater levels of living by the century's end.

Moreover, the remainder of the world, all but the seven large nations singled out above, may have reached an aggregate population of some 3 billion in the next 31 years, and they also will be seated at the world's table for food and require the other necessities of life. In consequence, it may be expected that at least during the remainder of this century there will be increased, not decreased social unrest; more, not less, political instability; greater, not lesser threats to world peace; and intensified, not diminished cold war between capitalist and communist blocs or between have and have-not nations. Given the world population, economic and political outlook, it is reasonable to expect increased rather than decreased military and security expenditures, increased rather than decreased taxation.

Given the present outlook, only the faithful who believe in miracles from heaven, the optimistic who anticipate super-wonders from science, the parochials who expect they can continue to exist in islands of affluence in a sea of world poverty, and the naive who can anticipate nothing can look to the end of this century with equanimity.

Irene B. Taeuber

3

Population Growth in Less-Developed Countries

In 1960, two billion people lived in the less-developed countries. In 1970 the number will be two and one-half billion. In the ten years from 1960 to 1970, five hundred million people will have been added to populations where levels of living are low, food insufficient, and life precarious.[1]

If the estimated populations for 1960 and 1970 reflect the facts of the decade, natural increase raised the populations of 1970 almost one-

---

IRENE B. TAEUBER *is Senior Research Demographer, Office of Population Research, Princeton University. She is a Past President of the Population Association of America, and a Past Vice President of the International Union for the Scientific Study of Population. Her books include, as co-author,* The Future Population of Europe and the Soviet Union (*1943*), Public Health and Demography in the Far East (*1949*), The Changing Population of the United States (*1958*), *and* The People of the United States (*in press*); *as author,* General Censuses and Vital Statistics in the Americas (*1943*), The Population of Tanganyika (*1949*), *and* The Population of Japan (*1958*).

[1] United Nations, Department of Economic and Social Affairs, *World Population Prospects as Assessed in 1963,* Population Studies No. 41 (New York, 1966), vii, 149 pp.

Countries with crude birth rates of 30 or more, gross reproduction rates of 2.0 or more, were classified as less-developed, those with lower fertility as developed. Unless specified otherwise, the projections used in this paper are those classified as medium.

34

fourth above those for 1960. The relevance of this estimate of decade growth for all the world's less-developed peoples to the evaluation of the economic, social and political problems inherent in growth in the individual countries is debatable. A dichotomy of countries as developed and less-developed is convenient, but it is no longer valid. Countries classified as less-developed on the basis of present rates of population growth vary widely among themselves in type of economy, social structure, political organization, culture and ethnic origin. Comparable vital rates in the present need not mean similarities in future growth.

The most difficult question in an analysis that includes all less-developed countries is that of the Peoples Republic of China. China is the world's most populous nation; its historic demography is so distinctive that assumptions of identity in process and response with other Asian nations are hazardous. There is general agreement that the Chinese are a less-developed people with a declining mortality that is braked by economic and political difficulties and a relatively high fertility that may or may not be in transition to lower levels. The difficulty is measurement. The official data of censuses, surveys and vital records have always been sparse. They have been lacking since the Great Leap Forward in the late fifties transformed the status and the outlook for development in all fields, including the demographic.

There are other diversities among the less-developed countries. The peoples of Tropical Africa are moving or hoping to move from tribal societies to modern economies. Historical data are conjectural and current data are sparse. Latin American countries differ widely from Asian ones, in status and in outlook. But discussions for fragmented groupings of countries where population growth is rapid could lead only to catalogs of specifics. The combination of size and differing dynamics justifies a separate consideration of the less-developed countries excluding Mainland East Asia.[2] In 1970, Mainland East Asia included 30 per cent of the people of the less-developed world. Most of the less-developed people other than the Chinese were concentrated in Middle South and South East Asia (58 per cent), Tropical Africa (13 per cent), and Mainland Middle and Tropical South America (12 per cent). Only 16 per cent lived in other less-developed countries.

[2] In the United Nations study, projections were presented for 24 regions. Mainland East Asia includes Hong Kong, Mongolia, Macao and Mainland China. Estimated populations as of 1970 were 742 million for Mainland China, 4,350 thousand for Hong Kong, 1,250 thousand for Mongolia, and 180 thousand for Macao. The population of Mainland China was 99.2 per cent of the total.

The rates of population growth are higher, the problems of growth more severe, in that 70 per cent of the world's less developed people who are living outside Mainland East Asia. The population of all these countries was 1.4 billion in 1960. It was 1.8 billion in 1970. The increase of almost 400 million was 29 per cent of the 1960 population. The numbers that were added were as large as the combined populations of Pakistan, Indonesia, Mexico and Brazil.

What can or should be said in a few pages on a subject as vast, as complicated, and as serious in its implications for the world of the present and the future as that of population growth in less-developed countries? The growth of world population was the topic of the preceding chapter; the interrelations of population growth and economic development are the topics of the next chapter. There are later chapters on population control and on population policy. The emphasis in this chapter will be placed on growth as an aspect of the scientific, economic and political changes and the social continuities of the last half century. The slowing of growth will be assessed in relation to the values, aspirations and motivations of people rather than as mechanical consequence of economic growth. The thesis is that the natural processes of change in birth and death rates that characterized the evolution of populations in the past are insufficient for the future.

Transitions into slowing and finally slow growth are essential if peoples are to move far in modernization. The questions are not whether but when, how, and at what costs. There are now measurable transitions to lower birth rates in some of the less-developed countries; birth rates may be declining in others. These are countries unique in their economic histories and their demographic characteristics, and they are generally small in size. There are few evidences of major declines in birth rates in the larger populations. If transitions are to be speedy enough to avert severe economic and political difficulties, a demographic revolution in birth control must follow the still ongoing demographic revolution in death control. Even if this new revolution occurs, it will contribute to slow resolutions rather than direct solutions of the difficulties of modernization in the less-developed countries. The problems of the massive populations that have been generated in the twentieth century are not likely to be solved within the century in many of the countries. If birth rates decline rapidly, widely, and to sufficiently low levels in the near future, continuing and high population growth need not be a heritage of the past to the twenty-first century.

Growth

Population growth did not begin in the present decade, or even in the recent years when the seemingly miraculous chemicals, inoculations, and antibiotics became available for the elimination or control of many of the great historic causes of death. Fifty years ago, as today, death rates were declining while birth rates were unchanging. The levels of the death rates were related to food and nutrition, environmental hazards, the folkways of the people, and health services. Birth rates were related to the traditions, the family institutions, and the values of the cultures. Death rates were responsive to environmental changes occurring within the traditional cultures; birth rates were not. In the years from 1920 to 1940 there were widening areas with slowly declining death rates. Famines were limited and epidemics were controlled. Rates of natural increase rose. The population problems were etched ever more sharply in the quarter century that preceded the demographic revolution in mortality control in the late forties and the fifties and the rapid increases in rates of population growth. The dislocations and insecurities of the wars from 1937 to 1945 were hardly perceptible in general reductions in rates of growth, though some populations in the Pacific area suffered severely.

As populations increased decade by decade, the bases for future growth became larger and larger. The population of the less-developed countries as a whole, including China, was 1.2 billion in 1920, 1.5 billion in 1940. An increase of 24 per cent added more than a quarter of a billion people within 20 years. The population of 1.5 billion in 1940 increased to 2.0 billion in 1960. The increase in the two decades was 37 per cent; the addition to the population was half a billion. The 2.0 billion population of 1960 increased to 2.5 billion in 1970. The increase in the single decade was 24 per cent, the addition to the population almost half a billion. These are not conjectures as to population size and growth, though there are elements of conjecture in them. They are not predictions of the future. They are the facts of a half century that is past. Wherever possible, they are based on censuses and vital statistics; where estimation was required, it was done by demographers in the countries or regions concerned or in the international organizations.

The amounts and the rates of increase for all the less-developed countries may be over-estimates or under-estimates, depending to a large extent on the unascertainable relations between external estimates and internal facts for China. Since rates of increase have been and probably still are substantially less than those in the other large countries, the rates of increase for all less-developed countries are too high for China, too low for most of the other countries. A section on those countries of the less-developed world where there is access and knowledge, however limited, precedes a more speculative section on the peoples of the Republic of China.

LESS-DEVELOPED COUNTRIES EXCLUDING CHINA

The populations of the less-developed countries excluding Mainland East Asia grew from 711 million in 1920 to 941 million in 1940 (Table 1). This increase of almost one-third in two decades seemed rapid as it was occurring. In retrospect, it was omen of the future. In the late forties and the fifties, new technologies, more widespread and efficient health administration, and increasing and regularized food supplies resulted in rapidly declining death rates. The timing and the extent of the declines differed from country to country, but declines were worldwide. None of the changes of these extraordinary decades were conducive to immediate reductions in birth rates, since they had no direct influences on traditional values or on marriage and family institutions. Insofar as improving health and declining mortality influenced fertility, the effect was likely to be increase rather than decrease.

The population of the less-developed countries outside Mainland East Asia had increased from 711 million in 1920 to 941 million in 1940, a growth of 32 per cent. It increased from the 941 million of 1940 to 1.4 billion in 1960. The increase of 425 million amounted to 45 per cent. Growth was somewhat slower in Middle South Asia, where numbers were large, agricultural pressures severe, and political stability and economic development difficult in initiation and slow in achievement. The increase in South East Asia reached the average for the less-developed countries, despite the involvement of several countries in the Pacific War and the struggles for independence and national unifications in some countries. In Latin America, the traditional fertility was high and the institutions and ways of living that sustained it were undisturbed. The pressures on agricultural resources were less than in most other countries, the health activities were more intensive, and war was remote. The increase from 1940 to 1960 was 68 per cent in Tropical South America, 74 per cent in Middle America.

In the historic pasts of the less-developed countries, high birth rates had been essential if some children were to survive to care for aging

Table 1. *Estimated and Projected Populations of the Less-Developed Countries, without Mainland East Asia, 1920 to 2000*

Selected Regions

Year	L.D.C.,[1] minus Mainland East Asia	Asia		Tropical Africa	America	
		Middle South	South East		Tropical South	Mainland Middle
Population (in millions)						
1920	711	333	108	100	46	19
1930	809	371	127	115	54	22
1940	941	422	150	135	67	27
1950	1,094	479	173	155	84	35
1960	1,368	587	219	189	112	47
1970[2]	1,762	747	283	237	154	65
1980	2,286	954	364	303	210	90
1990	2,919	1,177	472	395	280	125
2000	3,643	1,399	603	525	362	166
Decade Increase, Per cent						
1920–1930	13.8	11.3	17.4	15.0	19.4	15.5
1930–1940	16.4	13.8	18.7	17.4	22.5	19.6
1940–1950	16.3	13.5	14.7	14.8	26.0	29.2
1950–1960	24.9	22.6	26.9	22.2	33.7	34.9
1960–1970[2]	28.8	27.2	29.3	24.9	36.8	38.0
1970–1980	29.8	27.7	28.7	28.0	36.2	40.0
1980–1990	27.7	23.4	29.5	30.4	33.5	37.8
1990–2000	24.8	18.8	27.8	32.9	29.4	33.1

1. Less-developed countries excluding the Peoples Republic of China, Mongolia, Hong Kong and Macao.
2. Medium estimates, 1970–2000.
Source: United Nations, Department of Economic and Social Affairs, *World Population Prospects as Assessed in 1963*, Population Studies, No. 41 (New York, 1966), Tables A3.1 and A3.2.

parents and in their turn have the children who would insure the continuity of the generations. This functional role of high birth rates was reduced as death rates declined. The family, the community, or the nation with an over-replacement of its children, its youth, and its claimants to food and jobs faced serious and increasing difficulties. The logical irrationality of continuing high birth rates did not seem to be perceived as such by the people. Birth rates remained at their initial heights, whatever happened to death rates. Whether compared between or within regions, there were few associations between the levels of birth and death rates. The following figures are estimates of birth, death, and natural increase rates per 1,000 total population as of 1960–1965: [3]

Region	Birth Rate	Death Rate	Rate of Natural Increase
Middle South Asia	43.6	20.3	23.3
South-East Asia	41.9	15.9	26.0
Tropical Africa	40.0+	24.0+	16.0+
Tropical South America	41.9	10.9	31.0
Middle America	43.6	11.6	32.0

The growth that had become the critical if not the central problem of development in the fifties was even more rapid in the sixties. A population growth of 29 per cent in the less-developed countries outside Mainland East Asia added 400 million people within the single decade. Increase varied from a low of 27 per cent in Middle South Asia to a high of 38 per cent in Mainland Middle America. The great concentrations of people and poverty were developing in Asia. In 1970, the population of Middle South Asia reached three-quarters of a billion people; the population of Middle South and South East Asia went beyond one billion.

The past is fact. The growth has occurred. The question is the future. The growth of the half century from 1920 to 1970 was product of the scientific advances and the economic, social, and political changes of that half century. The growth of the last third of the century will be influenced by the scientific advances and the economic, social and political changes of those decades. Past, present and future are interrelated, though, for the reductions in mortality and the persistences in fertility in the last half century produced the populations of the present from which those of the future will develop.

There are reasons other than the awe of numbers for assuming that the present rates of growth will not continue until rising mortality becomes the prime regulator of man's numbers. The associations between increasing population growth and lagging economic growth

[3] United Nations, *op. cit.*, Tables 7.1, 7.2 and 7.3.

have become apparent to demographers, economists, planners, legislators and administrators. Countries once food surplus became food deficit in the fifties and the sixties. One of the greatest armadas in history was not organized for war but to transport the food grains that would avert starvation. An increasing number of countries include family planning in health or related services; others are moving toward such inclusion. Some countries have programs to reduce birth rates by specified amounts or percentages in scheduled targets. National and international resources are being mobilized for scientific research in the many fields relevant to the control of human reproduction. By 1970 most of the people of the less-developed world lived in countries with policies to spread family planning or programs that made facilities for such planning available. Transitions were in process in some of the smaller countries, claimed in some of the larger ones. The bifurcated world in which there were developed and less-developed countries but no movement from the one category to the other no longer existed.

Prior to the sixties, hard questions underlay any even quasi-optimistic assessments of the future. The results of field surveys were demonstrating that the women in the peasant societies did not desire unlimited numbers of children. When questioned, they said that they would like to know about contraception.[4] But people were uneducated, life was difficult, and motivations were weak. The contraceptives of the period were quite inadequate. The outlook was improved in the sixties when the intra–uterine contraceptive devices and the pills became available; further scientific advances in the biomedical and behavioral sciences were anticipated. However, there were increasing fears that advances in science, administration and response in birth control programs would not come soon enough to avert food deficits and famines in great areas. The scientific advances in grain production that are called "the green revolution" give the technical possibilities for multiplying yields and so postponing the food-population crisis. In population control, as in food production, the questions concern the time required for the achievement of that which is technically feasible rather than technical feasibility itself.

What, then, is the outlook for the growth of population of the less-developed countries in the last third of the twentieth century? The

---

[4] Summary statements and analyses of these studies, plans and developments in population policies and programs, and achievements and evaluations of programs are included in the various issues of *Studies in Family Planning* (The Population Council, 245 Park Avenue, New York, N. Y. 10017).

population projections of the United Nations are based on an implicit assumption that the transitions in countries now less-developed will be similar in course and in speed to the historic transitions in countries now developed. In many of those countries, birth rates were reduced to half their initial levels within thirty years after decline began. If this also occurs in the less-developed countries, the main question of course is the simple one of when decline begins. Mortality is assumed to decline at slowing rates. In the medium projections, declines in fertility begin in India and Pakistan in 1970. They are assumed to have begun in South East Asia in 1960, but the time required for halving is taken as 60 years rather than 30. In Middle and Tropical America, declines begin in 1970 but reduction to half the present levels requires 45 years. No decline is projected for Tropical Africa within this century.

Thus the future populations that are presented in Table 1 are mainly those of countries that are assumed to be beginning the transition from high to low birth rates. Some complete the movement to birth rates half the present levels by the end of the century. In others, declines in birth rates continue in the early decades of the next century. In all, rates of decline are slow and the time of transition is long. Under these assumptions, the increase in the populations of the less-developed countries excluding Mainland East Asia is 30 per cent from 1970 to 1980, 28 per cent from 1980 to 2000, and 25 per cent from 1990 to 2000.

The total populations are 1.8 billion in 1970 and 3.6 billion in 2000; the difference is 1.8 billion. A projected doubling of the already massive Asian populations occurs in the decades when birth rates are being cut in half. The populations of the Latin American regions in 2000 are almost two– and one-half times those in 1970, despite a reduction of one-fourth or more in birth rates.

The numbers that have been cited are projections rather than predictions. They pose the dilemma of the future in a form that permits no evasion. Can all or most of the less-developed countries sustain their increasing populations while achieving those economic and social developments that seem to be essential for declining birth rates? Can economic and social development be initiated and continued without the declining birth rates that slow population growth?

CHINA

In 1920, the people of China were two-thirds as numerous as the other peoples of the less-developed countries combined, but population growth was slow and erratic. China was not colonial; no imposed system of government provided a bureaucracy, civil order, transport, regularized subsistence, or internal epidemic protection. Death rates were at premodern levels in normal times, while famines and epidemics were still episodic. Modern economic centers were mainly coastal, and they were oriented externally. Social change was occurring but its penetration of the traditional family system and its impact on values and reproductive habits was slight. The ancient culture of China still conditioned the marriage habits and the reproductive mores of the people. There were pragmatic controls of births and a reduction in numbers of surviving children in difficult times, a conformity to multi-generation ideals in favorable times. The consensus of observers, Chinese and outsiders, was that the birth rate was about 40, the average annual increase about one-half of one per cent. In the estimates of the United Nations, the population of Mainland East Asia which included China was 476 million in 1920, 533 million in 1940. The increase of 12 per cent in the period of two decades was far less than that in any other Asian region.

In 1953, an investigation and registration of the population of the Peoples Republic of China indicated a population of 582 million. If this figure is accepted, estimation of the population from 1953 to 1970 requires a constructed age distribution along with estimated birth and death rates from 1953 to 1970. Projections onward from 1970 to 2000 require estimates of future changes in hypothetical rates. The projections of the United Nations are based on the assumption that the initial birth rate was 38, that decline began in 1955, and that halving will be completed by 2000.[5] In numerical terms, the birth rate declines from 34.3 in 1960–65 to 20.4 in 1995–2000, while the death rate declines from 21.1 to 11.2 in the same period. The rate of natural increase declines from 13.3 in 1960–65 to 9.2 in 1995–2000. This is a low rate of increase, far lower than that occurring or anticipated in Middle South or South East Asia. However, a gigantic base population yields very large increases in numbers, even at the assumed slow rates of growth. The population that was little more than half a billion in 1940 becomes almost three-quarters of a billion in 1970 and more than a billion in 2000.

The assessments of the United Nations suggest that China will be

[5] United Nations, *op. cit.*, p. 57. The medium projection cited here is the average of two projections. In one, the expectation of life at birth reaches 42.5 years in 1965–1970 and 57.6 years in 1995–2000, while the birth rate is cut in half between 1970 and 2000. In the other, the expectation of life at birth is 42.5 years in 1955–1960 and 63.2 years in 1995–2000, while the birth rate is cut in half between 1955 and 1985.

first among the large less-developed countries to move through demographic transition, and that she will do so with relatively low birth rates and relatively high death rates. If so, the population of Mainland China will be a decreasing proportion of the Asian and the world population. A series of United States estimates of the past and future growth of the population of China include one based on assumptions of moderate economic development, fertility declining at intermediate rates, and halting increases in expectations of life at birth.[6] As contrasted with the medium estimate of the United Nations, initial fertility is somewhat higher, decline begins later, and it proceeds more slowly. The initial mortality is lower and declines are speedier. The differences in estimated and projected populations are cumulative over the thirty years from 1955 to 1985. In the United Nations estimate, the population of Mainland China is 883 million in 1985; in the United States estimate it is 1.1 billion. The United States estimate is 4 per cent above the United Nations estimate in 1955 but 25 per cent above it in 1985.

Although the reconstructions and projections of population growth in China differ, there is a fundamental concurrence. The traditional birth rate in the Chinese population is assumed to be lower than that in other less-developed Asian populations. The transition to declining fertility is assumed to be in process now, whether it began in 1955 or in 1965, whether it proceeds more or less slowly. If so, the Peoples Republic of China is in the forefront of demographic change among the large countries of the less-developed world.[7]

Transitions

Most of the historical periods of rapid population growth occurred under favorable circumstances and ended in rising mortality

---

[6] U. S., Bureau of the Census, *Estimates and Projections of the Population of Mainland China: 1953–1986* (International Population Reports, Series P-91, No. 17), prepared for the Foreign Demographic Analysis Division by John S. Aird (Washington, D. C.: Government Printing Office, 1968), Table 1, Model III, 1953–1965, and Table 2, Model B, 1966–1986. In this projection, the initial birth rate is taken as 40, the initial death rate as 20. A gross reproduction rate is assumed to remain unchanging at 2.654 from 1953 to 1965, then to decline to 2.209 in 1985. The expectation of life at birth for women, 46.0 in 1953, is assumed to increase to 51.7 in 1965 and 53.4 in 1985.

[7] If space permitted, alternate projections would have been examined for other regions, particularly tropical Africa. An analytic assessment by Etienne van de Walle, "The Population of Tropical Africa in the 1980s." Presented as the symposium, *Africa In the 1980s*, Adlai Stevenson Institute, Chicago, April 1969.

rather than in falling fertility. In the power-based industrial civilization of Europe, declines in death rates were associated or followed by declines in birth rates. Population growth slowed and the balance of numbers became that of low birth rates and low death rates. A comparable process of population change occurred among the Japanese. A half a century ago, even a quarter century ago, it was assumed that demographic transitions similar to those that had occurred earlier in European countries would occur in the less-developed countries as they, too, became industrialized and urbanized. Transitions were assumed to be by-products of economic development of an urban and industrial type. With the worldwide thrusts for political independence and economic advance in the last quarter century, theories of smoothly moving natural transitions became archaic. Health, freedom from disease, and longer lives were driving aspirations for people and major goals for governments. Scientific and medical advances combined with the many facets of the development process itself to yield declines of death rates in advance of the economic developments and the social changes that had been assumed to be the essential preconditions for low mortality. In the demographic revolution in mortality control, the reduced and still declining death rates of the new era existed alongside the high birth rates that were heritages of ancient orders.

The recognition of the existence of population growth and the problems associated with the continuation of that growth is widespread in less-developed and in developed countries, in regional and in global associations of countries. There is an advancing consensus that birth rates must decline soon and sharply if economic and social development and political stability are to be maintained. There is a widespread though far from universal acceptance of the thesis that governments must assume responsibilities in the area of birth reduction, as in earlier times they assumed responsibilities in the area of death reduction. Perhaps, though, recognition of the problems of growth and programs to provide contraceptive services come too late to solve the problems of increase in many of the countries whose populations are large, densely settled, and rapidly increasing. If so, a new demographic revolution may be required, this one to replace slow declines in birth rates with rapid declines such as those that occurred earlier in death rates. The search for an answer requires an examination of some of the demographic transitions that have been completed and some that are now occurring.

HISTORIC TRANSITIONS

The potentials for population increase under favorable conditions and the aspects of those conditions that lead to changes in birth rates are alike demonstrated in the history of the United States.[8] In 1790, when the first census was taken, 95 per cent of the four million people were rural. The birth rate was about 55 per 1,000 total population. Population was increasing at 30 to 35 per cent a decade. It was the experience of the American colonies that was so convincing to Malthus in the development of his theories concerning the potentialities of human reproduction. Malthusianism was prevalent among the intellectuals of early America.

In the century from 1790 to 1890 the increasing population of the United States occupied the land from the Atlantic to the Pacific, from the Canadian to the Mexican borders. Agricultural expansion and urban growth proceeded together. Millions of immigrants were added to the labor force of the growing economy. The birth rate declined decade by decade throughout the century and a half from the formation of the nation in the late eighteenth century to the mid-thirties of the twentieth century. Birth rates declined earlier and more consistently than death rates; rates of natural increase declined. By 1935 the birth rate was 18.7, the death rate 10.9. The net reproduction rate was below unity, that is, potentially the population was failing to reproduce itself.

Then, in a country that had presumably completed transition, age at marriage declined and the fertility of the married rose to levels above those of the early twentieth century. In 1957, the birth rate was 25.3, the net reproduction rate 1.8. A people who were largely metropolitan, educated and affluent, and who knew and practiced birth control, were reproducing at levels sufficient to yield an increase of 80 per cent a generation. This increase was due more to the overabundant reproduction of the affluent than to the unplanned childbearing of economically depressed groups, whether the natives of the Appalachian hills, the poorer and less educated blacks, the cultural

---

[8] Summary based on: Irene B. Taeuber and Conrad Taeuber, *The People of the United States*, a 1960 Census Monograph, prepared in cooperation with the Social Science Research Council (in press). Current data from: U. S., National Center for Health Statistics, Division of Vital Statistics, *Vital Statistics of the United States, 1966*, Vol. 1, *Natality* (Washington, D. C., 1968), Tables 1-2 and 1-4; and U. S., Bureau of the Census, "Estimates of the Population of the United States and Components of Change: 1940 to 1969," *Current Population Reports*, Series P-25, No. 418 (March 4, 1969), Tables A and B.

minorities, or the indigenous Indians. But the fertility of advanced transition did not remain unchanging at higher levels. The birth rate declined from 25.3 in 1957 to 17.4 in 1968, the lowest in American history. The ratio of births to women aged 15 to 44 had been 123.0 in 1957; it was 85.8 in 1968. The gross reproduction rate that had been 1.84 in 1957 was 1.34 in 1966. Portions of the gyrations in birth rates and more refined measures of fertility were due to changing age cohorts moving into and through the reproductive ages and to changes in the timing and the spacing of births. Three conclusions are obvious, however. First, fertility was responsive to the values and aspirations of the people, whether in the new world or the old, whether in the period of underdevelopment or in that of development. Second, trends in change that had persisted for a hundred and fifty years altered quickly, in speed and in direction. Third, the future of fertility and therefore of population was not predicted in the recent past, nor is it now predictable. Perhaps these conclusions that have been phrased in general terms are relevant both to the interpretation of declining fertility in the less-developed countries and to those of rising fertility in the more affluent countries.

The demographic transition in the United States cannot be replicated elsewhere in the world. There are no empty Americas available for occupation by prolific peoples. In this most favorable of physical settings in a period of time when advancing technologies, relatively abundant capital, and immigrants were all available, the birth rate declined for a century and a half before reaching replacement levels at the low mortality that had then been achieved. Famines were never present; death rates were always limited. Transition was indeed a natural process, one in which rural and urban birth rates alike declined, and one in which birth rates declined earlier than death rates. Recent problems of increasing numbers are those of the affluent rather than the disadvantaged society. American understanding of the depths of the problems of population, the intricacies of the interrelations, and the difficulties of solution cannot be derived from the American experience.

The demographic transition in the United States may seem singularly irrelevant to the future of the less-developed countries, while the experience of Japan may seem directly relevant.[9] Japan's transition

[9] Summary based on: Irene B. Taeuber, *The Population of Japan* (Princeton: Princeton University Press, 1958). Current data from: United Nations, Department of Economic and Social Affairs, Statistical Office, *Demographic Yearbook*, 1965 and 1967.

demonstrates that industrialization, urbanization, advancing education, increasing expectations of life, declining fertility, and reproduction insufficient for permanent replacement are not limited in continent, culture, or time. It does not demonstrate that natural transition
is inherent in the Asian future. Japan's experience, as that of the
United States, is not subject to replication.

In the early seventeenth century, the Tokugawa *shogun* closed
Japan to the trade and proselyting activities of the Europeans. In
the mid-nineteenth century, the 35 million people of Japan confronted
the industrial and imperial world outside their borders with a traditional economy, an archaic social and political structure, and a vital
balance in which problems of growth that could not be sustained
were resolved either in famine and epidemic or in *mabiki,* the thinning
of the newly born. However, there were positive aspects to the balance
sheet. The people were united and disciplined, without major diversities in culture, religion, or language. Opening to the West was an
ordered and peaceful process, without political or social revolution.
Neither the struggle for power through industrialization nor the
military expansion and final repatriation need be described here. The
fundamental point in the present context is that the transformation
from the feudal and largely agrarian regime of 1868 to status as the
most industrialized, metropolitan, educated and affluent of the populations outside the world of the Europeans occupied a century.

Japan's demographic transition was rooted in the distinctive demography of Tokugawa, formed in the Meiji Restoration, and
achieved during a period when no miracles of modern chemistry or
biology permitted truly low death rates. Mortality declined slowly
from the Meiji Restoration onward; fertility probably began a slow
decline in the eighties or the nineties of the last century. Annual
natural increase never reached 2 per cent until after the Second World
War when a baby boom coincided with the introduction of modern
medical technologies.

The period of high growth was brief. Declines in death rates were
swift, but they were swiftly overtaken by even more rapidly declining
birth rates. The gross reproduction rate had been 2.3 in 1930 and 2.0
in 1937–1940. It rose to 2.26 in 1947, then declined to 1.44 in 1952,
.99 in 1957, and .96 in 1963. The net reproduction rate was above 1.7
from 1947 to 1949. It has not been above unity in any year since 1956.
Today the crude birth rate fluctuates around 17 to 18 per 1,000 total
population. The central problems of population still include those
of change, but now change is smaller numbers of children entering

school, an insufficiency of labor, and increasing proportions of the aged.

Japan's demographic transition was natural in the sense that there were no policies or programs of government designed to reduce birth rates prior to the period when the birth rate reached low modern levels. In the early postwar years the government legalized sterilization, induced abortion, and contraception for eugenic and health reasons, but the induced abortions thus legalized were available in the private rather than the public sector. The precipitant declines in the birth rate were products of the determination of most of the families of Japan to have only two children, not more and usually not less. The development came after almost a century of industrialization and urbanization. It accompanied a rate of economic growth even more miraculous than the rate of demographic transition.

Japan's experience does demonstrate that industrialization, urbanization, education, and wider areas of contact and communication are conducive to declining fertility in an Asian culture, as in a European one. If Japan's demographic transition is to be a model for countries now less developed, that model has to involve the total transformation of Japan rather than simply its family ideals and its reproductive performance.

TRANSITIONS IN PROCESS[10]

The increasing and increasingly recognized pressures of population growth on food, living space, employment and education are forces of change in the motivations of people and the policies of governments. The time, the speed, and the efficiency in the consideration and development of programs are related to traditional values, social structure, and political form as well as the state of economic development and the rate of social change. Objective and definitive measurement of status, achievement, and prospects is difficult, whether measured as a change of attitudes and receptivities or as a decline in numbers of births.

The initial impacts of programs may be largely the intangibles of a spreading awareness and a deepening motivation. Reorientation in the many attitudes, institutions and goals influencing daily living are

[10] Bernard Berelson, et al., eds., *Family Planning and Population Programs, A Review of World Development*, Proceedings of the International Conference on Family Planning Programs, Geneva, August, 1965 (Chicago, Ill.: The University of Chicago Press, 1966), xvi, 848 pp. Also, the country analyses and summaries in: *Studies in Family Planning* (The Population Council).

not clearly separable by the spheres of activity to which they pertain. Neither health, family planning, nor birth control programs operate in isolation. If government activities stimulate changes, those changes are likely to be more widespread than the area of direct impact. Furthermore, it is difficult to measure the early changes in fertility that presage future changes of larger magnitudes and greater speed. Since demographic statistics are aspects of government functioning, early steps in demographic transition are not likely to be measurable in the still approximate data of census and vital records.

Birth rates are now declining in all the areas of the Western Pacific where the peoples are Chinese or related to the Chinese in culture and in historic associations. The changes in crude rates evident in the data of Table 2 mirror the interrelated influences of changing age structures, increasing ages at marriage, and declining fertility among the married. They are indicative of the forces of transition to lower fertility rather than precise measures of it. It is probable that birth rates are declining in Korea, but vital rates are not available.

These areas of transition in the Western Pacific are distinctive in economic history, present rates of economic growth, and metropolitan

Table 2. Crude Birth Rates in Selected Western Pacific Countries, 1945–1949 to 1967

Year	Japan	Ryukyus	Taiwan	Hong Kong	Singapore
1945–1949	30.2	36.1	40.2	—	46.4
1950–1954	23.7	35.5	45.9	34.2	45.5
1955–1959	18.2	29.2	42.8	36.3	42.8
1960–1964	17.2	23.7	37.1	32.8	35.6
1958	18.1	28.7	41.7	37.4	42.0
1959	17.6	27.4	41.2	35.2	40.3
1960	17.2	25.0	39.5	36.0	38.7
1961	16.9	25.2	38.3	34.2	36.5
1962	17.1	23.4	37.4	32.8	35.1
1963	17.3	23.8	36.3	32.9	34.7
1964	17.7	22.2	34.5	30.2	33.2
1965	18.6	22.3	32.7	27.7	31.1
1966	13.7[1]	18.5	32.4	24.9	29.8
1967	19.3[2]	—	28.5[1]	23.0	25.8[1]

Source: United Nations, Department of Economic and Social Affairs, *Demographic Yearbook;* 1965, Table 7; and 1967, Table 7.

1. The year of Horse and Fire, when girl babies have dubious futures, particularly as wives.

2. Provisional.

dominance, or in some combination of these factors. The Ryukyus are a prefecture of Japan. Taiwan and Korea were colonies of Japan and subject to economic developments that became more industrial in type prior to the Second World War. Hong Kong and Singapore are metropolitan countries. All these areas now have rapid rates of economic growth. There are traditions of infanticide or related practices to limit the numbers of children, and abortion is generally ethical and widely acceptable. In areas outside Korea, perhaps in Korea, government programs speeded declines already in process. In Korea, an extensive and intensive program to reduce births operates in a milieu of rapid urbanization and advancing education, along with widespread unemployment. Here, as elsewhere in the Chinese cultural area, abortion is available and acceptable to implement decisions not to have a child, perhaps after intra–uterine devices have been removed or pills have not been taken.

There are many countries in the less-developed areas where economic and social change should be conducive to advancing age at marriage and declining childbearing among the married.[11] There are many programs of government that should influence the numbers and the spacing of births and thus the birth rates and the rates of growth. The program of Pakistan is particularly relevant to the broader questions of direct and intensive crusades to reduce birth rates rapidly so that rates of growth become manageable soon rather in some remote future period.[12] There are targets for the reductions of birth rates in the five year plans. There is a separate administration for family planning, with a use of specifically trained but non-medical young women under the supervision of, or with access to, doctors and nurses. The extent of the program's operations and some data from surveys and studies corroborate official beliefs that there is some reduction of numbers consequent on the program, but there are no definitive measurements, census or vital statistics to sustain estimates of decline.

The decade of the sixties may be viewed as preparatory for the population programs of the seventies. It is late for a preparatory decade. In many countries, continuing growth at present rates well into the

[11] The developments in India and the program there are perhaps the most crucial in terms of the size of the population that is involved, the urgencies of resolution, and the relevance of developments in India to Asia and the world. Simple statements would contribute little; adequate description of the status and the prospects is not possible in the space available here.

[12] Pakistan Family Planning Division, *Proposals of the Family Planning Division for Family Planning Sector during the Fourth Five Year Plan* (1970–75), (Islamabad, Government of Pakistan, 1969.)

seventies may create economic deterrents and political hazards so severe that orderly evolutions of future populations through declining fertility are threatened.

The Problems of Growth

The problems of growth include not alone increasing total numbers but increasing numbers of children who need schools, increasing numbers of youth who need jobs, and increasing numbers of adults who must support families. We shall not discuss these problems in generalizations concerning the rest of the century. Rather, we shall discuss growth in India, Pakistan, Indonesia, Mexico and Brazil in the years from 1960 to 1975 (Table 3). That growth is largely determined, little subject to the effects of present activities or future programs, for all those who will be aged 6 or over in 1975 are already born. The populations and the increases in the different ages are those of the period in which we are now living. The estimates of the populations and the growth were made a decade ago; both are too low. It was assumed that fertility would not change but that mortality would decline. Fertility did not decline but the level of the fertility was underestimated; mortality declined, but the rate of the decline was underestimated. And, finally, the actual populations as of 1960 were larger than the ones assumed. The populations and their increases are illustrative data, biased in the direction of understatement.

The increases in total populations need no further emphasis. They were rapid in rates and large in amounts. Countries already struggling with problems of growth and development in 1960 had populations 40 to 60 per cent larger within the brief span of 15 years. These are not small countries. India has the world's largest population apart from China. Pakistan and Indonesia each exceed 100 million in total numbers. East Pakistan and Java are areas of extraordinary pressures on resources, insufficient food production, few opportunities for increasing youth within or outside agriculture, precarious internal order, and political instability. In Mexico, economic development, increasing agricultural productivity, and urbanization coincide with a growth rate that yields an increase of three-fifths in total numbers in fifteen years. Brazil is a continental country with the largest population in the Western Hemisphere outside the United States of America.

The age structures of the five countries are weighted with youth. In 1960 some 16 to 17 per cent of the total populations were aged 0 to 4, while 40 to 45 per cent were below age 15. The ratios of those

Table 3. Projected Increases by Age in Five Countries, 1960 or 1961 to 1975 or 1976, on Assumptions of Continuity in Fertility and Declines in Mortality

Variable and Country	Total	Selected Age Groups		
		5–14	15–44	45–60
Population (in 000)				
India: 1961	423,600	100,100	187,600	45,700
1976	600,600	150,300	252,400	64,200
Pakistan: 1961	95,387	24,323	41,045	9,092
1976	145,630	38,752	60,404	13,632
Indonesia: 1960	93,344	21,363	41,479	10,042
1975	137,376	34,666	57,205	15,084
Mexico: 1960	34,119	9,181	13,854	3,356
1975	54,462	14,035	22,539	4,552
Brazil: 1960	66,085	16,701	28,642	6,483
1975	98,297	25,809	41,541	9,422
Amount of Change (in 000)				
India	177,000	50,200	64,800	18,500
Pakistan	50,243	14,429	19,359	4,540
Indonesia	44,032	13,303	15,726	5,042
Mexico	20,343	5,454	8,685	1,196
Brazil	32,212	9,108	12,899	2,939
Per cent of Change				
India	41.8	50.1	34.5	40.5
Pakistan	52.7	59.3	47.2	49.9
Indonesia	47.2	62.3	37.9	50.2
Mexico	59.6	59.4	62.7	35.6
Brazil	48.7	54.5	45.0	45.3

Sources of Data: United Nations, Department of Economic and Social Affairs, Population Division, *Future population estimates by sex and age*: Mexico, Report I, *The population of Central America (including Mexico). 1950–1980*, Table 2, p. 42 (New York, 1954), 84 pp.; Brazil, Report II, *The population of South America, 1950–1980*, Table 4, p. 73 (New York, 1955), 139 pp.; Indonesia, Report III, *The population of South-east Asia (including Ceylon and China: Taiwan), 1950–1980*, Table 6, pp. 138–139 (New York, 1958), 166 pp.; Pakistan, India, Mainland China, Report IV, *The population of Asia and the Far East, 1950–1980* [Pakistan, Table xvii, p. 109; India, Table viii, p. 100 (high fertility projection)].

in the productive ages to youthful and aged dependents were high in 1960 and they will increase between 1960 and 1975.

Is it correct to assume that rates of population growth of 40 to 60 per cent in the years from 1960 to 1975 constitute major population problems in the South Asian and Latin American countries? The answer is unequivocal, and it is affirmative. The justification of this statement begins with the numbers and the changes in the numbers of those in the productive ages.

The prime activity of men in the productive ages from 15 to 59 years is labor, whether in agriculture or industry, in country or city, in modern industry and commerce, or in the production and distribution sectors of traditional economies. The activities of women are more diversified, for these years include homemaking and child rearing along with participation in economic activities. Men and women in the central years of life maintain both themselves and those in the younger and the older ages. This is the economic responsibility. They produce the younger generation for whom they provide—thus meeting their fundamental demographic responsibility. They care for the aging and the aged—thus fulfilling the familial responsibilities of the ancient societies.

The demographic situation in which numbers of adults in the productive ages are increasing rapidly dictates a commensurate increase in jobs. The depth of the interrelated problems of population increase and labor force expansion in the years from 1965 to 1970 is apparent in some rather arbitrary computations. All men aged 15 to 64 are assumed to be in the labor force, and no position is vacated except through death or retirement at age 65. All young men aged 15 to 19 enter the labor force. Under these assumptions, the number of entrants to labor force ages for each 100 departures is now about 225 in India, 285 in West Pakistan and Indonesia, and more than 300 in East Pakistan and Mexico.

Changes in the numbers of girls in the late teens suggest the changes in marriage and families. In India, Pakistan and Indonesia, as in Mexico and Brazil, young women aged 15 to 19 will be half again as numerous in 1975 as in 1960. If age at marriage and the prevalence of marriage remain unchanged, new families formed in 1975 will be half again as numerous as those formed in 1960. Given unchanging rates of childbearing, numbers of births in 1975 will also be half again as numerous as those in 1960.

The education of youth is an aspiration of families and a goal of governments. There are not only hopes to improve the quality of living but desires to provide the more skilled and professional manpower essential to economic development. But in the projections cited, numbers of children aged 5 to 14 increase 50 to 60 per cent within the fifteen year period in India, Pakistan and Indonesia, as in Mexico and Brazil. An increase of at least 50 per cent in facilities and teachers is needed to maintain educational institutions at the levels that had been attained in 1960. The expansion required to train the more efficient labor force and the homemakers of the future is over and beyond this 50 or 60 per cent increase that is essential if retrogression is to be avoided.

The children who were less than five years of age in 1960 will be 15 to 19 years of age in 1975. If these youth of 1975 are not educated, the workers and the parents of the following decades will not be educated. The advance of education is perhaps the most critical factor beyond economic viability itself, and the two are interrelated. The self-perpetuating mechanisms of traditional societies are nowhere more apparent and more serious than here, for the large families, the severe burdens on families and communities, and the deterrents to economic growth are part of a complex of forces that preserve traditionalism and illiteracy. These in turn perpetuate early marriages, abundant child-bearing, and high rates of population growth.

Continuities and Changes

Technologies of death control spread quickly; the wish to live rather than to die exists among all people, all cultures, and at all stages of development. There are almost universal desires for less than maximum sizes of family, but there are few evidences of universal motivations sufficient to insure rapid and continuing declines in birth rates, even when technologies are available. In this area of decision and action, as in economic and social change in general, there are major differences among the countries in readiness for development and in the capabilities for the design and implementation of development plans. There were differences in the intensities of the awakened aspirations and the aroused expectations in the early hopeful years when improving levels of living and upward economic and social mobilities were assumed to be imminent. Today there are differences in the extent and volatility of the frustrations.

A coincidence of pervasively high fertility and pervasively low mortality cannot endure indefinitely. Continuing expansions in health services and continuing economic growth are essential to the continuing downward movement of death rates. In a period of time that cannot now be determined, continuity in economic growth, increasing health services and declining death rates will be dependent on reductions in birth rates.

As death rates move downward with convergences in levels among the countries and the regions, the rates of population growth become tied ever more closely to the rate at which new life is produced. Present diversities in rates of growth reflect the levels of the birth rates in the countries. Birth rates are likely to move downward, but the declines are not likely to be uniform among the countries. The relations become current levels and future declines are not predictable. It is likely that there will be increasing diversities in birth rates and therefore in rates of population growth.

The deepest resistances to reduced family size and hence the slowest transitions to low birth rates might be expected in Latin America and the Philippines. There are major indigenous components in populations and in cultures; resources are believed to be sufficient for future growth; and religion is Catholic. But the countries of temperate South America are in the developed sector in the demographic dichotomy of developed and less-developed countries. Catholicism has not been inconsistent with low fertility, whether in Europe or in Latin America.

The central population problem of the world is the Asian one. Here there are diversities in present status and in anticipated future paths to and speeds of transition. Japan has few competitors in the world in industrialization, urbanization, advanced education, and demographic transition as aspects of comprehensive modernization. Transitions are now occurring in Taiwan, the Ryukyus, Hong Kong, Singapore, and probably in Korea. There may be transition in the Peoples Republic of China.

The faith of Islam may be neutral with reference to fertility control but the ethical ideals, the family values, and the roles assigned to women are conducive to early and continuing childbearing. Fertility is very high in the great crescent from North Africa through the Middle East to Pakistan and down across the subcontinent through Malaya and on eastward to Indonesia and northward to Mindanao. But today there are programs or interests in programs to reduce birth rates in Islamic countries from Nigeria and North Africa to Indonesia.

The most difficult and hazardous of all population questions are probably those of recently nonliterate peoples suddenly sovereign in complex environments for which they are ill-prepared. In the scattered islands of the Southwest Pacific, solutions other than education and out-migration were once difficult to envision. Today there are family planning programs and drives for such programs. Hawaii stands as symbol of the potentialities of all island and mainland peoples to achieve advanced modernization within one or two generations, given the opportunity to do so.

The demographic outlook for sub-Saharan Africa is difficult to envision. Given political stability, feasible developments for the masses of the people would seem to lie in advancing agriculture. If so, the demographic path might lead toward Asian-type population pressures. The goals of the countries are advanced modern rather than peasant traditional, though, and industrialization requires direct movement from tribal to modern technologies.

Population projections indicate the hazards inherent in the future unless birth rates decline. They suggest the growth inherent in the continuation of high or even slowly declining fertility along with still declining mortality. But how will the populations of the future develop? Will there be increasing uniformities or widening differences in India and Pakistan, in Indonesia and the Philippines, in North Africa and the Middle East, in Western and in Eastern Africa? Will Brazil, the Indian nations of the Andean highlands, and Mexico move along similar paths? What is the present and future population of mainland China?

Perhaps the greatest social and political process of our times is the advance of aspirations among the ordinary peoples of the world, whether Latin American, Asian, or African. The corollary of aspirations in a milieu of population growth, precarious economic advance, and rigidities in social structure is frustration. Political instability, internal disorders and revolution may be associated with economic retardation and contribute to further retardation in the advances that are needed.

The population growth that now jeopardizes economic development, social continuity and political order in many less-developed countries is a heritage of the unchanging birth rates and the declining death rates of the last half century. The acceleration of growth and the increasing sizes of the populations have changed deepening problems into crises. If birth rates should decline rapidly in the seventies and thereafter, the acute difficulties in production and distribution, education and employment that are associated with the increasing numbers of those in the ages of childhood, youth, labor and homemaking would be reduced in time.

There are no scientific bases for determining whether declines in birth rates will come soon enough and rapidly enough. The predictions of increasing or decreasing rates have often been erroneous in developing and less-developed countries alike. The sharply declining death rates of recent decades that were mainly responsible for the increasing rates of growth were not predicted in advance. No one within or outside Japan predicted the swift decline in birth rates in the early postwar years. That which is not predictable from past trends may occur.

The urgency of the problems of population growth may contribute to dedications in research, administration, plans and programs that achieve those swift reductions in rates of growth that now seem almost unattainable. The years of lethargy, postponement, and procrastination cannot persist on assumptions that there can be continuity in high birth rates and declining death rates for indefinite periods of time in the future. Those revolutions that are needed in fertility control and in food production are technically possible. The decade of the seventies is critical not alone for demographic transition to lower birth rates but for human survival.

Ansley J. Coale

4

Population and Economic Development

Anyone examining estimates of per capita incomes or other indexes of material well-being must be impressed with the wide difference —by a factor of ten or more—between the wealthiest and the poorest countries. The countries with the highest average incomes are those that have undergone industrialization or modernization; and the countries with lowest incomes are those that retain traditional techniques of production and modes of industrial organization (with a predominance of agriculture in most instances) that have persisted without essential change for generations. The disparity between the prosperity of the industrialized countries and the poverty of the pre-industrial countries is an increasing irritant to the pride and ambition of the leaders in the underdeveloped areas and to the conscience of the modernized countries.

Demographic Characteristics of Poverty Areas

It is the purpose of this chapter to consider how the demographic characteristics of the low-income countries are related to their poverty, and how their population trends will influence their modernization.

ANSLEY J. COALE *is Professor of Economics and Director, Office of Population Research, Princeton University. From 1961 to 1969 he served as United States Representative on the Population Commission of the United Nations. He is a former president of the Population Association of America, a Fellow of the American Statistical Association, and a member of the American Philosophical Society. Among his publications is (with E. M. Hoover)* Population Growth and Economic Development in Low Income Countries.

Other chapters in this book have described the nature of the population in the underdeveloped areas of the world and current population trends in these areas. Among the demographic characteristics of low income areas today are:

High fertility—Most underdeveloped areas of the world have birth rates of forty per 1,000 or higher and an average number of children born at the end of the fertile period—at age of forty-five or fifty—of at least 5. This fertility contrasts with experience in Europe, where birth rates are, with only two or three exceptions, below twenty per 1,000, and total fertility is two to three children. The fertility of Japan is at the low end of the European scale. Other highly industrialized areas outside of Europe—the United States, the Soviet Union, Australia, New Zealand and Canada—have birth rates between eighteen and twenty-two per 1,000 and a total fertility of two and a half to three and a half children.

Low or rapidly falling mortality—As a consequence of the invention and application of low cost techniques of public health, underdeveloped areas have recently experienced a fall in mortality more rapid than ever seen before. They have not had to wait while the gradual process of developing medical science took place; nor have they had to depend on the possibly more rapid but still difficult process of constructing major sanitary engineering works and building up of a large inventory of expensive hospitals, public health services and highly trained doctors. Instead, the underdeveloped areas have been able to import low-cost measures of controlling disease, measures developed for the most part in the highly industrialized countries. The use of residual insecticides to provide effective protection against malaria at no more than twenty-five cents per capita per year is an outstanding example. Other innovations include antibiotics and chemotherapy, and extend to the discovery of relatively low-cost ways of providing a safe water supply and adequate environmental sanitation in villages that in other ways remain little touched by modernization.

Accelerating population growth—The result of a precipitous decline in mortality while the birth rate remains essentially unchanged is, of course, a rapid acceleration in population growth, reaching in some instances rates of three to three and one-half per cent per year. The underdeveloped areas with more moderate growth rates of one and one-half to two and one-half per cent per year are typically in the midst of a rapid decline in death rates, and are experiencing steep increases in the rate of growth of their populations.

A very young age distribution—The high fertility of low-income countries produces a large proportion of children and a small proportion, in consequence, of adults in the economically most productive ages. The underdeveloped countries have forty to forty-five per cent of their population under age fifteen, in contrast with a maximum of twenty-five to thirty per cent in the highly industrialized countries. Differences in mortality among countries, whether industrialized or not, have only slight effect on the distribution of the population by age, and specifically on the proportion of the population that children constitute. Indeed, the effect of a lower death rate on the proportion of children is in a surprising direction. Mortality is typically reduced the most in infancy and early childhood; and if fertility remains unchanged, a reduction in mortality of the sort usually occurring increases the proportion of children and reduces rather than increases the average age.

Density ranging from low to high—There are great variations in population density from one low-income area to another, with fewer than ten persons per square mile in Bolivia, and nearly 800 in South Korea.

In this chapter we shall consider how these characteristics of the population affect the process of industrialization or modernization to which the low income areas aspire. Their populations at present suffer from inadequate diets, enjoy at best primitive and overcrowded housing, have a modest education or no formal education at all (if adult) and rarely attend school (if children), and are often productively employed for only a fraction of the year. These populations suffer all of the misery and degradation associated with poverty. They naturally wish to enjoy the universal education, adequate diet, housing equipped with modern amenities, the long and generally healthy life, the opportunity for productive work and extensive voluntary leisure that the highly industrialized countries have shown to be possible. To do so the underdeveloped countries must modernize their economies.

The changes in social and economic structure that make up the process of modernization or industrialization are many and profound. More productive techniques must displace traditional methods of manufacturing, agriculture, trade, transport and communications. Economic activity must become more diversified and more specialized. The emphasis in production must shift from extractive industries, especially agriculture, to manufacturing, trade and communications. The interchange of goods through a monetary medium on widespread markets must replace local consumption of goods produced on the farm or exchanged only in small village markets. The labor force must be transformed from illiteracy to literacy. A sufficient supply must be found and trained of what has come to be known as "high talent manpower"—doctors, lawyers, engineers, entrepreneurs and managers. Production must shift from small, family-oriented enterprises into large, impersonal, professionally supervised organizations. However, many of these essential changes are related only indirectly to demographic characteristics such as growth and age distribution.

To explore in detail these indirect relationships would go far beyond the scope of this chapter. Here only two important aspects of industrialization or modernization will be considered. One aspect is increasing income per person as a consequence (and an index) of industrialization, and the other is the attainment or maintenance of productive employment for the labor force.

Population and Income Per Head

Examining the implications of population change for the growth of real income we shall consider nations rather than areas within nations. The selection of the nation as the unit for analysis implies that gains or losses of population through migration can generally be considered of negligible importance. There are a few exceptions (perhaps four or five small countries that can expect gains or losses from migration of important magnitude compared to natural increase), but for the majority of underdeveloped countries and certainly for the larger ones there is no such realistic likelihood.

For somewhat different reasons, the possibility of alternative courses of mortality can also be ignored, at least for a generation or two. The basis for paying little attention to different possible courses of mortality is that the technical feasibility of reducing mortality to lower levels— of increasing expectation of life at birth at least to some fifty or sixty years—has been widely demonstrated in the underdeveloped areas themselves. Unless the effort to start and continue the process of modernization fails completely, or unless there is a breakdown in world order, the attainment and maintenance, at least for a short time, of low mortality rates seems potentially within the reach of most low-income countries. It does not appear that widespread famine or even severe increases in malnutrition are a necessary consequence in the next few decades, even if the low-income countries experience population growth rates of two to three and one-half per cent.

The agricultural and industrial technology that can be introduced into low-income countries is, in a sense, parallel to the medical technology that can be imported to achieve a rapid reduction in mortality rates. Rates of increase in agricultural output of at least three or four per cent a year appear technically feasible, even in such a densely settled, highly agricultural country as India. If the birth rate in India is not reduced, the population will probably double in the next generation from about 450 million to about 900 million persons. Agricultural experts consider it feasible within achievable limits of capital investment to double Indian agricultural output within the next twenty or twenty-five years. In the short run, then, it can be assumed, provisionally at least, that mortality reduction can be achieved and maintained.

Finally, if sickness can be reduced and death postponed within the resources available to the health authorities in the underdeveloped countries, assisted by the World Health Organization, UNICEF, and directly by the industrialized countries, it is scarcely imaginable that by deliberate policy these opportunities would be foregone. In other words, the only factor that can be realistically considered as variable in causing population change by deliberate policy is fertility. We shall be concerned here with the implications, for the growth in per capita income and for the provision of productive employment, of alternative possible future courses of fertility. The specific alternatives to be considered are the maintenance of fertility at its current level (which would involve in most underdeveloped countries the continuation of an essentially horizontal trend that has already continued for generations) and, as the contrasting alternative, a rapid reduction in fertility, amounting to fifty per cent of the initial level and occupying a transitional period of about twenty-five years.

We will inquire what effects these contrasting trends in fertility would have on three important population characteristics: first, the burden of dependency, defined as the total number of persons in the population divided by the number in the labor force ages (fifteen to sixty-four); second, the rate of growth of the labor force, or, more precisely, the annual per cent rate of increase of the population fifteen to sixty-four; and third, the density of the population, or, more precisely, the number of persons at labor force age relative to land area and other resources. Then we shall consider how these three characteristics of dependency, rate of growth, and density influence the increase in per capita income.

ALTERNATIVE POPULATION PROJECTIONS

It is possible to translate assumptions about the future course of mortality and fertility in a specific population into numerical estimates of the future size and age composition of that population. Table 1 presents the projection one hundred fifty years into the future of a hypothetical initial population of one million persons with an age distribution and fertility and mortality rates typical of a Latin American country. The current birth rate is about forty-four per 1,000; the current death rate is about fourteen per 1,000, so that the population is growing at three per cent per year. The current expectation of life at birth is about fifty-three years, and the average number of children born by age forty-five is slightly over six. It is assumed that in the next thirty years the expectation of life at birth will rise to approximately seventy years, so that mortality risks at each age become closely comparable to today's experience in the most highly industrialized countries. Once the expectation of life reaches seventy years, no further improvement is assumed. If this projection of one million persons is multiplied by 90, it would fit Brazil; by 48, it would fit Mexico, starting in 1969.

The initial population and the expected mortality risks at each age in the future are the same for the two projected populations. However, two contrasting assumptions are made with regard to the future course of fertility. In one projection, it is assumed that the current rates of

Table 1. Illustrative Projections of the Population of an Underdeveloped Area

(Initial population 1,000,000 persons. Initial age distribution, fertility, and mortality typical of Latin America north of Uruguay. Mortality rapidly improving.)

Projection A—Fertility continues unchanged.

Projection B—Fertility falls linearly by fifty per cent in twenty-five years, thereafter unchanged.

				Population in Thousands					
	Year	0	10	20	30	40	50	60	150
Projection A	0–14	434	616	870	1,261	1,840	2,655	3,848	110,700
	15–64	534	718	996	1,406	2,003	2,901	4,204	120,800
	65+	32	43	65	90	132	180	245	14,000
	Total	1,000	1,377	1,931	2,757	3,975	5,736	8,297	245,500
Projection B	0–14	434	567	637	676	783	901	994	3,014
	15–64	534	718	985	1,287	1,573	1,869	2,181	6,613
	65+	32	43	65	90	132	180	245	850
	Total	1,000	1,328	1,687	2,053	2,488	2,950	3,420	10,477

child-bearing at each age of women continue indefinitely into the future. In the other projection, it is assumed that fertility rates are reduced each year for twenty-five years by two per cent of their initial value, so that in twenty-five years fertility is reduced by a total of fifty per cent. After twenty-five years, this projection is based on a continuation of fertility at fifty per cent of current levels. Note that there is no difference in the first fifteen years in the projected population over age fifteen. Differences in fertility such as are assumed between these alternative projected populations inevitably affect the child population before the adult population is affected. In fact, at the end of twenty-five years, when fertility for one population has fallen by fifty per cent, the population fifteen to sixty-four is only four per cent greater in the high fertility projection. It is nine per cent greater after thirty years. In the more distant future the divergence becomes increasingly rapid. After about sixty-two years the high fertility population would have twice as many people in the labor force ages, and by 150 years it would have eighteen times as many.

The three population characteristics whose implications are to be examined here are of differing relative significance in the short run, over an intermediate period, and in the long run. In the first twenty-five or thirty years the age distribution effect, or the difference in burden of dependency, is almost the sole factor at work. There is a rapidly widening difference between the projected populations in the burden of dependency during the first generation (Figure 1). This difference in dependency once established then continues more or less unchanged. Starting in about twenty years there develops first a slight and then a widening difference in the rate of growth of the population aged fifteen to sixty-four. This difference in rate of increase reaches a maximum value, at which it thereafter remains, in about sixty-five to seventy years (or forty to fifty years after fertility levels off). The period of widening differences in the growth rate will be considered as an intermediate one separating the short and the long run. The two projections have essentially constant differences in age composition and rate of growth in the long run (from sixty-five to seventy-five years on). During the intermediate period there develops an increasingly conspicuous difference in the size of the two labor forces, and therefore in the density of the labor force relative to resources. In the long run the difference in density assumes overwhelming dimensions. For example, in something less than three hundred years the high fertility population would be a thousand times bigger than the low fertility population.

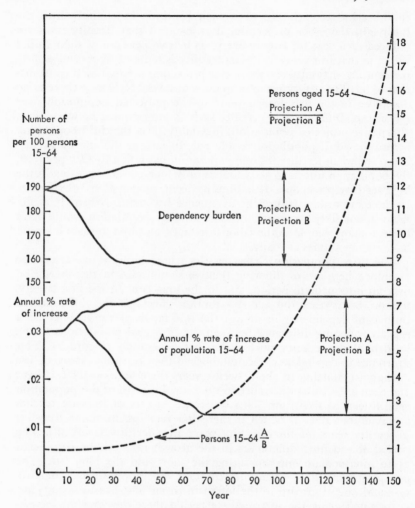

FIGURE 1. Dependency Burden (Total Number of Persons 15–64); Relative Size of the Population 15–64; and Annual Rate of Increase of Population 15–64 in Two Model Projections (Projection A, Fertility Unchanged, Projection B, Fertility Reduced Linearly by 50% in 25 Years, Thereafter Constant)

Source: Office of Population Research, Princeton University.

To sum up: In the short run there is a reduction in the burden of dependency in the low fertility relative to the high fertility population. This difference reaches a stable maximum in some thirty years. In addition to this effect there begins to develop in the intermediate period a widening difference in the rate of growth of the population of labor force age. This difference attains a maximum (thereafter maintained) within seventy years. The cumulative effect of differences in rates of growth of the labor force in the long run produces overwhelming differences between the high fertility and low fertility population in the size or density of the labor force.

ECONOMIC DEVELOPMENT AND DEMOGRAPHIC VARIABLES

We shall consider primarily the implications of our demographic variables for the capacity of the economy to divert effort and resources from producing for current consumption to producing for the enhancement of future productivity. In other words, it will be assumed that to accelerate the process of modernization an economy must increase its level of net investment. Net investment here means additions to factories, roads, irrigation networks, fertilizer plants and other productive facilities. It also can include in a broad definition resources and effort devoted to education and training. It is not an intended implication that merely stepping up the rate of new investment automatically insures a major speed-up in industrialization, or assures the attainment of the fastest possible pace of modernization. Resources mobilized for productive purposes must be wisely allocated. Adequate leadership must be found for the new forms of productive organization that an industrialized society requires. Long-standing customs and traditions must be altered if new and more effective techniques of production are to be employed. In other words, a high level of net investment is a *necessary* but not a *sufficient* condition for a rapid pace of industrialization. In the ensuing analysis it will be assumed that the other crucial elements in modernization are present.

AGE DISTRIBUTION AND INVESTMENT

At the end of twenty-five years there is only a four per cent difference in the size of the labor force or, more precisely, a four per cent difference in the number of persons fifteen to sixty-four. Let us suppose that productive employment can be found for all males of labor force age seeking employment and for all females who are not bound to housekeeping duties by lack of education, tradition, and the necessity to care for small children and who also are in search of productive employment. Let us assume further that twenty-five years from now the progress toward modernization has included the establishment of virtually universal primary education, so that the effective age of entry in the labor force is not before age fifteen. Let us also make the provisional assumption, which we shall re-examine shortly, that national income is, in the twenty-fifth year, the same for the two projected populations. If the reader objects that this provisional assumption seems unrealistic because the high fertility population would have some four per cent more persons of labor force age, let him consider the offsetting fact that the low fertility population would contain only about half as many young infants and half as many pregnant women. If allowance is made for the greater number of women free to work outside the home, the number of persons actually available for productive employment would not really be four per cent less in the low fertility population but might actually be slightly greater. It is certainly reasonable to disregard the small difference in size of population over age fifteen.

If there were the same total national income to be utilized by the two projected populations, the pressure toward utilizing nearly all of it for consumption would be substantially greater in the high fertility population, as a direct result of the greater burden of dependency that must be borne by the labor force. In the high fertility population after twenty-five years, there would be ninety-six persons in the dependent ages for every one hundred persons in the productive ages, while in the low fertility population there would be only sixty-five dependents for every one hundred persons fifteen to sixty-four.

The pressure to spend a higher fraction of national income on consumption can take many forms in different kinds of economies. In a capitalist economy, where investment is financed out of private savings, the fact that families with a large number of children find it more difficult to save reduces the volume of savings and hence the level of investment. When low-income families are not an important source of savings, higher fertility creates social pressure to increase the share of national income received by the poorest earners (the non-savers) in order to maintain minimum standards of consumption.

High fertility can depress private savings in two ways: (1) by reducing the volume of savings by individual families when such savings are an important component of the national total; (2) by increasing the proportion of national income that must accrue to non-savers if standards of consumption play any part in determining the earnings of low-income families.

When it is the government rather than individual entrepreneurs that provides a large proportion of national investment, fertility affects the level of investment through its effect on the capacity of the government to raise money through taxation. Suppose the government attempts to maximize the fund it mobilizes for net investment. For any given level of deprivation that it is prepared to impose, it can raise more taxes from a low fertility population than from a high fertility population with the same national income and the same number of adults in each. Even if the government does not calculate the maximum revenue it can assess, the existence of such factors as exemptions for children would automatically reduce income tax revenues.

After this lengthy review we reach a simple conclusion. Given the same labor force and the same total national income, a low fertility population will achieve a higher level of net investment than a high fertility population. It will therefore be able to make larger additions to the productive capacity of the country and achieve a higher national product in the next year. In addition, the population with a higher burden of child dependency feels a constant pressure to divert investment funds to less productive or at least to less immediately productive uses. To meet given target dates for achieving universal literacy or universal primary education, more funds must be spent on education. In a population of large families rather than small, more construction must be diverted to housing rather than to factories or hydroelectric plants.

During a short-run period of twenty-five to thirty years, the age-distribution effect of declining fertility enhances the capacity of the economy to increase its net investment, and to utilize investment in more immediately productive ways. The labor force available for productive employment during the short-run period is the same, or perhaps a little larger during the first fifteen years because persons over fifteen would be the same in number and more women could participate in productive employment. Actual numbers available for employment probably become equal in the two projections some time between twenty-five and thirty years after the decline of fertility starts. The resources available would presumably be identical. In consequence, there emerges a conclusion that may seem paradoxical. During a period of twenty-five or thirty years, at least, after fertility reduction begins, the population reducing its fertility would produce a more rapidly growing national product than a population which kept its fertility unchanged. This more rapid growth would cumulate into a consequentially higher total product at the end of the thirty-year period. In other words, in the short run not only does a population with reduced fertility enjoy the benefit of dividing the national product among a smaller number of consumers, it enjoys the additional benefit of having a larger national product to divide.

EFFECTS OF LABOR FORCE GROWTH

After twenty-five or thirty years declining fertility begins to cause major differences in the growth rate, and later on major differences in the size of the adult population. The difference in dependency burden reaches a maximum by about forty years, thereafter remaining unchanged. The high fertility labor force must continue, as in the short run, to share what it produces with a distinctly greater number of dependents, and this necessity continues to impair the capacity of the economy to attain a high level of investment. But after the short run a new element, the different rate of growth of the labor force itself, assumes important dimensions.

The significance of the growth of the labor force for income per head is that higher rates of growth imply a higher level of needed investment to achieve a given per capita output, although there is nothing about faster growth that generates a greater supply of investible resources. A larger labor force requires a larger stock of productive facilities in order to have the same productivity per head. The per cent of national income that must be invested merely to keep productivity from declining is some three times the annual per cent rate of increase of the labor force. In other words, if the labor force were growing by three per cent a year, a level of net investment of nine per cent of national income would be required to prevent declining productivity, while if the rate of growth of the labor force were one per cent a year, the needed level of investment for this purpose would be only three per cent of national income.

This rule of thumb assumes that the stock of capital must increase as much as the labor force to prevent a decline of productivity, and assumes further that the stock of capital is roughly three times as large as the current level of national income. Yet the faster growing labor force has no intrinsic advantages in achieving a high level of savings to finance the needed higher level of investment. It needs more investment but has inherent advantages in achieving more.

Another way of presenting the difference between a rapidly growing and a slowly growing labor force is to consider the effect of net investment at the respectable rate of fifteen per cent of national income. A population with a rate of growth of three per cent in its labor force can with such a level of net investment add about two per cent per year to the endowment of capital per worker. If the labor force were growing at one per cent, the annual increase in the stock of capital per worker would be four per cent.

An economy where additional members of the labor force settle on empty land, a "frontier society," is a partial exception to the above line of reasoning. If frontier settlement provides an outlet for the growth in the labor force, it is possible that new members provide most of their own capital—by clearing land, constructing roads, building log houses, etc. Under these hypothetical circumstances the rate of capital formation might be automatically higher with a more rapidly growing labor force. However, it is uncertain whether there are genuine instances of this kind of frontier settlement in the world today. Indonesia has attempted to resettle families from densely populated and rapidly growing Java to the relatively empty land in Borneo. However, the Indonesian government has felt impelled to make a generous capital investment in the form of tools and equipment for each family, the numbers involved have been at most a trivial fraction of the annual increase in Java's population, and many of the pioneers have returned to Java after a short period.

Most underdeveloped countries find it difficult to invest as much as fifteen per cent of their national incomes, and hence will find it necessary for the next generation to utilize more than half of their investment merely to provide capital for the growing labor force. In the short run a reduction of fertility would not affect this necessity. However, even in the short run the age distribution advantages of reduced fertility would increase the level of net investment that would be attained. During the intermediate period, when reduced fertility results in a substantially slower growth of the labor force, the age distribution advantage would continue. A greater capacity to allocate output to investment would be combined with a less imperative necessity to invest merely to keep up with the growth of the labor force.

EFFECT OF DENSITY

The question of population density tends to be the dominant concept in most casual thought about the population problems of underdeveloped areas. The notion of excessive density is certainly implicit in the term "overpopulation." The underlying idea is that when there are too many workers relative to the available resources, per capita output is smaller than it would be with a smaller number of workers. Given gross enough differences in the numbers of workers being compared, it is certainly possible in principle to establish that overpopulation in this sense exists. For example, in 150 years the high fertility population that we projected would be eighteen times as large as the population that would result from fifty per cent reduction in fertility. Even the labor force with reduced fertility would imply a density more than twelve times greater than at present, while the population with sustained fertility would involve a density more than 200 times greater than at present. There is little doubt that in most countries a density 200 times greater would have a depressing effect upon per capita output compared to a density twelve times greater.

There are, however, two reasons for doubting the immediate usefulness of the concept of density in considering population problems of underdeveloped areas. The first is that in this period of human history few countries have any genuine freedom of choice of policy that would have an important effect on population density (or, more specifically, on the density of the labor force) in the short run. There are few areas where realistic alternatives of promoting or retarding international migration would have an important effect upon density. It is unlikely, and I would argue strongly undesirable, that an underdeveloped country should contemplate a deliberate restraint on its public health programs in order to retard the decline of mortality and thus prevent an increase of population density. As is shown in Figure 1, a reduction in fertility does not have an important effect on density for a long time in the future. The difference in the size of the labor force is less than ten per cent thirty years after a rapid and extensive decline in fertility begins. After thirty years, however, the difference in density between sustained and reduced fertility rapidly mounts, reaching a factor of two in about sixty years, a factor of three in seventy-five years, and a factor of eighteen after 150 years. In other words, so far as acceptable and attainable policies are concerned, only in the relatively distant future can the density of the labor force relative to resources be affected. In the meantime the policy that would have a long-run effect on density, namely one that reduces fertility, would through changes in dependency and differences in the annual rate of growth of the labor force have produced major economic effects.

A second reservation about the relevance of density is that it is of clearcut importance only in a closed economy—i.e., one that does not trade extensively—or in an economy where the principal industry is extractive. Only in extractive industries—mining, agriculture, and forestry—are resources as related to numbers of workers a dominant element in productivity. For example, if India were compelled to continue to employ seventy per cent of its labor force in agriculture, increasing density would inevitably mean smaller average holdings. The average holding today is only about two acres per person aged fifteen to sixty-four dependent on agriculture, and the possibility of bringing new areas under cultivation is limited.

In non-extractive industries international trade can greatly reduce the effect of limited resources. In all industries, extractive or otherwise, productivity is determined to a large degree by the stock of capital per worker. The underdeveloped areas have in common a small endowment of productive equipment per worker relative to the industrialized countries; in other words, the underdeveloped countries all have a "high density" of workers relative to capital, whether the country appears to be sparsely or densely settled relative to land and other resources.

Two examples indicate the dubious relevance of the concept of overpopulation where non-extractive industries are dominant and a large volume of trade is possible. One is the narrow strip of territory extending from Boston to Washington along the east coast of the United States. There is a 400 mile long line of contiguous counties with an aggregate area of about 14,000 square miles and an aggregate population in 1960 of about 28,000,000, or a population density of more than 2,000 per square mile. There are few if any areas of similar extent in the world with a higher density. The median family income of this strip was $6,600 in 1960, just a thousand dollars more than the median for the United States as a whole. Is it overpopulated? It would certainly be difficult to demonstrate that per capita output would be greater if the population density were less. Of course this area belongs to a large market—the United States and its territories—where trade is unrestricted. Extractive industries play a trivial role in the output of this area. It can readily import the raw materials and semi-finished products that it requires in exchange for the finished goods and services it produces.

The second example, Hong Kong, shows that the possibility of importing raw materials and semi-finished goods in exchange for finished goods and services is not limited to a region within a country. Hong Kong has a population of nearly 4 million on a land area of 398 square miles, with a resultant density of about 10,000 persons per square mile. Land for new buildings on Victoria Island is dredged from the harbor. After the war Hong Kong had a very low per capita income, and its density was inflated by an influx of refugees. Nevertheless Hong Kong has achieved increases in national produce of seven to ten per cent per year and has probably doubled its real output in a decade. It obtains its needed imports (including food) on the world market. Imports from Mainland China constituted only 22 per cent of Hong Kong's imports from all countries in 1967. Hong Kong has very important special advantages, especially in terms of human capital, as data from the 1961 census show. The refugees that swarmed into Hong Kong were not illiterate peasants but had an average educational attainment well above what must characterize China as a whole. Among the immigrants were experienced entrepreneurs from Shanghai. In short, Hong Kong was endowed with an energetic, literate and partially trained labor force and had no scarcity of organizational and entrepreneurial skills. It nevertheless remains a fact that an extraordinarily high density of population relative to resources has not prevented an extraordinary rapid increase in per capita income.

In the normal course of industrialization the proportion of the population engaged in agriculture and other extractive industries steadily declines. In the history of every highly industrialized area a period was reached during which the number of persons dependent on agriculture was stabilized so that all increases in population of labor force age caused increases only in non-agricultural employment. The period of unchanging numbers engaged in agriculture has typically been followed by a shrinkage in the absolute number. This sequence has been typical both in countries where the initial density of agricultural settlement was very high, such as Japan, or where it was relatively low, as in the United States or New Zealand. The implications of this sequence for employment in industrializing countries will be considered later. Here its relevance is that for countries in the earlier stages of economic development some of the increases in the labor force must seek employment in extractive industries. If the agricultural population is already densely settled (as in India), this necessity undoubtedly constitutes a greater hardship or barrier to rapidly increasing incomes than in a less densely settled country.

As was noted earlier, the underdeveloped countries all suffer from what might be called a high density of population relative to *capital*. Therefore the effects not only of the age distribution but also of the rate of growth of the labor force (with their respective implications for the ease with which capital formation can proceed and for the rate at which it must proceed to attain given objectives in per capita output) operate in sparsely settled as well as in densely settled countries. In very sparsely settled countries the adverse effect upon the possible reduction of density relative to capital of rapid growth of the labor force may be partially offset by an increasingly advantageous relationship between numbers and land area and other resources. A larger population may, when original density is unusually low, permit the use of more efficient large-scale operations. This possibility does not imply, however, that the more rapid the rate of growth the better. Additional capital for the additional labor force is still essential, and rapid growth prevents an increase in the capital worker rates. Moreover, from a strictly economic point of view the most advantageous way to attain a larger labor force is through immigration, because it is possible by this means to obtain additional labor without incurring the expense of childhood dependency.

DECLINING FERTILITY AND PER CAPITA INCOME: SUMMARY

A reduction in fertility has the immediate effect (during the first generation after the decline begins) of reducing the burden of child dependency without any major effect on the size of the labor force. After twenty or twenty-five years the decline in fertility begins to effect a major reduction in the rate of growth of the labor force. In the more remote future, beginning after forty or fifty years and with increasing importance with the further passage of time, reduced fertility produces a population of lower density—with a smaller labor force relative to the available resources. The age distribution effect of reduced fertility operates to produce during the first generation a larger total national product than would result if fertility had not been reduced. The greater rise in total output results from the fact that the same number of producers—the same number of persons eligible for participation in the labor force—is accompanied by a smaller number of consumers. The smaller number of consumers decreases the fraction of national output that must be allocated to current consumption, and thus promotes the mobilization of resources for economic growth. Both private savings and the ability of the government to raise funds for development are increased.

In addition, a smaller number of consumers (especially children) permits the expenditure of savings and tax receipts in ways that raise national output more (or more immediately) than other uses. Less must be spent for primary education, housing and "social overhead" purposes generally.

Another indirect effect of reduced fertility is that, as a result of larger per capita consumption, the labor force is perhaps more productive because of better nutrition, and because of the effects of rising consumption in combatting apathy, and in providing better work incentives. These effects of a reduced number of consumers relative to the producers in the population caused in the short run by a decline in fertility continue into the future so long as fertility remains below its former level. Starting after twenty-five or thirty years is the additional effect of reduced fertility in slowing down the growth of the labor force. A reduced rate of growth of the labor force means that a given level of net investment can be used to add more to the per capita endowment of the labor force in productive equipment than if the labor force were growing more rapidly.

In the long run the slower rate of growth that reduced fertility brings would result in much lower density of population than with the continuation of high fertility. Even with a fifty per cent reduction in fertility, the population in most underdeveloped areas would grow very substantially during the next two or three generations. For example, in the projection presented earlier showing typical prospects for Latin American countries, with fertility falling by one half, density would be multiplied by 2.46 in thirty years and by 1.71 in the ensuing thirty years, a total increase of 4.2 times in sixty years. In spite of greatly reduced fertility, the density of workers relative to resources would increase by a factor of something like four in the next two generations.

Brazil is often cited as a country that might derive economic benefits from more dense settlement. Even with a fifty per cent reduction in fertility, the population of Brazil aged fifteen to sixty-four will have increased from 38 million to 161 million in the next sixty years. This would give Brazil a population at these ages sixty years from now forty-two per cent larger than that of the United States today. It is hard to argue that this density would be too small to achieve an efficient exploitation of Brazil's resources, especially since much of Brazil's vast area is of uncertain economic value. Not all underdeveloped areas have as high a current growth potential as Latin America. Current fertility is in many instances below that found in Mexico or Brazil, and in other instances success in reducing mortality is somewhat behind the achievements of the more advanced Latin American countries. In India, for example, where current fertility is probably lower than that of Mexico, Brazil, or Colombia and current mortality higher, the increase in the labor force in the next two generations, if fertility were to be cut in half in the next twenty-five years, would be only two and a half to three times rather than more than four times. It should be added that any increases in density are scarcely advantageous to India's economy.

In sum, the population density that would result from a fifty per cent reduction in fertility in the next twenty-five years would in almost every underdeveloped area be at least adequate for the efficient exploitation of the resources available. The much *higher* density that would result from sustained fertility, a margin of higher density that would increase with ever greater rapidity the further into the future one looks, might in the most favorable circumstances cause no insuperable difficulties for a few decades. It might be possible, for example, to offset a high density of population in some areas, as Hong Kong has done, by engaging in trade, provided there remain areas of the world prepared to supply agricultural products and raw materials in exchange for finished goods and services. But in all areas, a prolonged continuation of rapid growth would lead to intolerable overcrowding.

GAINS IN INCOME PER HEAD

It is possible to estimate roughly the cumulative advantage that reduced fertility brings in the form of more rapidly increasing income per head. Such calculations have been made at the Office of Population Research utilizing alternative population projections and concomitant economic projections based on the demographic and economic data of two countries, India and Mexico. In each instance we assumed that increases in savings per consumer were proportional to increases in income per consumer. In calculating the number of "consumers" each child under fifteen was counted as only one half. Thus the calculations make a conservative allowance for the effect of the burden of childhood dependency. These calculations take account of the estimates of government authorities and economists in each country with regard to such matters as the expected productivity of new investments and of the allocation of funds to education, housing, and other social overhead categories. On the basis of precisely equivalent assumptions about the determination of the future growth of national output, national output was projected into the future, in conjunction with two alternative population projections. These alternative population projections were analogous to the illustrative projections that have served as the basis of our discussion here. The contrasting projections for each country assumed a continuation of past trends of declining mortality, and assumed two alternative future courses of fertility: unchanged on the one hand, and reduced in a linear fashion by fifty per cent in twenty-five years on the other.

In spite of different initial economic and demographic conditions—Mexico has higher fertility and lower mortality than India, a substantially higher initial per capita income, and is further advanced in most aspects of industrialization and modernization, having for example a relatively larger manufacturing sector and a relatively smaller agricultural sector in the economy—the estimated proportionate gains resulting from reduced fertility were almost identical in the two countries. Table 2 shows the ratio of income per consumer with reduced fertility

Table 2. Income per equivalent adult consumer in Projection B (fertility reduced), income per consumer with sustained fertility = 100

Income per consumer in Projection B, income per consumer in A = 100

					Time in years							
0	10	20	30	40	50	60	70	80	90	100	...	150
100	103	114	141	163	186	209	235	264	297	334	...	596

to income per consumer for sustained fertility at various dates following the initiation of the fertility decline. The difference is small at first but amounts to forty per cent after thirty years and more than one hundred per cent in sixty years. After 150 years the low fertility population would have an income per consumer six times as high as the faster growing population with unchanged fertility.

These calculations make no allowance for any adverse effects caused by high density. They allow only for the effect of differences in age distribution and of different rates of growth in the labor force. These projections of the advantages of reduced fertility implicitly assume a world of unlimited resources, and thereby understate the gains a lower birth rate would bring.

DELAYING REDUCTION IN FERTILITY

There is a persuasive *laissez-faire* position on population policy in the pre-industrial countries, based on the following argument. Every country that has become highly industrialized has experienced a decline in fertility amounting to at least fifty per cent of the pre-industrial level. Therefore, the argument runs, public policy should be concentrated on achieving the maximum pace of industrialization. The decline in fertility will take care of itself.

The generalization upon which this argument rests is well founded. All countries that have become predominantly urban, that have shifted away from agriculture as the source of employment for as much as half of the labor force, and that now have adult populations that are at least eighty-five per cent literate have experienced at least a fifty per cent decline in fertility. Included among these countries are: all of Europe (except for Albania); the overseas industrialized countries with predominantly European populations—Australia, New Zealand, Canada and the United States; Japan and the Soviet Union. However, it is far from clear precisely what aspects of industrialization have been instrumental in causing the decline in fertility in these countries. In some instances industrialization had preceded for a long time and had effected major changes in the economy and society before any tangible reduction in fertility occurred. For example, a marked decline did not begin in England and Wales until the 1880's, nor in Japan until about 1925. For countries that are as yet in the early stages of modernization, having very low current per capita incomes, it might take at least thirty to sixty years to attain a state of industrialization that would in itself cause a rapid decline in fertility. In fact the adverse effects of continued high fertility in the interim might in itself postpone the attainment of the needed state of advanced industrialization. Table 3

Table 3. Income per equivalent adult consumer, with immediately reduced fertility, income per consumer with fertility reduced after 30 years = 100

Income per consumer in Projection B, income in projection with delayed decline in fertility = 100

					Time in years							
0	10	20	30	40	50	60	70	80	90	100	...	150
100	103	114	141	158	163	149	144	141	141	141	...	141

shows the ratio of income per consumer in a population where a fifty per cent decline in fertility spread over twenty-five years begins immediately to output per consumer in a population where fertility remains unchanged for thirty years and then begins a fifty per cent reduction in twenty-five years. Note that the advantage of the early reduction in fertility reaches a maximum in about fifty years and then settles back to a permanent advantage of about forty per cent (the gain previously noted at the end of thirty years from a decline in fertility).

The calculation underlying this table was based on the assumption that the relative advantage to be gained by fertility reduction shown in Table 2 would apply no matter when the reduction began. Again as in Table 2 itself no allowance is made for the adverse effects of higher density. The long-run population resulting from a reduction in fertility postponed by thirty years would be sixty-four per cent larger than the population arising from an immediate reduction in fertility. Table 3 makes no allowance for the possibility that a population sixty-four per cent bigger would because of greater density tend to have lower per capita output.

In sum, the advantages of an early reduction in fertility shown in Table 3 are a minimum estimate. To wait for an automatic decline in fertility (if a program of family planning could cause an earlier reduction) is to forego *at least* the relative gains in income per consumer shown in this table. Any allowance for the deleterious effects of greater density would serve to increase the estimated cost of postponement. There is moreover the possibility that the slower progress of industrialization with sustained fertility, especially when great increases in an already high density are involved, might postpone the expected attainment of an "automatic" fertility decline.

Population and the Labor Force

It is of course a drastic oversimplification to treat industrialization and modernization wholly in terms of increases in income per head. Such increases are surely a valid and necessary objective of economic development, but there are other goals widely shared in the underdeveloped areas, including better health and improved and more widespread education, rightly viewed as values in themselves, as well as means of achieving larger incomes. A nearly universal goal is that of providing productive employment for male adults and for a proportion of adult women that steadily increases as modernization proceeds. This goal, like those of better health and education, is considered as valuable in its own right, because of the degrading effect of unemployment or of unproductive employment.

The problems of "unemployment" and "underemployment," which are the subject of so much comment in the underdeveloped areas, are essentially reflections of the poverty and low productivity to which these areas are subject. Underemployment is sometimes defined as a situation in which a reduction in the number of persons engaged in a given activity would not cause an important reduction in total output from the activity in question. Examples are the presence of more porters in a railway station than are needed to carry the normal load of luggage, farming operations where a traditional set of tasks are divided among whatever family members have the responsibility for operating the farm, or a cluster of small retail shops carrying essentially identical merchandise in which the clerks or proprietors are idle most of the day because of the scarcity of customers. In most underdeveloped areas such examples are common. The existence of essentially redundant man-power that these examples indicate is called "underemployment" rather than "unemployment" because the redundancy does not show itself in the form of large numbers actively looking for work. The measurement of unemployment (and the technical definition of unemployment) has become increasingly a matter of determining the number of persons actively seeking jobs.

In most underdeveloped areas a major increase in the number of productive jobs would be needed to make serious inroads into current underemployment and unemployment. The prospective rapid growth in the labor force that such countries face adds greatly to the difficulties of achieving satisfactory employment goals. During the first generation the number of additional productive jobs that must be provided is scarcely affected by the course of fertility. The labor force thirty years following the start of a fifty per cent reduction in fertility spread evenly over a twenty-five year period is less than ten per cent smaller than the labor force resulting from a continuation of unchanged fertility. In a typical Latin American population the labor force would increase in thirty years by a factor of 2.44 should fertility be reduced, and 2.67 should fertility remain unchanged. In either case the provision of adequate employment opportunities is a job of frightening proportions. An annual increase of about three per cent or more in the number of jobs is required if unemployment and underemployment are not to increase.

In underdeveloped areas the barrier to more adequate employment opportunity is not primarily that lack of sufficient effective demand which many economists see as the source of the apparently chronic problem of attaining full employment in the United States. The simultaneous existence of unemployed persons and idle capital equipment in the United States (a conspicuous example is the steel industry) is not the situation typical of the underdeveloped countries. The absence of opportunities for productive employment is primarily the result of insufficient productive equipment and resources for labor to work with, compounded by the lack of education and training on the part of the labor force itself.

In the earlier discussion it was seen that a population with reduced fertility has important advantages in its capacity to accumulate capital. It also can more readily provide a rapid attainment of specified educational standards. Consequently, even during the first twenty-five or thirty years following the start of fertility decline, when the number of new jobs needed each year is not much affected by reduced fertility, the advantages in reduced dependency that lower fertility brings would, by enabling higher levels of investment, permit the more rapid expansion of employment opportunity. In the longer run the reduced rate of growth of the labor force resulting from lower fertility would make the achievement of adequate employment opportunities much easier. After sixty years, for example, the rate of increase in the labor force in our model projection for a Latin American country would be 3.7 per cent if fertility were sustained, and only 1.3 per cent if fertility were reduced. By that time the number of persons sixteen to sixty-four in the lower fertility projection would be nearly 4.2 times as great as today, and with sustained fertility it would be eight times as great.

The magnitude of the problem of providing future jobs in the underdeveloped countries can be better appreciated when one considers the typical change in the composition of employment that accompanies the process of industrialization. In general terms the change in patterns of employment is one of increasing diversity, with reduced proportions in the traditional occupations, especially in agriculture. If the employment history in the industrialized countries is examined, the universal trend during the process of industrialization is found to be a steadily decreasing proportion in agriculture. In fact all of the more highly industrialized countries have reached or passed through a phase in which the *number* in agriculture remains constant, so that all of the increases in the population of labor force age are absorbed in the nonagricultural sectors of the economy. This phase has then typically been followed by a decline in the absolute number of persons dependent on agriculture. It is not surprising that such a decline has been experienced in countries such as England and Wales, known for their emphasis on manufacturing and for their exports of manufactured products and imports of agricultural products. It is somewhat unexpected that a decline should have occurred in Denmark, a major exporter of agricultural produce. Decreases in the absolute number in agriculture have also been recorded in countries of very different densities, ranging from England and Japan on the one hand to the United States, the Soviet Union, and New Zealand on the other.

At some stage, then, an industrializing country must, if it follows the sequence common to the history of the now industrialized countries, look to the non-agricultural sector of the economy for the provision of employment opportunities sufficient for the whole increase in the labor force. This pattern of employment must occur even if modernization of the economy consists to a large extent of increases in agricultural output through improvement in agricultural organization and technique. A modernized agricultural economy employs more persons in transportation, processing, marketing, and services than in agriculture proper. Only when agriculture remains in a primitive state of subsistence can the labor force remain predominantly in agricultural employment. Table 4 shows the magnitude of this goal with two

Table 4. Average annual per cent increase in non-agricultural employment required if all of the increased labor force is to be employed outside agriculture

Required annual per cent increase in employment

Per cent in agriculture at t = 0	Projection	Period					
		0–10 years	10–20 years	20–30 years	30–40 years	40–50 years	50–60 years
70	A	7.3	5.9	5.1	4.6	4.4	4.2
	B	7.3	5.7	4.0	2.7	2.2	1.9
60	A	6.2	5.3	4.8	4.4	4.3	4.1
	B	6.2	5.1	3.8	2.6	2.1	1.8
50	A	5.3	4.8	4.5	4.3	4.2	4.0
	B	5.3	4.7	3.5	2.5	2.0	1.8

model population projections and three illustrative different starting points in terms of the proportion of the labor force now engaged in agriculture. In most underdeveloped countries it will be impossible to achieve these rates of increase in non-agricultural employment. They will be forced to continue to increase the number of persons engaged in agriculture. Such continued increases are at best a necessary evil. In fact these unavoidable increases in agricultural employment show the cost of an initial high level of density in a country that has a high proportion of its labor force engaged in agriculture. Such countries cannot provide non-agricultural employment opportunities for the whole of the increase in their labor forces, and because of the small land holdings that high density implies, additions to the labor force in agriculture add mostly to underemployment in this sector.

It is a reasonable, almost an essential objective that within a generation or two most countries should plan to provide non-agricultural employment for the whole of their additions to the labor force. Table 4 shows how greatly eased is the task if fertility is reduced rather than allowed to remain at current high levels.

This sketchy analysis is sufficient to show that the reduction of fertility would play an even more crucial role in attaining the goal of adequate employment opportunities than in the closely related but not identical goal of insuring a more rapid increase in income per consumer.

Summary

The underdeveloped areas in the world for the next fifty years or so have a choice at best between very rapid growth and moderately rapid growth in population. Any low-income country that succeeds in initiating an immediate reduction in fertility would in the short run enjoy a reduction in the burden of child dependency that would permit a higher level of investment and more immediately productive uses of investment.

After twenty-five or thirty years the advantage of reduced dependency would be enhanced by a markedly slower growth of the labor force, making it possible to achieve a faster growth in capital per worker from any given investment, and making it easier to approach the goal of productive employment for all who need it.

In the long run, the slower rate of growth that fertility reduction causes would reduce the overwhelming multiplication of density that continued rapid growth implies.

The additional gains in per capita income resulting from a fifty per cent reduction in fertility occurring within twenty-five years would be about forty per cent in thirty years, 100 per cent in sixty years, and 500 per cent in 150 years, neglecting the effects of density. To postpone the reduction by thirty years is to add sixty-four per cent to the size of the population in the long run, and to suffer a loss in potential long-range gains from the interim reduction in dependency of forty per cent. In sum, a reduction in fertility would make the process of modernization more rapid and more certain. It would accelerate the growth in income, provide more rapidly the possibility of productive employment for all adults who need jobs, make the attainment of universal education easier—and it would have the obvious and immediate effect of providing the women of low-income countries some relief from constant pregnancy, parturition and infant care.

Philip M. Hauser

5

The Population of the United States, Retrospect and Prospect

The United States is perhaps the world's most dramatic example of explosive population growth—combining high natural increase over the years with heavy immigration. The first census of the nation, taken in 1790, recorded fewer than 4 million inhabitants. The population had doubled 5 times by 1950, and may well have doubled again by this century's end. The first three doublings each required about 25 years so that by 1860 the nation had achieved over 31 million inhabitants. The fourth doubling required the 35 years between 1865 and 1900. At the end of the nineteenth century population had reached almost 76 million. The fifth doubling took 50 years. By 1950, United States population exceeded 150 million. The sixth doubling, in prospect, is also likely to take 50 years—for by 2000 the population of the nation may approximate 300 million persons.

This remarkable chronicle of population growth spans the settlement and development of a largely uninhabited and unexploited continent, largely by immigrant Europeans who migrated across their own national boundaries for a variety of reasons, largely economic. In the period from 1820, when the federal government first began to count immigrants, to the present, some 45 million persons came to this nation mainly from Europe. They managed to achieve unparalleled economic growth in developing the resources of the nation and, in the process, prodigiously to increase their numbers.

Despite the heavy immigration, during no intercensal period did net immigration exceed natural increase in the United States—the excess of births over deaths. In 1800, the birth rate has been estimated to have been as high as 55 (births per 1,000 persons per year), a level about as high as ever reached by any nation. But in the early history of the country death rates were also relatively high, probably close to 30 (deaths per 1,000 persons per year). Hence, natural increase, the difference between the two, was about 25, giving an annual growth rate, without immigration, of about 2.5 per cent per year. This historical rate of population increase is not far different from that of contemporary India. With immigration the United States grew at an annual average of over 3 per cent during most of the nineteenth century. In fact, the average annual percentage population increase of the nation exceeded 3 per cent in the first six decades of the nineteenth century but fell to levels of 2.1 to 2.7 per cent during the last four decades of that century.

The peak in immigration was reached during the decade 1901 to 1910, when about 8.8 million immigrants were admitted. Immigration, of course, greatly diminished during World War I. Furthermore, with the passage beginning in the 1920s of laws controlling the admission of persons from abroad, immigration became a relatively minor factor in natural growth. Under present legislation immigration is, in general, restricted to about 400,000 persons per year.

During the nineteenth century the birth rate as well as the death rate of the nation began to decline. The United States was thus among the first nations to experience declining fertility, second probably only to France. The national birth rate tumbled from 55 in 1800 to a low of about 18 during the depression thirties. From the depression low in the 1930s, the birth rate rose in response to economic recovery in the late thirties and early forties—a recovery augmented by the role of the United States as arsenal for the Allied Powers. With demobilization both the marriage and birth rates soared so that the birth rate averaged about 25 (births per 1,000 persons per year) from 1947 to 1958. The birth rate has been declining since 1957 to reach an all time low of 17.4 in 1968.

The death rate of the nation has also declined considerably since 1800. From perhaps the level of 30 in 1800 (deaths per 1,000 persons per year) the death rate had fallen to 17 by 1900, and to less than 10 at the present time. As a result, the rate of natural increase declined from 25 (excess of births over deaths per 1,000 persons per year) to about 7 at the bottom of the depression. It then rose again with the postwar baby boom to a level of about 15 only to fall again with decreased fertility to about 8 in 1968. Thus the national growth rate by reason of natural increase alone, excluding immigration, fell from 2.5 per cent per year in 1800 to .7 per cent during the depression 1930s; rose to 1.5 per cent per year after World War II demobilization; and dropped again to about .8 per cent in 1968.

The decline in the birth rate of the United States since 1957 has led some to believe that the population explosion in the United States has run its course and that we no longer have a problem of excessive growth. Indeed not only laymen but, also, an occasional demographer has heralded the slowdown in growth rate which the nation has experienced between 1957 and 1968. Yet, the fact is that the United States is still faced with enormous population growth during at least the remainder of this century, and that the nation is also faced with the prospect of continuing to pay a high price in human as well as monetary terms for the growth which is still in prospect.

The Total Population Outlook

To understand the population prospect of the nation it is necessary to examine the immediate past and especially the decline in fertility and growth rate since 1958. The birth rate of the nation, after a 12 year postwar "baby boom" initiated with demobilization in 1946, began a decline in 1958 which has persisted to at least July of 1968. The "general" or "crude" birth rate, peaking to 26.6 births per 1,000 total population in 1947, remained at a level of about 25 through 1957. Then in 1958 it began to drop to reach an all-time low of 17.4 in 1968.

A better measurement of month-to-month or year-to-year changes in births is given by the "fertility rate," the number of children born to women of childbearing age, 15 to 44 years. This is a better measurement of changes in natality because in this rate persons below and above reproductive age and males are eliminated in the calculation of the rate. The fertility rate which reached a peak of 122.7 in 1957, has declined steadily since to a level of 84.8 in 1968. However, it is to be noted that at this level the fertility rate was well above the lows of 76 to 79 recorded during the depression years 1933 to 1939.

Downturns or upswings in the birth rate have generally been accompanied by a plethora of pronouncements about their profound implications for the future. What is responsible for the plummeting of the birth rate since 1958 and what is the population outlook over the coming years? What are the implications of population changes taking place?

To begin with, consider the effect on total national population growth of the fertility changes which have occurred and which may be in prospect. Between 1950 and 1960, the population of the nation increased by some 28 million, or by 18.5 per cent, an average annual increase of 1.8 per cent. Since 1960, the decrease in births, in absolute number as well as in rate, has depressed the population growth rate. From an increase of 1.7 per cent per year in 1960 and 1961, the growth of the total population diminished to a 1.0 per cent increase from 1967 to 1968. In absolute numbers the increase in total population which averaged about 2.8 million per year during the fifties declined to an annual average of 2.6 million from 1960 to 1968.

Before proceeding to an examination of the implications of the changes in fertility for future population, let us examine the factors involved in variations in the birth rate. It has been demonstrated by demographers that year-to-year changes in the crude birth rate or the fertility rate provide a quite inadequate basis for assaying fertility trends or making projections into the future. The reason for this is to be found in the almost universal control of family size in the United States. Only about 1 in 20 couples in the nation report they never have employed methods for regulating the number of their children. With birth control is it possible for couples to postpone births under conditions they regard as unfavorable and to draw an advance on the future under conditions regarded as favorable. Since the reproductive period of women spans some 30 years, 15 to 44 years of age, year-to-year measurements of birth rates obscure what may be happening to the total number of children born per couple during the entire reproductive period. This number, called variously "average size of completed family," "mean marital parity" or "cohort fertility," provides a much sounder basis for analyzing fertility trends and making future projections.

One eminent demographer, Professor Norman Ryder of the University of Wisconsin, has calculated that 43 per cent of all the variations in year to year or "period" fertility for cohorts of women born from 1893 to 1938 were attributable to "tempo," that is changes in timing of births rather than to changes in "quantity," that is the number of births during the entire reproductive span. He attributes as the major reason for the decline in the birth rate from 1957 to 1966 "a reversal of tempo," a rise in age of marriage and of age of mother at births.

The reason for the increased age at marriage and at childbirth since 1957 can be traced to the consequences of the postwar baby boom. The tidal wave of babies between 1946 and 1958 has produced a huge

bulge in the number of persons now reaching labor force and reproductive age. It is mainly by reason of their relatively great numbers
that youth unemployment rates have skyrocketed. The number of
young persons under 25 years of age entering the labor force averaged
about 200,000 per year in the quinquennium from 1955 to 1960; and
it soared to triple that number during the 1960s—to about 600,000
per year. The unemployment rate for whites of this age in the 4th
quarter, 1968, was 10.8 and for nonwhites 25.8. Inability to obtain
employment together with the impact of the Vietnam war have operated to reverse the downward movement in age at marriage and at
births, and these changes in tempo have been a major factor in the
depressed birth rates since 1957. Since such changes do not necessarily
affect average size of completed family, it is a grave mistake to use
the declining "period" crude birth rate or "period" fertility rate as a
basis for future population projections.

Future Total Population

The Bureau of the Census in early 1967 projected the population
of the United States to 1990 with age, sex and color detail, and to
2015 for total population. As is the usual practice of demographers,
the Census Bureau calculated "range" projections rather than a "point"
projection. That is, the Bureau of the Census calculated what the
future population would be at varying assumptions of "average size of
completed family" rather than making one projection based on one
fertility assumption. Since the assumptions in respect of mortality and
net in-migration are constant in the projections and are subject to
much less variation, these will be ignored in the discussion which
follows.

The Census has published four projections of future population
varying from a high projection labeled "A" to a low projection labeled
"D". Projection "A" assumed that average completed family size
would gradually move toward a terminal level of 3.35 children per
woman, the number which would be generated if the 1963 birth rate
of women at each age persisted throughout the reproductive period.
Projection "B" assumed a completed average family size of 3.1 children per woman, the level which would be generated with the average
schedule of birth rates at each age of women which obtained in 1964–
65. The "C" projection assumed a completed average number of 2.78
children per woman, that based on experience in 1966. Finally the
"D" projection assumed an average of 2.45 children per woman, that

which would result from the experience of the early 1940s, before the onset of the baby boom.

The estimated population of the United States under each of these assumptions is given below in millions of persons:

	1970	1980	1990	2000	2015
Projection A	208.6	250.5	300.1	361.4	482.1
Projection B	207.3	243.3	286.5	336.0	430.2
Projection C	206.0	235.2	270.8	307.8	373.5
Projection D	204.9	227.7	256.0	282.6	324.5

The difference between the high projection "A" and the low projection "D" by the year 2000 would produce a United States population ranging from about 283 million to about 361 million, or a difference of 78 million persons in the next 32 years. The difference between the high and low projections could reach 157 million by the year 2015, the difference between 482 million and 325 million persons. To consider the shorter run range, note that by 1980 the difference between the high projection of 251 million and the low projection of 228 million totals 23 million—a population greater than the Pacific States combined in 1960 (Washington, Oregon, California, Alaska, Hawaii).

The Bureau of the Census made these population projections before the year-to-year birth rates, the "period" rates, dropped to their postwar low during 1968. How does present fertility compare with the fertility assumptions on which the projections are based? How do these projections compare with the actual population growth which has occurred since they were made?

In 1965, the completed average family size which would be generated by the schedule of birth rates at each age of woman was 2.96 children per woman; and in 1966, it was 2.76. It is estimated by the Census Bureau that the completed average number of children per woman could have dropped to 2.52 in 1968 (for the year ending July 1). This number is well below that assumed for 1968 in Census projections, "A", 3.14 children per woman; and even projection "C", 2.76 children per woman. Moreover, it is only slightly above that assumed in the lowest of the Census projections, "D", 2.60 children per woman by 1968, and 2.45 by the end of the projection period.

Does this mean that the future population of the nation will be below the lowest of the published Census projections? The answer is not necessarily so. Moreover, in all probability the answer is decidedly no.

The reason for these answers is to be deduced from the discussion about "period" and "cohort" fertility above. Just as one swallow does not make a summer, so a decline in period fertility does not necessarily mean a reversal of trend in completed average family size. Period fertility, as has been indicated, is affected by "tempo," age at marriage and age at childbearing as well as by the "quantity" of children born. In consequence, period birth rates have greater swings, up and down, than cohort fertility. That is, year-to-year changes in births, whether measured by the crude birth rate or more refined measurements may be much more affected by changing conditions than the cohort fertility rate—the average number of children born throughout the reproductive span. Thus, it is likely that the Census Bureau's projections will encapsulate the actual population of the nation in the longer run even if the lowest of the projections proves to be too high in the short run. This conclusion is certainly reinforced by three considerations. First, a great increase in women of heaviest childbearing age has just begun. Although both women now in the older and younger childbearing ages have lower fertility rates than did women of the same ages in the 1950s, the number of young women, product of the postwar baby boom, is now rising rapidly. The number of women in the ages of heaviest childbearing, 20 to 29 years, was 13.6 million in July, 1967. But these relatively prolific women will reach 18.3 million by 1975, an increase of 35 per cent. The great increase in women of heaviest childbearing age could produce another tidal wave of babies even if their birth rates at each age declined.

Second, recent national surveys report that, although marriage has been delayed and also birth of first child, women expect to have families as large as their recent predecessors, 3.0 children. Third, there has been a pronounced increase in marriages. The number of marriages began to increase in 1959 and the marriage rate in 1963. Between 1963 and 1967 the increase in the marriage rate averaged 2.7 per cent per year. Between 1967 and 1968 the increase more than doubled reaching 6.2 per cent. It may also be significant, especially since the number of births for 1968, 3,470,000, was the lowest number recorded since 1946, that beginning in October 1968 and for each month through February 1969 (the latest month available as this is written) the number of births has exceeded that for the same month in the preceding year. Thus, it is possible, but not yet established, that the year 1969–1970 could mark the beginning of an upturn in natality and the beginning of a new baby boom which could persist for some 12 years—the length of the postwar baby boom.

In the light of the above considerations which of the Census Bureau's projections is to be considered the "best" one if one must choose only one of the projections—if one must act on the basis of the most likely course of events? This may be necessary for public and private purposes. The United States Office of Education, for example, must make plans on the basis of best judgment of future school population; and industry and business must, similarly, make plans for investment, production and marketing on the basis of the best estimates of the future.

In 1967, the "best" estimate was generally agreed by demographers to be the "B" projection—the projection which gives a population of 243 million by 1980 and 336 million by 2000. By reason of the decline in fertility which has occurred the "D" projection is certainly closer to the facts for children under 5 years old for 1968, only 0.2 per cent above the current Census estimate, compared with excesses of 2.3 per cent for the "C" projection, 4.8 per cent for the "B" and 9.2 per cent for the "A". The Census Bureau's estimate of total population for July 1, 1968 of 201.2 million is below the "A", "B", and "C" projections but above the "D" projection.

Should the number of births turn upward, as succeeding month's statistics may show, then in the shorter run, to perhaps 1975, an average of the "C" and "D" projections may well be the "best" projection. After these dates, it is possible that the "C" projection may prove to be the most realistic; but should fertility rates turn upward as the number of women in the heaviest childbearing ages increases it is possible the best estimate will be above the level of the "C" projection. For practical purposes, then it would at the present time be a conservative procedure to use the average of the "C" and "D" projections for the next decade or so. But it is possible, and in the judgment of the writer, probable, that this projection may prove to be too low by 1980; and it may prove to be too low before 1980 if age at marriage and age at birth of first child stops rising as postwar babies enter well into their twenties. Professor Ryder has estimated that the cohort of women born 1941–45 who are still bearing children may average 2.98 children per woman, a figure well above the present level of 2.51 for all women. It is not unreasonable to assume that a level of at least 2.73, that assumed in the "C" projections, may be achieved by the postwar baby boom cohort yet to be heard from.

To assume that the population explosion in the United States has come to an end or that the nation will reach a "stationary" population at a level of 220 million, as has recently been stated by Dr. Donald J. Bogue, is decidedly a premature and unwarranted conclusion as is also his statement that we will not reach a population of 300 million "within the next 100 years." Such a conclusion assumes a further decrease in completed average family size and fails completely to take into consideration the great increase in women of heaviest childbearing age which will occur between now and 1977. Moreover, it discounts completely the recent national surveys to which reference has been made above. The high improbability of these conclusions is further attested to by the following considerations. Even with the average number of children for woman approaching replacement value, 2.11, as soon as possible which would be in about 15 years, the population of the nation would be about 260 million by the year 2000. Since a drop in completed average family size from 2.45 assumed in projection "D" to replacement level (a zero rate of growth) would give a population for the nation only 23 million lower by the end of the century (the difference between the 283 million of projection "D" and the 260 million indicated above), it is in the realm of the fantastic to assume that the population could level off to a maximum of 220 million by the end of the century.

By reason of the uncertainties in respect of the course of future fertility, discussion of the characteristics of the population of the nation are restricted to the year 1990 in the analysis which follows; and are based on projection "C" which assumes a terminal completed average family size of 2.78 children per woman, a number below the level of 3.0 "expected" by American women but above the number of 2.52 which would be generated by 1968 birth rates at each age of woman. Under the "C" projection the total population of the nation would be some 271 million in 1990, but it could range, under the other assumptions made by the Census Bureau from a low of 256 million to, now, an improbable high of 300 million, a difference of 44 million. That is, the actual population in 1990 could be 29 million higher than the "C" projection or 15 million lower.

The Changing Age Structure

With the great fluctuations in birth rate which have been experienced during this century under the impact, among other things, of World War I, the depression of the 1930s, World War II, and the postwar aftermath, dramatic short run changes have taken place and will continue to take place in the age structure of the American people. This is shown in the table which follows:

	Per Cent Change			
Selected Ages	1950–60	1960–70	1970–80	1980–90
All Ages	19.9	14.7	14.2	15.1
5–14	46.9	15.4	—2.0	27.1
15–19	26.8	41.8	9.3	3.7
20–24	—3.2	55.3	21.6	—7.6
25–64	9.9	8.1	17.2	17.4
65 and over	35.8	17.6	17.8	17.1

Between 1950 and 1960 total population increased by 19.9 per cent. The assumptions of relatively low fertility on which projection "C" is based produces a decline in growth to a level of 14 to 15 per cent per decade in the next three decades, to an average increase of from 1.4 to 1.5 per cent per annum from a level of almost 2.0 per cent per annum during the 1950s.

The changes experienced and anticipated in specific age groups show remarkable differences from decade to decade. Consider first the changes in the age group 5 to 14 years, roughly the children of elementary school age. During the fifties these youngsters increased by about 47 per cent inundating the primary schools of the nation to the undoubted detriment of the quality of education. For there was no corresponding increase in well trained and experienced teachers or school facilities. From a growth of 47 per cent in the fifties, children in this age group will have increased by only 15 per cent during the sixties, reflecting the plateau in the postwar boom birth rate. Even more dramatic is the anticipated decrease of 2 per cent in youngsters 5 to 14 during the 1970s reflecting the decline in births during the late 1950s and 1960s. The impact of the increased number of women of childbearing age is evident in the data for the 1980s when the age group will increase by 27 per cent, even with the assumed lowered fertility of projection "C".

The need for drastic readjustment in primary school teachers and facilities over these four decades is paralleled by similar adjustments required throughout our society and economy for these children are also consumers, citizens, church goers, and the like. During the 1970s the relatively small change in this age group, albeit a decline, will require less adjustment in the schools and other elements of society and the economy for the nation as a whole than in the preceding several decades. But the nation will be confronted with a substantial increase in this age group again during the 1980s. However, it is to be noted that individual local areas may be faced with either great increases or decreases depending on migration patterns and local trends.

The age group 15 to 19 years corresponds roughly to secondary school population and is also the age group which, by definition, produces most of the juvenile delinquency. Youth of this age increased by 27 per cent during the 1950s and will have grown by 42 per cent during the 1960s. By the 1970s in response to decreased natality in the late 1950s and the 1960s they will register an increase of only 9 per cent, and by the 1980s an increase of only 4 per cent. Although the table does not show what is in store for the 1990s and subsequently, it is clear that this age group will again show a steep increase as babies born to the larger cohort of postwar born women reach these late adolescent years.

As a result of these changes the secondary schools were under great pressure to expand during the 1950s and especially the 1960s. This pressure will be considerably relaxed during the 1970s and 1980s but, it may be anticipated, will be greatly augmented again in the 1990s. The change in the number of post-adolescents is a major factor in understanding the increase in juvenile delinquency during the 1950s and especially the 1960s. Even if delinquency rates had not increased, the volume of delinquency would have increased by some 42 per cent during the 1960s by reason of the increase in the size of this age group. The changes in the number of post-adolescents has, among other things, also played a major role in the increased importance of the "teen-age" market, in the supply of youths seeking employment and entering the labor market, and in the young manpower available for national defense.

Changes in the age group 20 to 24 years are of special significance because this is the age group of heavy marriage and family formation. It may be astonishing to observe that during the 1950s this age group, in contrast to the experience of the younger groups, actually decreased by over 3 per cent! The reason for this decrease is traceable, of course, to the decline in the marriage and the birth rates as well as the stock market during the depression of the 1930s. From a drop of 3 per cent these young adults will have increased by over 55 per cent during the

1960s! They will still show a substantial increase during the 1970s, a growth of 22 per cent. Then in the 1980s, reflecting the small cohort of depression babies together with the decreased fertility assumed by projection "C", they will again decrease—this time by almost 8 per cent.

The impact of the great changes from decade to decade in the number of young adults 20 to 24 years is a profound one. Even if the marriage rate remains stable the differential growth rates generate ebbs and tides in the number of marriages and new households and in the broad range of social, economic and political phenomena affected thereby. New household formation significantly affects many markets —housing and construction, automobiles, furniture, appliances, the mass media, insurance, medical care and so on through virtually the entire range of goods and services. New household formation also profoundly affects the course of fertility and population growth.

The changing age structure has precipitated a "marriage squeeze" which is another factor in the rising age at marriage. The marriage squeeze refers to the disparity in the number of young women now reaching marriageable age and the number of men 2 to 3 years older who normally are their prospective mates. Young women reaching age 21 in 1967–68 will number about 1,854,000 as compared with 1,386,000 in 1966–67, an increase of approximately one half million. But the number of males 23 years of age in 1967–68, the product of a lower birth rate will be only about 1,424,000 and of males 24 years of age will be only about 1,418,000. The relative shortage of males will force young women to turn to men more nearly their own age for marriage, and the necessary readjustment of age patterns at marriage probably has contributed to increased age at marriage of women.

Two additional dramatic consequences of changes in the number of young adults may be noted. The age group 20 to 24 contributes materially to the number of more serious crimes. Great changes in the number of young adults, therefore, produces great changes in the volume of crime even if the crime rate for the age group remains unchanged. Failure to understand this fact has produced many distortions in the discussion of crime in the United States and especially naive have been the comparisons of increases in crime with increases in total population instead of the population which commits the crime (or juvenile delinquency). Another dramatic effect of changes in the size of this age group is afforded by changes in automobile accidents. Young men under 25, as is indicated by insurance rates, have relatively high automobile accident rates. In consequence, even if accident rates for the age group remained unchanged, the number of automobile accidents would have increased by about 55 per cent during the 1960s by reason of the increase in the size of the age group alone! This has been a decade during which automobile insurance companies have learned what reserves are for!

Finally, it may be observed that young persons under 25 entering the labor market have, as has been noted above, tripled during the 1960s over the last quinquennium of the 1950s by reason of age structure changes. This rise is not unassociated with high youth unemployment and rising age at marriage and birth of first child. The increase in youth 15 to 24 has required new job creation which constitutes a major challenge to the economy. Thus far, as indicated in the high youth unemployment rates, the economy has not proved to be as elastic as the reproductive behavior of the American people.

Although significant changes in the age structure have occurred and are in prospect within the age group 25 to 64, in the interest of brevity persons of these ages are considered as a single group. Adults in this age class during the 1950s and 1960s increased less than either the persons of younger or older age. During the 1950s they increased by about 10 per cent and during the 1960s by about 8 per cent. This broad age group will begin to show the impact of the postwar baby boom during the 1970s and 1980s as well as in subsequent decades. Since this is the age group which encompasses the major portion of the labor force it has a special significance for the economy in indicating the size of the labor supply and the need for job expansion.

Finally, important changes have occurred and are in prospect in the number of elders 65 years of age and over. Senior citizens registered an increase of almost 36 per cent during the 1950s, but will show rates of increase of about 17 per cent in each of the three following decades. The decline in the rate of growth of persons 65 and over after the 1950s is attributable, of course, to the long run decline in fertility— a decline over the last 65 years and more. But it is inevitable, short of the catastrophic, that beginning in the year 2011, 65 years after the beginning of the postwar baby boom, that senior citizens will show a substantial increase as survivors of the post-war boom in babies.

The great increase in persons 65 and over during the 1950s and in earlier decades has greatly affected our society. The needs of older persons who increased from 4.1 per cent in 1900 to 9.2 per cent in 1960 have been responsible for such major changes as those represented by Old Age and Survivor's Insurance and Medicare as part of the Social Security System, of many of the categoric forms of welfare including Medicaid, for the general heightened interest in gerontology, and for the development of many programs oriented to the needs of elders in housing, recreation, education, religion and other realms of life.

One final observation is in order in respect to the changing age structure of the population. It has been noted that the low birth rate of the depression and the high birth rate following World War II have generated significant age changes observable in the successive decades considered. This effect on the age structure will, indeed, persist for generations to come. For small cohorts of the type generated by the depression and large cohorts of the type generated by postwar conditions have an "echo effect" over the course of many generations; and they may portend contrasting life experiences for the respective cohorts.

For example the depression babies, who were in short supply, were able to obtain employment relatively early, set up their own households relatively early, experienced decreased age at marriage and at first birth, and had careers relatively little affected by unemployment and characterized by relatively good opportunity for promotion.

In contrast, the postwar babies, in relatively large supply, are experiencing difficulty in obtaining employment, are remaining in their parental households longer, are experiencing increased age at marriage and at first birth, and all other things being equal, may be afflicted with relatively high unemployment rates and low promotion rates throughout their careers. These differential experiences may well have significant political repercussions, one of which is now manifest in the "revolt of youth" which has just barely begun.

The postwar baby boom superimposed on the long-run decline in the national birth rate, since 1800, has resulted in younger and older people increasing more rapidly than persons of intermediate age. In consequence both the proportion of younger and older persons has been increasing. The median age of the population (the age below and above which one half of the population is distributed) has been decreasing since about 1955. In 1950, the median age was 30.2 years, in 1960, 29.6 years. In 1968, the median age was 27.7 years. Depending on the number of births in the years ahead the median age could either rise or fall. Under projection "C" median age will remain relatively constant until about 1973 and then begin to rise to a level between 28 and 29 years by 1990. At no recent time, however, despite the fact that it has been frequently stated, was it true that more than half the population was under 25 years of age. Moreover, this is not likely to be the case in the decades which lie ahead.

Future Sex Composition

In 1910, by reason largely of immigration, heavily male, the sex ratio of the nation was 106.2—that is, there were 106.2 males for every 100 females. With the restrictions on immigration imposed during the 1920s the sex ratio dropped below 100 during the 1940s. By 1950, women outnumbered men, there being only 98.7 males for each 100 females. By 1967, the sex ratio had further declined to 95.6. The excess of women which has resulted since the cessation of heavy immigration is generated by the higher mortality of males, a mortality high enough to offset the sex ratio at birth which tends to be 106.

The sex ratio varies greatly by age. In 1967, for example, for persons under 15 the sex ratio was 103.7. For persons 15 to 24 years old, however, it was only 97.8 and for persons 25 to 44, 95.6. For persons 65 and over the sex ratio was only 75.7.

In the decades which lie ahead the sex composition of the total population is not likely to change much; the sex ratio is likely to remain at a level of from 96 to 97. But the sex ratio may be expected to decline further at the older ages as the survivors of previous immigration decline in number, and as the difference between female and male longevity further increases. In 1960, only 19 per cent of the men 65 and over were widowed but 52 per cent of the women. By reason of the trends described the disparity in the proportions of men and women widowed is likely further to increase by 1990.

Future Non-White Population

About 92 per cent of the non-white population is Afro-American. Non-whites are growing much more rapidly than whites by reason of rapidly declining death rates, still above white levels, and persistent high fertility. Between 1955 and 1965, non-whites increased by 27 per cent while the total population increased by only 17 per cent. By 1985, non-white population could number some 34 million under projection "C" as compared with about 24 million in 1967–68. Thus, the proportion of non-white population would increase from about 11 per cent in 1966 to about 14 per cent in 1985.

Although the projections assume a narrowing of the gap between white and non-white birth rates, non-whites will continue to increase more rapidly in the years ahead because by reason of their higher birth rate they are a younger population and the number of young non-white women in the childbearing ages will increase more rapidly than corresponding whites. Between 1966 and 1985, while white women of childbearing age will increase by about 40 per cent, non-white women of childbearing age will increase by about 65 per cent.

Non-whites are considerably younger than whites. Half were under 21.4 years in 1966. In contrast, half the white population was under 28.7 years old. By 1985, depending largely on births, the median age of non-whites could vary between 19 and 25 years, whereas that of whites could vary from 27 to 30 years. By 1985, non-whites could make up from 16.3 to 17.4 per cent of the total population under 20, as compared with 14.5 per cent in 1966.

Between 1960 and 1985, on the basis of calculations made by the writer with his colleague, Patricia L. Hodge, the non-white population could increase by 68 per cent while the white population registered a gain of 37 per cent (based on an average of projections "B" and "D" necessary to estimate metropolitan distribution which will be discussed below). Non-whites under 15 years of age would increase by almost 60 per cent, compared with an increase of whites under 15 of only 26 per cent. Non-whites of labor force age, 15 to 64 years, could increase by 75 per cent compared with an increase of only 41 per cent by comparable whites. Finally, non-whites 65 and over could increase by 63 per cent, compared with an increase of 50 per cent for white senior citizens.

Within the labor force ages, 15 to 64, the disparity between non-white and white growth rates would be much greater for younger persons than for the older. Non-whites 15 to 44 years would increase by 124 per cent, much more than double, while whites of this age increase by only two-thirds, 67 per cent. The older non-whites of working age, 45 to 64, would increase by 60 per cent, as compared with a 28 per cent increase for whites.

These projected differential rates of growth by age of the non-white and white populations will have tremendous impact and probably operate to exacerbate present racial tensions. They will result in an increase in the proportion of non-whites of college age as well as of primary and secondary school age which will augment present problems of integration and quality in education. They will constitute a major challenge to the economy to absorb a much larger proportion of non-white and especially young non-white workers.

Future Regional and Metropolitan Distribution

Within the framework of the Bureau of the Census projections the writer, with his colleague Patricia L. Hodge, has calculated future white and non-white population by regions and metropolitan distribution to 1985. These calculations averaged the "B" and "D" projections of the Census, the only projections by States, to approximate the "C" projections.

Between 1960 and 1985, it is estimated that the population of the United States will increase by 73 million or by 41 per cent. But the West will increase by 21 million or 75 per cent; and the South by 24 million or 44 per cent. Growing more slowly than the national average will be the Northeast with a gain of 14 million or 31 per cent, and the North Central States, also with a gain of about 14 million but a growth of only 27 per cent.

The relatively rapid growth of the West is a continuation of the pattern of growth and population redistribution which has characterized the settlement of this nation. The relatively rapid increase in the South is the product of high fertility associated with its relatively rural and economically underdeveloped state, and a significant change in internal migration patterns which, since the mid-1950s, has converted the South from a region of out-migration to a region of in-migration.

The slow growth rates of the Northeast and North Central regions are the product of both relatively low birth rates and internal migration patterns. Since the mid-1950s the North Central States for the first time in their history have become areas of out-migration, in response apparently to better economic opportunity in the other regions. The Northeast, long an area of out-migration, since about the mid-1950s has become an area of in-migration. Since internal migratory movements are largely movements from areas of lesser economic opportunity to areas of greater economic opportunity bolstered by movements from relatively unfavorable to more favorable climates, the states of greatest attraction to migrants in the decades ahead will more specifically, in order of estimated in-migration, be: California, Florida, New Jersey, New York, Arizona, Maryland, and Connecticut. The states with anticipated greatest out-migration, in order of anticipated greatest out-migration, will be: Pennsylvania, Michigan, Kentucky, West Virginia, Mississippi, South Carolina, North Carolina, and Iowa.

The United States will continue to become increasingly metropolitanized between now and 1985. In 1960, about 113 million people, or 63 per cent of the total, lived in the Standard Metropolitan Statistical Areas—cities of 50,000 or more and the counties in which they were located. Between 1900 and 1960, the metropolitan areas absorbed 78 per cent of the total growth of the nation—testimony to increasing concentration of population and economic activities.

Between 1960 and 1985, while the total population is projected to increase by 41 per cent, metropolitan population, if trends persist, would increase by 58 per cent, whereas non-metropolitan population would grow by less than 12 per cent. In consequence, by 1985, 71 per cent of the population would be resident in metropolitan areas. By 1985, the West would have replaced the Northeast as the most metropolitanized region, with 82 per cent of the population resident in metropolitan areas. In the Northeast 81 per cent would reside in metropolitan areas, in the North Central region 68 per cent, and in the South 59 per cent.

The continued concentration of the American people into metropolitan areas is attributable to the great economic and social advantages of metropolitanism as a way of life. Adam Smith long ago observed that the larger the aggregation of population, the greater is possible the division of labor. This leads to increased specialization, easier application of technological advances and the use of non-human energy, economies of scale, external economies and minimization of the frictions of space and communication. In brief, there will be continued concentration into metropolitan areas because such areas are the most efficient producing and consuming areas which man has yet devised. They are also the areas of greatest social lure—embodying the most advanced levels of education, science, art and general recreational and cultural facilities.

Metropolitanism as a way of life, however, has also generated severe problems—physical, economic, personal, social, racial and governmental! The nation must, therefore, be prepared to deal with increasingly severe problems associated with metropolitan living. Physical problems which will be almost certain to grow worse will include problems of air and water pollution, waste removal, housing—both supply and quality, traffic congestion, urban design and the management of natural resources. The economy will probably require more not less government intervention, more not less control of labor-management strife, greater not lesser problems of income maintenance and poverty. Personal and social problems which will be exacerbated will include problems relating to delinquency and crime, alcoholism, drug addiction, quality of education, recreational facilities, religion. Problems of governance will also become more severe on the federal, state and local levels and in their inter-relationships. Problems of taxation and sources of revenue for government at the three levels will grow more severe and the anachronisms of governmental structure and process will become more apparent and more difficult to live with. Preponderant urban and metropolitan majorities will increasingly wrest control of the Congress and State legislatures from disproportionate rural influence.

Among the most difficult of the problems with which the nation will be confronted will be those stemming from the trends in the distribution of non-white population. Significant shifts are in prospect both in the regional and metropolitan redistribution of non-whites. As recently as 1910, 86 per cent of non-whites were concentrated in the South. By 1960, largely by reason of the impact of World Wars I and II which attracted non-whites to the North with job opportunity, the proportion of non-whites in the South had declined to 60 per cent. Should the trends continue, by 1985 more than half of non-whites would be in the North and some 49 per cent would remain in the South. Moreover, by 1985, 78 per cent of all non-whites would reside in metropolitan areas as compared with 69 per cent of whites.

Of even greater significance would be the distribution of non-whites within metropolitan areas—in the central cities and suburbs, respectively. The concentration of non-whites in central cities within metropolitan areas would by 1985 rise to a level of 58 per cent from 50 per cent in 1960. In contrast, white population in central cities would decrease to 21 per cent by 1985 from 30 per cent in 1960. In consequence, 75 per cent of the non-whites would be in central cities and only 25 per cent in suburbs by 1985. In contrast, 70 per cent of whites would reside in the suburbs and only 30 per cent in central cities. The trend is definitely in the direction of continuation and further separation of white and non-white populations—toward the perpetuation of an apartheid society about which fears were expressed by the President's Commission on Civil Disorder. By 1985, almost one-third of all central city residents, 31 per cent, will be non-white, as compared with 18 per cent in 1960. The list of central cities with a majority of non-white population is, with present trends, certain to be greatly increased.

The outlook set forth above is dependent on the continuation of trends prior to 1966. Census data based on a sampling survey indicate that the number of blacks in central cities may have declined between 1966 and 1968, although they still constitute 12 per cent of the central city population. Should this represent a change in trend the proportions of Afro-Americans resident in metropolitan areas who are in central cities would be somewhat lower than those contained in the above projections.

In summary, the projections of regional and metropolitan population indicate the redistribution of the population with the greatest absolute and relative gains in the West and South. The projections also indicate increased concentration of the population into metropolitan areas with the West replacing the Northeast as the most metropolitanized region of the country. By 1985, there will be increased residential separation by color as between the central cities and suburbs, with central cities becoming increasingly black and suburbs remaining predominantly white. The projections clearly indicate that the "racial crisis" is likely to worsen during the coming years.

Concluding Observations

Despite the recent decline in birth rates the United States will continue to experience large population increases to, at least, the end of this century. Such growth, while desirable in some respects, will be attended by many frictions and by the worsening of many chronic and acute problems—physical, economic, personal, social, racial and governmental. Examples of the physical problems include air, water, and general environmental pollution; traffic congestion; slums, and problems of public housing and urban renewal. The personal and social problems include the augmentation of delinquency and crime rates, the revolt of youth, the Black Rebellion, and deteriorated standards of education, each of which has been vitally effected by population factors. The economic problems include youth unemployment and great fluctuations in demand for housing and for durable and non-durable goods with rapidly changing age structure and family formation. The problems of governance include malapportionment of city and stage legislative bodies and of the federal House of Representatives, by reason of rapid urbanization and the reluctance of rural populations to give up political control; the chaotic conditions in local government in respect of authority and financing which heighten "the urban crisis"; and the growing concentration of functions and power in the federal government as the urban population, ignored by rural-dominated state legislatures, have turned to the Federal government for the resolution of their problems.

It would be a great mistake to assume that the much discussed slump in the national birth rate spells the end to the population explosion in the United States, or heralds any imminent stationary population level. On the contrary, there is great need to continue to decrease the birth rate and growth rate of the nation, even as we mobilize efforts to deal with the challenges of the population increase and the many population changes which confront us in the coming decades. Problems of policy raised by the trends which have been summarized are considered by Dr. Frank Lorimer in chapter 8.

Joseph L. Fisher and
Neal Potter

6

Natural Resource Adequacy for the United States and the World

Introduction

The question of natural resource adequacy has always been significant; it will not become less so in the future. Throughout history people have been concerned about the relationship between themselves and the land and other resources available to them. As geographic boundaries of regions and continents became known, and as statistical trends of population and agricultural production became established, this concern found more sophisticated and comprehensive expression. Malthus propounded one far-reaching proposition: population tends to outrun the means of subsistence, making preventive checks to population increase desirable and ultimately positive checks necessary. However, the working out of the consequences of the industrial revolution so increased the output of goods and services that

JOSEPH L. FISHER *is President of Resources For The Future, Inc. He has served on several university faculties of economics and as economist and administrative officer of the Council of Economic Advisers. He has published widely on the economics of natural resource development and regional economic analysis.*

NEAL POTTER *is a staff member of Resources For The Future, Inc. He previously served on the faculties of Carnegie Institute of Technology and State College of Washington.*

Malthus' gloomy prediction has not come true, at least in the Western world.

In more recent times the "population explosion" in the underdeveloped countries and very rapid increases in most of the more developed places have led to a reawakening of concern about the capacity of the natural environment and its resources to sustain desired rates of economic growth. Science, technology, and the economic adaption of their accomplishments are seen as pitted against the sheer increase of population, which in many less developed areas is now running at 3 per cent a year. Continuation of this rate would mean a doubling every 24 years.

Clearly the population problem is not simply one of numbers of people, but also of natural resources and how they are used. Much light can be thrown on this concept by trying to project resource trends into the future and bringing them into juxtaposition with population trends. Of key importance in determining the outcome of the population-resources (or man-land) situation are the prevailing levels of technology and culture, including organizational and institutional elements. Population projections, from Malthus to those of the recent past, have been notoriously wide of the mark. Projections of natural resources, if anything, have been worse, largely because of the difficulties of projecting technology and institutional adjustments. Nevertheless, some understanding may come from a look at comparative trends in the past, present levels of resource use, and at a few projections into the future even though the projections have to be strictly hypothetical and are altogether a hazardous and uncertain undertaking.

We shall examine resource problems principally in terms of certain indicators of whether natural resources and resource products are becoming scarcer in the United States and other major countries of the world. Five indicators of scarcity will be examined:

1. Production and/or consumption trends for major resource products, especially per capita trends. Special attention will be given to food and energy.
2. Employment per unit of output, as a measure of labor productivity trends in resource industries.
3. Relative price and/or cost trends for resource commodities as compared to trends of prices and/or costs in general.
4. Trends in exports and imports, or net foreign trade.
5. Trends in the rate of production and use of resources compared to estimated stocks, reserves, or potentials.

What the Indicators Can Show

A few general observations may help to clarify the relationships between these indicators and the problem of scarcity.

Scarcity in the most obvious sense always increases as population grows, for the physical content of the globe never changes significantly, and scarcity might thus be defined as the reciprocal of population. Such a definition of scarcity puts aside most problems of interest or significance, however, and points ultimately to the absurd conclusion that the Red Indians were better off materially before 1492 than Americans are today.

The actual output or consumption of resource commodities, stated in per capita terms, provides a crude measure of "welfare." This, however, takes no account of the cost or effort of obtaining supplies. The relationship between the labor inputs and the outputs of resource commodities gives a measure of the human cost of making resources available for consumption. This is the measure to which Malthus and the classical economists devoted their attention; it was their expectations of a rise in the labor cost of food and other resource commodities that led them to a gloomy view of a world with increasing population.

It may be argued that advances in technology rather than increases in the plenitude of resources account for declines in the ratio of labor input to resource output. This, of course, may be true, but as long as this process continues, scarcity of resources cannot become a threat to the level of living. It is also of interest that the ratio between labor inputs and outputs in the resource industries has not only declined, but has done so in the United States at a rate nearly the same as that in manufacturing, in which resource scarcity poses very few direct problems.

Labor inputs per unit of output reflect not only technology and availability of resources, but also capital inputs and inputs of fuel, fertilizer, and other materials. For this reason the relative prices of resource commodities, which reflect the costs of all inputs relative to the general price level, are useful as a check on the trend of employment/output ratios.

In addition, the percentage of consumption supplied by net imports is significant, since in many cases imports relieve the pressure for higher prices and employment/output ratios which increasing scarcity would otherwise cause. It must be remembered, however, that this measure too is incomplete, for it is "comparative advantage" which directs the flow of foreign trade: the ratio of the costs of domestic and foreign resource industries, compared to the ratio of the costs at home and abroad for the nonresource industries. Thus, either a discovery of low-cost oil in Venezuela or a rise in the efficiency of an American manufacturing industry that would make it more attractive than domestic extraction of natural resources could account for a rise in U.S. oil imports; and tariffs, quotas, and monopolies also play their part.

Finally, one may compare the trends in the rate of use of resources with estimates of stocks or reserves. This would perhaps be the most satisfactory test of scarcity, but it is just here that the data are most unsatisfactory. Ultimate reserves of most materials are many times larger than are likely to be used in the foreseeable future; and the limitations on resources available in the near future are not fixed, but highly dependent on the technologies and prices which one projects for that future, so that we are carried back to our second and third indicators, labor productivity trends and relative cost or price trends.

In the next section, we examine the statistics for the five resource-scarcity indicators for the United States. In the section following, we examine such data as we could bring together readily for other countries and for the world as a whole. It will be seen that the indicators, both for the United States and for other parts of the world, do not show that resources have become scarcer during recent decades. The indicators are not conclusive, however, for many countries. The data and the methods of measuring scarcity should be used with caution; both need improving.

Following this review of the past, we make some projections for the next few decades, based on existing trends in population and productivity, and what little is known about natural resource reserves, to see whether resources are likely to be scarcer or more plentiful in the foreseeable future.

The Case of the United States

It is self-evident that natural resources and their immediately derived products and services are essential to economic growth and well-being. Enough of these things must be available within a country or by way of imports. In a more highly developed country such as the United States, dependence upon resources may not always be obvious because of the overlay of processed items and the variety of economic services with no very close connection with resources. But the ultimate dependence on natural resources remains, never far below the surface. Many particular resources are a wasting asset; discovery of new sources and the development of substitutes may continue to avert the consequences of this characteristic, but for how long no one can say for certain.

Despite the possibility of altogether new developments, the history of what has happened in the past remains our most reliable guide to future likelihood. Statistics that trace the trends of production, con-

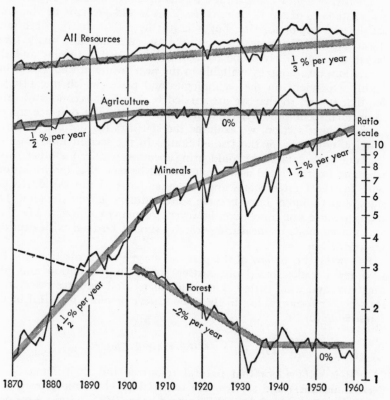

FIGURE *1. U. S. Resource Sectors: Per Capita Consumption, 1870–1960*
Source: Neal Potter and Francis T. Christy, Jr., *Trends in Natural Resource Commodities* (Baltimore: The Johns Hopkins Press for Resources for the Future, 1962), Chart 23.

sumption, prices, productivity, and net foreign trade have been assembled for resource commodities of the United States.[1] The data from 1870 to 1960 are reasonably consistent and reliable and can be used in applying the first four indicators of scarcity mentioned in the preceding chapter.

PER CAPITA CONSUMPTION

The first indicator of resource scarcity or abundance in the United States is provided by the historical trend of consumption of resource commodities on a per capita basis. Figure 1 shows the trends from 1870 to 1960 for the major resource categories. The over-all trend appears to be steadily upward; only for forest products has the trend been downward.

The aggregates cover up much significant detail. Within the minerals category, for example, oil, natural gas, bauxite for aluminum, and other items have risen steeply, while anthracite and bituminous coal have declined generally since the First World War period. Among the agricultural products, per capita consumption of wheat and hogs has fallen over the 90 years, while beef, milk products, and notably citrus fruits have risen. Lumber has declined; pulp and paper have increased.

In terms of the amount of resource products consumed by each man, woman, and child in the United States over nearly a century, scarcity has not been increasing. Instead it has decreased persistently at about ⅓ of 1 per cent a year, with the only major interruption occurring in the early 1930s.

EMPLOYMENT PER UNIT OF OUTPUT

The employment/output ratio[2] for the resource or extractive industries taken as a whole has been falling consistently for many decades with only an occasional and short-lived interruption, as shown in Figure 2. Since the mid-1930s the downward trend has been particularly marked. This has been true of each of the major resource categories with the notable exception of forest products and possibly also

[1] Neal Potter and Francis T. Christy, Jr., *Trends in Natural Resource Commodities* (Baltimore: The Johns Hopkins Press for Resources of the Future, 1962).

[2] We use the employment/output ratio instead of the usual output/employment (productivity) ratio because we are concerned with the real cost of obtaining a certain output in terms of labor input and with the factors underlying changes in real prices.

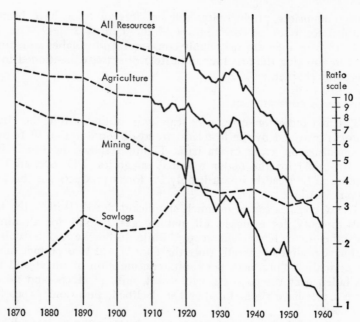

FIGURE 2. U.S. Resource Sectors: Employment/Output, 1870–1960
Note: The dashed lines indicate periods for which the data are available 'less frequently than on an annual basis.
Source: Potter and Christy, Chart 45. (For full source reference see Figure 1.)

of fish. Increases in productivity in agriculture and mining have outstripped those in manufacturing during the past 25 years or so.

The number of workers engaged in all the resource industries was just about the same in 1960 as in 1870, 7 million. But the value of their output in constant dollars had increased by more than five times. During the same long period the value of the total national product rose by more than twenty times, with more complex fabrication of raw materials and a larger services component in the expanding economy. About 10 per cent of the nation's labor force, instead of over 50 per cent as in 1870, was producing 20 per cent more in resource products for each member of the population. This second indicator of scarcity thus shows diminished rather than increased scarcity; fewer workers, working shorter hours, produced much more than 90 years earlier.

RELATIVE COSTS AND PRICES

The third indicator is the relative cost or price trend. If a resource is becoming scarcer, one would expect the cost of developing or producing resource products derived from it to rise in comparison with costs generally. Over the long run, prices usually reflect costs fairly accurately. Because price data are easier to come by than cost data, they can be used as a measure of both relative cost and price. Statistics in the early period are not thoroughly reliable, but the general picture which emerges is that for extractive industries as a whole, prices have not shown any marked tendency to rise or fall over the long run since 1870. They have moved erratically with many short-term ups and downs and possibly some slight general tendency upward. The component to move upward most noticeably has been forest products, for which relative prices recently have been nearly four times what they were in 1870 and twice those in 1930. But the overall picture does not indicate that resource materials have become scarcer on any general or alarming scale over a good many decades in the past.

NET IMPORTS

The fourth indicator relates to the resources position of a single country relative to the rest of the world. In more recent years the United States has been relying to an increasing degree upon imports of many raw materials, particularly oil and certain metals. Around 1930 the historic position of the United States as a net exporter of resource products shifted to that of net importer. This country continues to export basic agricultural commodities such as wheat and cotton, and to import noncompeting products such as coffee, cocoa, and natural rubber. But especially since the Second World War, the United States has also become a fairly large net importer of such items as crude oil, copper, lead, zinc, iron ore, and lumber; while its already considerable imports of manganese, nickel, chromium, asbestos, diamonds, and paper have continued upward. For the 1965–67 period imports of crude oil were 19 per cent of domestic consumption and imports of iron ore were over 29 per cent.

Without increased imports of particular commodities, cost and prices of certain items in the United States would probably have risen (or have risen more than they did), especially since the Second World War. In some cases new sources or techniques undoubtedly set ceilings on both price rises and amount of imports; for example, oil can be produced from ample reserves of oil shale in the Colorado plateau at only a little above existing oil prices, and low-grade taconite ores, of which there are large reserves in the Lake states, can be beneficiated. Nevertheless, the fact remains that ready access to foreign supplies has gained in importance to this country.

Looked at from a national viewpoint and without detailed analysis, this indicator suggests decreasing plentitude of raw materials. Its significance is limited, however, by the fact that its movement is due to changes in the comparative cost advantages of other industries as against raw materials production, both in the United States and in other countries. Government controls and subsidies also affect imports.

The first three tests indicate either lessening scarcity, or at least no increase in scarcity, for most items. There are some exceptions, notably lumber (sawlogs), among the more basic materials. Trends in per capita consumption of resource products, labor productivity trends, and deflated price and cost movements for raw materials—each of these seems to point to the unlikelihood of any general running out of resources in this country for some time to come. The import test indicates increasingly scarcity of resources, but it is a very mixed sort of indicator, requiring deeper analysis before firm conclusions can be drawn.

RESERVES AND POTENTIALS FOR MEETING REQUIREMENTS

The fifth indicator, necessarily more speculative than the others, involves the trend of rates of production and use of resources compared to estimates of stocks, reserves, or potentials. For the United States a comprehensive appraisal made five or six years ago attempts to review the historical data and to look into the future in terms of foreseeable new sources of supply, new technology, population trends, and expectations for a rising level of living.[3] Based on an estimated increase in population from 180 million in 1960 to 330 million in 2000 and in gross national product in 1960 dollars from $504 billion in 1960 to $2,200 billion in 2000, and also taking into account other demand and supply factors related specifically to each item, Table 1 shows the projected increases in a few basic resource and raw material requirements.

In the study from which these estimates are taken, a range of re-

[3] Hans H. Landsberg, Leonard L. Fischman, Joseph L. Fisher, *Resources in America's Future* (Baltimore: The Johns Hopkins Press for Resources for the Future, 1963).

quirements is presented: high, medium, and low. The figures in Table 1 are the medium estimates and should be regarded as projec-

Table 1. *U.S. Requirements of Selected Natural Resources and Resource Products, 1960 and Projected 2000*

	1960	*2000*
Cropland including pasture (million acres)	447	476
Wheat (million bushels)	1,110	1,385
Cotton (billion pounds)	7.0	16
Timber (billion cu. ft.)	11	32
Fresh water withdrawal depletions (billion gal. per day)	84	149
Oil (billion bbls.)	3.2	10
Natural gas (trillion cu. ft.)	13.3	34.9
Coal (million short tons)	436	718
Nuclear power (billion kilowatt-hours)	—	2,400
Iron ore (million short tons)	131	341
Aluminum, primary (million short tons)	2.1	13.3
Copper, primary (million short tons)	1.7	4.5

Source: Landsberg, Fischman and Fisher. (See n. 3.)

tions on the basis of assumptions of population, production, income, and the like which are as realistic as so broad an approach would allow.

The study found that there apparently will be enough cropland, assuming yields per acre continue to increase in line with recent trends. Meeting the increased demand for lumber will strain the country's capacity to produce saw-timber; and probably the United States will have to resort to additional imports and further substitutions, especially during the latter part of the period between now and 2000. Water problems are primarily regional; their solution will require more investment in conserving and developing supplies and reducing pollution, and more efficient management and use. Petroleum, now in oversupply here and in the world generally, may be short toward the end of the century. Fortunately there are good possibilities of supplementing underground liquid sources with oil shale and tar sands. Coal reserves remain plentiful. Very large nuclear sources await further reductions in cost. Costs of extracting and refining many nonfuel minerals are high, even though the minerals themselves are abundant in the earth's crust. But many areas of the world from which imports can be obtained have not been very well explored, some not at all, and the possibilities of using lower grade ores are reasonably bright based on the U.S. experience of recent years. For the minerals especially, it will be important to this country that import capacity not be reduced and that technological progress continue.

World Trends in Resources

Having taken this glimpse at the relatively complete historical picture available for the United States, we shall now look at selected statistical information available for other countries and areas of the world, which in most instances is far more limited.

CONSUMPTION OR OUTPUT

Food—In the critical area of food production, it is encouraging to find a Food and Agriculture Organization [FAO] study concluding that there has been for the whole world an 18 per cent increase in per capita food output since the 1930s.[4] At first glance, this would seem to indicate an improved future for the world's hungry people.

When we examine the picture more closely, however, we find serious problems. Per capita food output in Latin America, Asia, and Africa is no greater than it was thirty years ago—progress has occurred principally in North America, Western Europe, Japan, and the Soviet Union. The areas which have lagged contain two-thirds of the world's population, and have notoriously poor diets. The lag seems to be due partly to rapid rates of population growth, and partly to failure of these areas to participate sufficiently in the agricultural revolution that has brought such large increases in output per man and per acre in North America and Western Europe. However, there are signs of significant progress in several of the less developed countries. Mexico and Venezuela increased their per capita output 25 per cent in the last decade, and in 1968 India and Pakistan (and some other Asian nations) appeared to be starting on the agricultural revolution. Improved agricultural practices and new varieties of grain in that year raised the outputs of wheat and rice 30 per cent above the previous record, and total food grains 12 per cent above the record.[5]

The rate of increase is only part of the picture, and should be complemented by data on levels of consumption. The well-fed areas, like the United States and Western Europe, consume about 50 per cent more calories per capita than do the poorest areas. This difference means partial starvation for many in the poorer areas of the world,

[4] *State of Food and Agriculture 1962*, p. 14, and *1968*, p. 155 (Rome, Italy: The Food and Agriculture Organization).

[5] Lester R. Brown, "The Agricultural Revolution in Asia," *Foreign Affairs* (July 1968), pp. 688–89.

but the calorie gap is small relative to that in proteins and vitamins, for which consumption figures in the richer countries run several times those in the poorer.

As one means of combining divergent measures of diet, Figure 3 is reproduced from an FAO study. This chart portrays the diets in different areas in terms of their values, that is, the sums of the price-weighted farm commodities used for food. This way of looking at food facts gives the Far East a diet about one-sixth as valuable as that in North America (indexes of about 51 and 312, respectively, where 100 equals the world average for the years 1948–52). Western Europe, which on a calorie basis is 94 per cent as well off as North America, is by this "value" comparison only about 60 per cent as well off. As can be seen by the shaded portions of the bars in the chart, most of the differences arise in the values of livestock products (meat, milk, eggs, etc.) consumed. Large increases in the proteins supplied by such products are required for an adequate diet in the under-developed parts of the world, even though minimum nutritional standards can be met by a level of consumption well below the average for North America.

To summarize the food output picture, the past thirty years have shown a moderate improvement but there is still a long way to go, and progress is largely lacking where it is needed the most.

Energy—The second most important resource material is energy. The rates of growth in per capita energy available are much more encouraging than those for food. The trends of the past fifteen years incline more steeply upward (3.2 per cent per year instead of $\frac{1}{2}$ per cent per year), and growth seems generally greater in areas where consumption is lowest. Thus Western Europe and the United States show increases of 60 per cent for 1937–65 while non-Communist Asia and Africa show about 120 per cent, Latin America 157 per cent, and the Soviet Union over 200 per cent increase in this period. It is well to note, however, that the range of disparities in energy consumption among different countries is 200-to-1 (U.S. annual consumption 10 tons per capita, Nigeria .05 tons), whereas in food values they are only of the order of 6-to-1 (Figure 3).

NONFUEL MINERALS

Variations in rates of growth for non-fuel minerals have been wide among countries. The increase in world output[6] of iron ore

[6] The remainder of this section covers only output, because the U.N. data do not include consumption. Aggregate figures are given instead of per capita, because

FIGURE 3. *Estimated Values of Food Supplies Per Capita by World Regions, Prewar to 1958–60 (Price-Weighted Indices World[1] Average for All Food, 1948–52 = 100)*

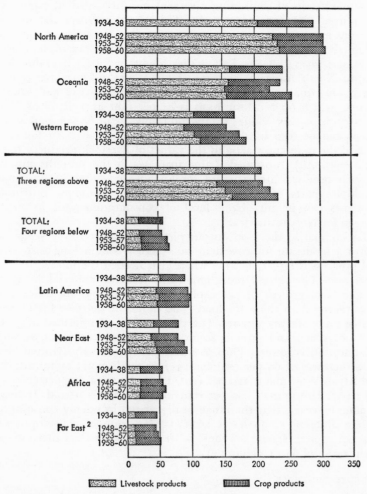

[1] Excluding U.S.S.R., eastern Europe and Mainland China.
[2] Excluding Mainland China.

Source: Food and Agricultural Organization, *State of Food and Agriculture 1961* (Rome: The Food and Agricultural Organization), p. 30.

from 1953 to 1966 was above 100 per cent, whereas the increase in world population was only 28 per cent. Rates of increase in some of the less-developed areas, such as Latin America and non-communist Asia, ran as high as several hundred per cent while Western Europe and the U.S. were essentially unchanged. It is well to note, however, that these increases followed a war and postwar period in which the rate of increase was quite low—about 15 per cent per decade, or a little less than the increase in world population. For the period 1937–66 taken as a whole, the world increase was about 50 per cent per decade, as against a population increase of 16 per cent per decade. For all metals taken together, the world price-weighted index of output rose about 74 per cent from 1953 to 1966. Output of every important metal, as well as of every important non-metallic mineral, increased faster than world population during this period, with the exceptions of tin, gold, and silver.

Forest products—Wood output increased about 40 per cent between 1946 (the earliest year for which the FAO presents a table covering most of the world) and 1965, about the same as the increase in population. Largest increases in timber output appear to have occurred in Asia and Africa, and probably in the Soviet Union. Increases in Northern America and Western Europe were only 17 to 35 per cent in 1946–65.

EMPLOYMENT/OUTPUT RATIO

Our second index for indicating scarcity is trends in the productivity of labor. Data collected by the United Nations Food and Agriculture Organization for agriculture, though not always consistent for the earlier years, show encouraging trends particularly for the last decade, when our data as well as agricultural technology have improved. While the figures reflect most strongly the upsurge in productivity in North America and West Europe from the impact of the agricultural revolution which has occurred in the past 30 years, declines in labor required per unit of output also appear to be substantial in Latin America and in a number of Asian countries.

Mining labor per unit of output also declined an estimated 29 per cent on the average between 1938 and 1953.[7] By 1963, an additional

---

outputs of most minerals have very little relation to population, or to the welfare of the population, since foreign trade constitutes such a large percentage of output and consumption for many countries. Thus in 1960 Venezuela produced 1.7 metric tons of iron per capita, the United Kingdom only .09 tons; Latin America produced over 8 pounds of copper per capita, Western Europe a little over ½ pound.

[7] United Nations, *Patterns of Industrial Growth, 1938–1958.*

decline of about 30 per cent was indicated by the 16 national indexes we were able to estimate.

RELATIVE PRICE TRENDS

Relative prices are our third indicator of scarcity trends. It is difficult to find series that are not seriously impaired by changing value standards, fluctuating exchange rates, and artificially fixed or supported prices. However, a few series are available which appear to be reasonably good indicators; they relate chiefly to standard commodities which have been traded on a fairly free world market over the past 50 years or so. The relative price of sugar has fallen by at least one-half since the pre-World War I period (1900–10); wheat has fallen over 25 per cent, cotton about 30 per cent, while copper, though undergoing erratic price movements, appears to be at about the same level as sixty years yearlier. These few price series do not indicate increasing scarcity but rather the opposite.

NET IMPORT TRENDS

Fourth, the growth of trade in raw materials may be examined for its indications of scarcity in particular countries or particular materials. FAO data show a 70 per cent increase in total world imports of food and feedstuffs since the 1930s. The biggest changes came in the shift of North America from a small net import balance, due largely to the droughts of the 1930s, to large net exports, and the shift of the Near East and Asia from small net exports to large net imports.

In foodgrains—wheat, rye, and rice—little change took place in the balance of trade between 1934–38 and 1966 for West Europe or Oceania. But North America increased its exports very heavily (in 1967 U.S. and Canadian net exports of wheat were 50 per cent of output), while Asia imported nearly half the increased exports, the U.S.S.R. and East Europe about one-fourth, and South American and Africa absorbed small amounts. In feed grains (corn, barley, oats, millet, and sorghum) Europe has absorbed the bulk of the increased exports of Northern America, while Asia has absorbed about a quarter.

The 150 per cent increase in imports of food and feedgrains by the non-communist Far East in the last decade reflects a growth in dependency on outside resources, though the absolute volume of imports is still below that of Europe, and is not more than 18 per cent of the grain output in this part of Asia.

Do these growing imports reflect increasing scarcity of agricultural resources in these countries? The answer cannot be clear-cut because the recent growth in imports has been in considerable part a result of increased availability of monetary exchange from the U.S. foreign aid program and oil exports from the Near East, and the subsidies given to agricultural exports by the United States. Western Europe, the heaviest importer of foods and feedstuffs, has actually reduced its dependence on food imports: 1966 food imports were only 20 per cent above prewar, while population had increased 30 per cent.

Trade in other raw materials is considerably smaller than that in agricultural products. In 1966 fuel imports, the second largest group, totalled $16.7 billion, as compared to $52.6 for food and raw materials. However, the rate of increase in fuel trade is steep: the 1966 quantity of fuel traded was nearly ten times that of 1938, and was 52 per cent above 1960.[8] Moreover, a number of nations are almost wholly dependent on imports for their energy supplies, while other nations are thoroughly dependent on exports for their national prosperity. In 1965, Italy, for example, produced only 20 per cent of her energy needs, Sweden 17 per cent, and the Philippines 4 per cent. Venezuela's 1965 exports were 93 per cent petroleum and products, Iraq's 94 per cent, and Libya's 99.4 per cent.

Net imports as an indication of resource scarcity, therefore, present a variety of pictures, country by country, but generally of increasing dependence on sources or markets in other countries. For the world as a whole increasing dependence, or linkage, among the countries for their raw materials should work in the direction of lower costs generally speaking and, therefore, increases in living levels, as fuller advantage is taken of more favorable international locations of resources.

CONCLUSIONS

Historical data on resource trends in the other world areas is not as systematic or comprehensive as for the United States. Available evidence is far from conclusive, but it does warn against easy generalizations that the rest of the world is about to run out of raw materials or, conversely, that the less-developed areas are going to take off right away into rapid improvements in living levels because of plentiful supplies of food, energy, and raw materials. The picture is mixed: quite favorable for energy commodities, much less so for food. For some less-developed but heavily populated countries the race between food and people apparently will be a close one. As with the United States, only more dramatically, much will depend on the rate at which

[8] United Nations, *Statistical Yearbook 1967*, p. 66.

technological advances already proven can be broadly applied, and on keeping open the channels of world trade. One hopes that data on resource commodity trends can be improved as time goes on; if so, our scarcity indicators can be improved as guides for policies and actions.

Projections of Resource Demands

Let us now take a look at levels of demand for resources and raw materials which would arise by the year 2000 under a few simple assumptions. Taking the high population projections of the United Nations' 1966 study as shown in Table 2,[9] we have made rough esti-

Table 2. Population Trends: Historical 1920–65, and Projections for 1980 and 2000, by World Areas (Millions)

	1920	1938	1950	1965	1980	2000
World*	1860	2170	2517	3295	4551	6994
Northern America	116	142	166	214	275	376
Latin America	90	125ᵉ	163	246	383	686
Western Europe	233ᵉ	260ᵉ	286	324	350ᵉ	390ᵉ
East Europe and U.S.S.R.	250ᵉ	300ᵉ	285	352	440ᵉ	570ᵉ
China, Communist Asia	490ᵉ	520ᵉ	580ᵉ	730	1010ᵉ	1400ᵉ
Non-Communist Asia	530ᵉ	670ᵉ	800ᵉ	1100	1600ᵉ	2700ᵉ
Africa	143	186ᵉ	222	311	463	864
Oceania	8.5	11.0ᵉ	12.7	17.5	23	35

* Total will not add due to rounding
e—Rough estimate by the authors
Sources: United Nations, *Demographic Yearbook*, *1960*, *1966*; U.N. Department of Economic and Social Affairs, *World Population Prospects*, *as Assessed in 1963* (United Nations, New York, 1966: Population Studies, No. 41), Table A3.3 and others. The "high" variant is used throughout.

mates of the materials which would be consumed in the year 2000 under each of the following assumptions:

1. The trends in resource consumption during the past decade continue for the next 35 years in the several parts of the world.

[9] In thus casually taking a population projection for the year 2000, we make no assumption that that *will* be the population, for this depends on a multitude of social attitudes and adjustments relative to birth rates and the availability of resources, among many factors. Our purpose is simply to set up a reasonably high target and then to examine the difficulties which resource scarcities may pose in reaching it.

2. The average per capita level of consumption for the world as a whole in the year 2000 is at the level attained in the United States in 1965.
3. The average level of consumption in the world is at the level attained by Western Europe in 1965.

FOOD PRODUCTS

Applying each of the three assumptions in turn to the available data on food [10] results in the following projected increases:

1. FAO data, though somewhat fragmentary, indicate an increase in world per capita food consumption of 7 per cent between the average for 1951–53 and that for 1963–65. In 35 years, this rate of increase would compound to 21 per cent. The total increase in food consumption, taking into account the projected 112 per cent increase in population, would come to slightly over 150 per cent.
2. To raise the average calorie consumption of the world by the year 2000 to the level attained by the United States in 1965 would involve a 34 per cent increase per capita. The increase in proteins and other food elements would be much larger, but we shall discuss this later.
3. The increase in average world consumption of calories to attain a West European 1965 level would be 28 per cent per capita.

Table 3 summarizes the number of calories that would be consumed under each of the above assumptions. This is done by combining the projected changes in per capita consumption with the population projections of Table 2. For example, in column (1) for Latin America, per capita consumption in 2000 would be 32 per cent above the 1965 levels and population 179 per cent over 1965. Combined, these percentages give an increase of 268 per cent. The 640 billion 1965 Latin American daily calorie intake, increased by 268 per cent, equals the 2350 billion calories shown in column (1) for Latin America.

It is most interesting that the consumption trends of the past decade should give us a projection for year 2000 which is only 10 per cent below the "target" U.S. level of 1965. This does not mean, however, that an adequate diet is fast approaching for the world's hungry people, because:

[10] This appears to omit an allowance for rising standards in the United States, but in terms of world totals the omission is not large, since U. S. population is projected at less than 5 per cent of the world total and increases in per capita consumption of raw materials in the United States have been only about 1/3 per cent a year.

1. Continuation of the recent trend for some areas would carry them past the point of satiation by the year 2000. Note, for example, that column (1) is higher than column (2) for Latin America and Western Europe. Clearly, these areas in 2000 will not consume calories at a per capita rate higher than Northern America in 1965. Thus our total of 19,400 billion contains some over-inflated figures; we can be sure trends will change, and the result will be a lower total than shown in column (1). Exports to deficit areas could utilize the excess food in the surplus areas, but the sheer size of the shipping and distribution problems would probably prevent complete utilization of this potential output, if quotas, tariffs, and exchange controls did not.

2. There may be great difficulties in maintaining for 35 years the rate of increase in output achieved between 1951–53 and 1963–65, particularly because the 1950's included a significant amount of recovery from wartime damage and neglect in Europe, the Soviet Union, and Japan,

Table 3. Projections of Calorie Consumption in the Year 2000 Compared to Prewar and 1965 Actual Consumption (billions of calories per day)

	Actual		Calorie consumption in year 2000 if:		
	Prewar	1965	Trend of 1952–56 to 1963–65 continues (1)	World is at U. S. 1965 per capita consumption level (2)	World is at West Europe 1965 per capita level (3)
World	5200	7800	19,800	22,100	21,100
Northern America	460	680	1,190	1,190	1,130
Latin America	280	640	2,350	2,170	2,060
Western Europe	750	980	1,440	1,230	1,170
East Europe and U.S.S.R.	800e	1100e	2,600e	1,800	1,720
Communist Asia	1100e	1400e	2,900e	4,400	4,200
Non-Communist Asia	1400e	2200e	7,000e	8,500	8,100
Africa	400e	710e	2,200e	2,700	2,600
Oceania	36	60	110	110	100

e—Very rough estimate by the authors.

Sources: *Prewar and 1965 actual:* Population data of Table 2 multiplied by indicated consumption levels from FAO, *The State of Food and Agriculture 1968*, pp. 176–77; U.S. Department of Agriculture, Economic Research Service, *The World Food Budget 1970*, pp. 100–02; and FAO, *Production Yearbook 1958*, p. 239.

Columns (1), (2), and (3): Population projections of Table 2 multiplied by levels of consumption as indicated (see text).

as well as considerable impact from recent agricultural discoveries, such as DDT, 2, 4-D, and hybrid corn.

3. There are much larger and more serious deficiencies in proteins and vitamins in the world's average diet. While the world needs only a 20 to 30 per cent increase in per capita calorie intake, it needs a 40 or 50 per cent increase in its total protein supply to reach West European standards of 1965. The increase in animal proteins (milk, eggs, meat, etc.) required would be of the order of 200–300 per cent.[11]

ENERGY COMMODITIES

In Table 4 energy consumption for the year 2000 is projected on the basis of each of four assumptions given at the opening of the

Table 4. *Projections of Energy Consumed in 2000 Compared to 1938 and 1965 Actual* (*billions of metric tons of coal equivalent*)

| | | | Energy consumption in year 2000 if: | | |
	1938 actual	1965 actual	Trend in consumption from 1955 to 1965 continues (1)	World consumption is at U.S. 1965 per capita level (2)	World consumption is at West Europe 1965 per capita level (3)
World	1.79	5.5	40.5	67.6	23.7
Northern America	.71	2.04	6.45	3.64	1.27
Latin America	.039	.20	2.01	6.63	2.32
Western Europe	.56	1.09	3.84	3.77	1.32
East Europe and U.S.S.R.	.30	1.23	10.98	5.51	1.93
Communist Asia	.027	.32	6.42	13.5	4.74
Non-Communist Asia	.112	.39	9.94	26.1	9.14
Africa	.023	.093	.55	8.36	2.92
Oceania	.018	.061	.33	.34	.12

Sources: Special tabulations of world energy use done at Resources for the Future, Inc., from United Nations and other data sources.

chapter. These assumptions and their implications for energy are as follows:

[11] *The State of Food and Agriculture 1968* (Rome: The Food and Agricultural Organization), pp. 178–79.

1. Per capita consumption in each continental area continues to increase at the rate at which it increased in the decade 1955–65 [column (1) of Table 4]. This would result in an aggregate consumption in year 2000 a little over seven times that of 1965. This assumption looks quite possible, since it is based on a rate of growth that has actually been experienced. It should be noted, however, that the decade 1955–65 was one of booming economies in most of the world, so this may be a higher rate of increase than can be sustained to the year 2000.[12] On the other hand national economies in stages of rapid industrial development may well require as much as a doubling of energy input each ten to twenty years.

2. That the world average consumption in the year 2000 would be as great as that of the United States in 1965 [Table 4, column (2)]. This is a very generous assumption, as U.S. per capita consumption in 1965 was nearly six times the world average and three times that of Western Europe. On this assumption, the total consumption in the year 2000 would be twelve times that of 1965.

3. That world average per capita consumption would equal that of Western Europe in 1965. This is a much more modest assumption, and gives a world total a little over four times that of 1965 [Table 4, column (3)].

Taking these assumptions and projections together, it seems quite possible that in the year 2000 world consumption of energy will be about five times that of 1965, or, to speak more realistically in terms of a range, four to six times as great. World consumption of energy in 2000 at the 1965 U.S. level appears unattainable, although rates of increase in other parts of the world, especially the less-developed areas, are expected greatly to exceed that of the United States during the next 30 years.

NONFUEL MINERALS

Continuation for 35 years of the phenomenal growth in world iron ore output which occurred in the decade 1955–65 would produce an eight-fold increase, or a four-fold increase per capita.[13] Despite its steepness, this is a lower rate of increase than that attained by the U.S. during its 40 years of fastest growth of iron output, and it may be a possible rate of growth for some parts of the world. However, it seems unlikely that the recent rates of growth in output for Latin

[12] The figure for Communist China is surprisingly high for the year 1965, giving a rate of increase for the decade that would be almost impossible to imagine for the next thirty-five years; so we have used a rate of increase equal to that estimated for non-Communist Asia for this decade.

[13] Potter and Christy, *op. cit.*, pp. 37, 376.

America, the Soviet Union, and Asia can continue for 35 years. If it did, world consumption would be .4 ton per capita as compared to U.S. 1965 consumption of ⅓ ton (iron content). Extrapolation of the 1937–65 rate of increase yields a 4⅓-fold increase in aggregate output by the year 2000, and would provide a world per capita consumption of about ¼ ton.

The growth in output projected for copper at the 1955–65 rate would be modest compared to that of the United States during its "take-off" 45 year period—about six-fold compared to nearly forty-fold. Nevertheless, the fact that the older producing areas, like the United States, Chile, and Europe, show slower rates of growth, plus the fact that the 1937–65 growth was only 125 per cent (34 per cent per decade) suggest that even a six-fold increase may not be attained by the year 2000. Perhaps a three-fold increase is more likely; this would mean a world consumption of about 5 pounds per capita, as against 1965 consumptions of about 19 pounds by the United States, 14 pounds by Western Europe, 10 pounds by Japan, and 6 pounds by Russia.[14]

A number of other significant minerals may be mentioned briefly. It appears that growth rates for ferroalloys may be about as high as for iron, while a much higher rate of growth for bauxite seems inevitable as use of aluminum continues to expand rapidly in construction, transportation equipment, and electrical goods. Other metals may experience a slower rate of growth than during the recent past. Such non-metals as sulfur, phosphate, and potash may experience fairly high rates of growth—several hundred per cent over the 35 years as fertilizer and other chemical industries grow.

FOREST PRODUCTS

The increase in the rate of wood removals from the forests of the world between 1955 and 1965 was 21 per cent,[15] just sufficient to keep pace with the increase in population. To keep pace with the population increase assumed in Table 2, industrial wood output would have to more than double by the year 2000. In view of the downtrend in per capita consumption of sawlogs in the United States in the past 50 years, and the sharp rate of increase in prices, we feel no assurance that these world forest product projections will actually be experienced.

[14] American Metal Market, *Metal Statistics 1968*, p. 111. U.S. consumption is primary only; others appear to include secondary copper (about 10 per cent of total in U.S.).

[15] *The State of Food and Agriculture 1698*, p. 163.

Reserves and Alternate Supply Possibilities

Will it be possible to increase the output of food, energy, wood products, minerals, and other raw materials so as to reach the levels projected in the preceding section? By the year 2000 this would involve roughly:

1. A 160 per cent increase in aggregate food output, just to provide adequate calories, and considerably more to provide adequate proteins and vitamins.
2. A seven-fold increase in energy output, if 1955–65 trends continue, or over four-fold for the world to reach a level of consumption equalling that of Western Europe in 1965.
3. Perhaps a five-fold increase in output of iron ore and ferroalloys, and somewhat less in copper, but a much larger increase in bauxite-aluminum.
4. More than doubling world timber output.

FOOD

The most important of these increases and the most difficult to meet is probably that in food output.

The chief hope of reaching the food "target"—unless important new technologies are developed, such as synthesizing foods from cellulose or petroleum, or getting acceptable food from algae—lies in increasing crop yields per acre. The first three columns of Table 5 show increases in yields for some of the principal crops as estimated by the FAO for the period of 1948–52 to 1966. The average increase in yields on a world basis from these crops, chiefly grains, was something like 35 per cent for the period. Thus, increases in yields per acre seem to account for most of the increase of 61 per cent in the total food output for this period, as estimated by the FAO.[16] A rate of increase of 35 per cent in 16 years, if it were maintained for 35 years, would raise the output of food and feed crops over 90 per cent—well over half the increase needed for an output gain of 160%.

If, instead of extrapolating world trends in increased yields for the past 16 years, we consider what would be possible if the rate of progress in Europe and Northern America were extended worldwide and continued to the year 2000, we get much larger possibilities. Table 5 shows rates of increases in yields per acre running at 50 per

[16] *Production Yearbook 1967* (Rome: The Food and Agriculture Organization), Table 7. Mainland China not included in the data.

cent and higher for the important grain crops in this area of the world. If such a rate of improvement were maintained by the entire world for 35 years, the aggregate increase in crop output would be 145 per cent, which is nearly the 160 per cent needed to provide adequate calories.

Table 5. Changes in Crop Yields per Acre, by Major Crops for Selected World Areas

	Percentage of increase in yields 1966 over 1948–52			Yields in N. America and Europe ÷ Asia, Latin America, and Africa (1966)
	World	Europe	North America	
Wheat	43	52	57	2.2
Rye	34	25	78	2.0
Barley	46	59	45	2.6
Oats	39	31	31	1.7
Maize	46	141	58	2.8
Millet and sorghum	52	a	163	5.6
Rice	23	a	57	2.2
Potatoes	18	27	46	2.2
Cotton	42	a	84	2.5

a—Very small quantities produced.
Source: FAO, *Production Yearbook 1967*, Table 13A.

It might be possible that world agriculture could not only increase its yields at the same rate as Europe and North America, but that it might catch up with these advanced countries in yield per acre. The last column of Table 5 shows yields in the advanced countries more than double the levels in Asia, Africa, and Latin America, whose acreage is about 60 per cent of the total in the non-communist world. If this 60 per cent doubled its yields, the output of the non-communist world would increase 60 per cent; if the world also increased its yields each decade by 30 per cent, as did Europe and North America, the total crop output in the year 2000 would be four times that in 1965. Such large increases in yields could not only provide the larger population with an adequate supply of calories, but offer a very large increase in the grain available for animal feed, as an aid in securing human diets with more adequate proteins.

Crop production may be increased by increasing the acreage, as well as by increasing the yield per acre. The FAO *Production Yearbook* for 1967 reports about 150 million hectares (one hectare is equal to

2.2 acres) as "unused but potentially productive"; 4,000 million hectares as "forested"; 2,900 million hectares of "permanent meadows and pastures"; and nearly 5,000 million hectares of "built-on areas, wasteland, and other." Little more than 10 per cent of the world's land area is under crops. We may reasonably hope for substantial increases in the raising of crops on the more favorable parts of the remaining 90 per cent.[17] Some of this may be at the expense of pasture and timber land, thus diminishing the base for supplies of livestock products and lumber. But greater yields can also be obtained from the land which remains in pasture or timber, through the application of technology and investment.[18] What is required to achieve these large increases?

Whatever the possibilities of increasing acreage, the bulk of the needed output for meeting future food needs must come from increases in yields per acre. The matter is complex and includes some relatively unchangeable factors like climate and soil qualities; but large possibilities seem to center on the use of more adequate amounts of fertilizer, improved cultivation and harvesting practices, proper use of irrigation water, better drainage and soil demineralization, and use of better seeds and pesticides. More efficient tenure, credit, and marketing arrangements can also play an important part. Some of these factors, such as more fertilizer, require significant amounts of capital investment; others require institutional changes that may be even more difficult to achieve. Better extension services and a willingness to change long established farming practices can make significant contributions.[19]

Of these several factors, only water and fertilizer seem to present questions of the availability of resources. Water will probably con-

---

[17] Walter H. Pawley, *Possibilities of Increasing World Food Production* (Rome: The Food and Agricultural Organization, 1963), pp. 30–31, cites "reputable geographers" who have estimated the possibilities of increasing cultivated land as ranging from 35 per cent to 300 per cent.

[18] *Timber Resources for America's Future* (U.S. Forest Service, 1958), pp. 476ff., indicated that nearly a four-fold increase in output was possible in the United States through better management alone. R. O. Whyte, T. R. G. Moir, and J. P. Cooper, in *Grasses in Agriculture* (FAO, Rome, 1959), state on page 4: "The great future development of grassland agronomy as such is likely to take place in the tropical and subtropical regions where the potentials are considered to be enormous and increases in yield of the order of 100, 200, or 300 percent may be obtained by simple adjustments in management or the application of fertilizer."

[19] See, for extensive discussion of techniques and possibilities in this field, *Possibilities of Increasing World Food Production*, FAO Freedom from Hunger Campaign basic study No. 10 (Rome, 1963).

tinue to be a limiting factor in arid areas. Data are very limited, but a few generalizations are attempted later on in this chapter. With fertilizer, however, there seems to be no problem of availability, though the investments required for manufacture will be large. Reserves of presently usable phosphates and potash salts already known amount to about 50 billion tons each,[20] and the chief source of nitrogen is the practically infinite supply in the atmosphere. Against these supplies we may place estimates of 150–200 million tons aggregate annual requirements for the food outputs projected above. This gives an estimate of about a 300-year supply of phosphate and potash fertilizer at the year 2000 rate of use.

These calculations do not take into account another source of increase in the food supply, namely animal products. Increases in yields of output per unit of feed would be in *addition* to those given here for crops, since our discussion has implicitly assumed that no gains are made in the efficiency of conversion of grains and forage into animal products. Gains which have already occurred in the advanced countries indicate that outputs per unit of feed can be substantially increased. The contribution which the world's fisheries can make to better diets has never been adequately explored, but it is undoubtedly large. In 1966, about 33 per cent of the world's catch went into fertilizer and feed,[21] while many edible species went uncaught because they were not regarded as fit to eat. Some potentially rich fishing grounds in the Antarctic, in the Indian Ocean and off the west coast of Africa are hardly exploited at all, while others are probably fished far below their sustainable yields. Finally, much might be gained by breeding and caring for fish, for most species are still part of the primitive economy of free, competitive hunting.

ENERGY

The problem of increasing energy output is complicated by the fact that mineral fuels are wasting assets; that is, there are fixed quantities in existence and replenishment is at a geological pace, infinitesimally slow relative to the rate of use. Knowledge of reserves is quite scanty, chiefly because there is insufficient incentive to do expensive exploration work until there is prospective use or market within the next one to three decades. All future values in the market place are subject to discount at the going rate of interest; a 5 per cent

---

[20] U.S. Bureau of Mines, *Mineral Facts and Problems*, 1965 edition, pp. 704, 727.
[21] FAO, *Yearbook of Fishery Statistics 1966*, Table A1-1.

rate of discount makes a dollar 50 years hence worth only 9 cents today.

Speculative estimates, based on general knowledge of geological formations around the world, and on rates of occurrence of coal seams, oil and gas fields, and oil shale, indicate conventional energy resources equal to about 700 years of use at the 1965 rate of consumption, or 100–200 years of consumption at the rates we have projected for the year 2000.[22] Some investigators note that this does not include all discoveries which may be expected; if these are included total energy reserves might be four or five times as great.[23] Others regard such a 200-year forecast as optimistic, or at least they anticipate that many areas of the world will have to rely mainly on nuclear energy in less than a century if steeply increased costs and reductions in consumption are to be avoided.[24] In either case, the problem of any absolute world energy shortage is not foreseen until long after the year 2000.

Long before world shortages arise in fossil fuels, of course, atomic plants will be used for substantial amounts of energy. By the year 2000, 10 to 20 per cent of the world's energy consumption may come from atomic sources, principally as heating elements for the generation of electricity.[25] How adequate are the reserves of atomic fuels?

The U.S. Geological Survey is reported to have estimated potential uranium resources in this country, comparable in quality to ore now being mined, as representing more than twice the energy equivalent of all coal, oil, and gas resources now believed to exist in the country; by geological inference, the total energy content of world resources of currently minable uranium should also be larger than that of the fossil fuels.[26] This favorable view depends on the assumption that through "breeder" reactors it will be possible to convert the relatively abundant uranium 238 into fissionable plutonium. Further possibilities of abundant energy lie in the conversion of thorium into a fission-

[22] *Fossil Fuels in the Future,* by Milton F. Searl (U.S. Atomic Energy Commission, October 1960), pp. 1–9; Sam H. Schurr, "Energy" in *Scientific American,* September 1963, p. 114.

[23] Cf. Schurr, *ibid.,* p. 116.

[24] H. J. Bhabha (Chairman, Indian Atomic Energy Commission), address at the U.N. Conference on Applications of Science and Technology for the Benefit of Less Developed Countries, Geneva, 1963.

[25] Projections made recently for the United States show that by 2000 about 15 per cent of total energy may come from nuclear sources, and about half of all electricity generation. From then on nuclear energy is expected to furnish increasing proportions of both. See Hans H. Landsberg, Leonard L. Fischman, Joseph L. Fisher, *op. cit.,* pp. 282–92, 855, 858.

[26] Sam H. Schurr, "Energy," *op. cit.,* pp. 120–24.

able material, and in the development of processes for exploiting lower grade ores. If an atomic fusion process is developed to a practical stage, much greater abundance will be available.

Between now and 2000, therefore, more than sufficient high-grade uranium and thorium ore would appear to be available to meet projected demands of the order of 10 to 20 per cent of total energy. The principal difficulties concern reactor technology and economies, safety, and, for less-developed countries, capital requirements.

METALLIC MINERALS

As we have observed previously, discovery and "proving up" of reserves of minerals is rarely done for more than will be required within two or three decades. However, enough is known in a rough sort of way to provide fair degrees of assurance for supplies at least as far as the year 2000.

A recent study indicates that for iron, aluminum, and manganese the known and inferred reserves are large enough, worldwide, to supply projected demands for at least the next 30 years without significant increase in costs.[27] Doubts about the existence of unknown or inferred reserves may be moderated by noting that in recent years major new sources of iron ore, for example, have been discovered in Venezuela, Canada, Liberia, Brazil, and Australia, as well as other places. Techniques for beneficiating lower grade ores have also been improved. For copper, lead, and zinc the conditions of occurrence of deposits and the lack of published data make the prospects less certain, but major new discoveries continue to be made. It should be kept in mind, moreover, that there are satisfactory substitutes for these metals in most uses, and that substitution, technology, and probably discovery will proceed at an accelerated pace if costs and prices rise.

FOREST PRODUCTS

Whether the world's forests will be able to double output as projected above seems dubious, though much more information is required to make a conclusive judgment. In the United States the relative price of lumber has risen and per capita output has declined due not only to price but to the widespread introduction of substitutes. However, FAO data indicate that half the world's output of sawlogs and 37 per cent of its total wood came from Northern America and Europe in 1965, though forest acreage in these two areas was only

[27] Bruce C. Netschert and Hans H. Landsbert, *The Future Supply of the Major Metals: A Reconnaissance Survey* (Resources for the Future, 1961).

22 per cent of the world's total.[28] Thus, if sustained output per acre in the rest of the world could be brought to a European-American level, output would be doubled. Such an increase in output could result from the introduction of faster-growing species in some areas, or exploitation of the large potentials of tropical hardwoods, now awaiting solution of difficult economic problems.

Changes in management practices that would entail only moderate costs could yield a large increase even in United States output, especially in small private holdings.[29] In less-developed areas, where cutting practices are poorer than in this country, the gains from this source could be much greater.

WATER

Thus far in this study we have not gone into the outlook for water demand and supply for either the United States or the whole world. This is only because comprehensive historical data for the United States are limited; and for many parts of the world virtually nonexistent. Lack of data is among the most pressing problems in the water resource field. The high cost of supplying fresh water severely limits economic development in many arid and semiarid areas. Precipitation is irregular in most countries, both regionally and seasonally, and water is costly to transport, prohibitively so for long distances.

Estimates of water demand and supply by continents, or even by countries except for the very smallest, make little sense; the job has to be done by river basins and frequently by portions of basins. However, some rough estimates made recently for the United States indicate that withdrawal uses—by cities, industries, and irrigation farmers —have been rising fairly rapidly and will continue to do so in the future. In the East withdrawal depletions (the fresh water taken from streams and lakes and not returned) are projected to increase from 14 billion gallons per day in 1960 to 37 billion in 2000; in the more arid West from 60 to 92 billion gallons per day, and in the Pacific Northwest from 11 to 20 billion gallons per day.[30] Large additional amounts of water, not actually depleted but frequently rendered unavailable for other uses, will be required to dilute pollutants and carry them downstream. In the arid West, lack of enough water

[28] FAO, *Yearbook of Forest Products Statistics 1966*, Table S1.
[29] *See* Charles H. Stoddard, *The Small Private Forest in the United States* (Resources for the Future, 1961).
[30] Landsberg, Fischman, Fisher, *op. cit.*, p. 28.

could limit further expansion in agriculture; industrial growth in some areas might be blocked unless a larger share of the water supply is allocated to this use. In the East and in metropolitan and industrial regions, generally the chief problems are those of water quality.

A number of possibilities exist for augmenting supplies. Additional storage reservoirs can be constructed; evaporation and irrigation canal losses can be checked; water-consuming trees and plants can be reduced; water can be recycled in industry; salt or brackish water can be substituted for fresh water in cooling and some other uses; water prices can be raised to check increases in consumption; surface and groundwater sources can be integrated for more economic use; whole river systems can be interconnected. Pollution abatement on many streams would yield large amounts of higher quality and, therefore, more usable water than is now available. Large gains could be made by legal and institutional changes which would result in some reallocation of water use away from irrigation, toward industrial and other much higher value uses. For the United States, speaking generally, water requirements for the next three decades can probably be met, save for a few places, if a number of these supply-increasing and loss-reducing efforts are applied with reasonable success.

Western Europe, also a highly developed area, for the most part has ample rainfall so that with additional investment and careful management future needs of a relatively slow-growing population should be met. The same appears to be true for Japan, although in both these areas development will have to be intensive and management more careful. More effective institutional arrangements than in the United States have made possible heavy concentrations of population and water-using industries in the Ruhr valley of West Germany, despite limited amounts of fresh water.

For the less-developed areas information is still more scanty. Obviously water is short in some places and at some periods of the year, while it is too plentiful in other places and times. In many of the more arid areas, such as West Pakistan, North Africa, and Northeast Brazil, agricultural improvement will depend heavily on water developments of various kinds.

Cheap demineralization obviously would be a boon in such places as these; to date costs by various feasible methods are still much too high to permit large-scale application. However, for human consumption in a few high-cost places demineralized water is already being produced.

Some Concluding Observations

This survey of statistical evidence does not give a clear answer to the important question: Are resources becoming scarcer in the United States and the world? Limiting our forward look to the year 2000, we foresaw no general increase in scarcity in the more-developed areas; the opposite trend is likely to continue. In the less-developed areas severe problems will be encountered, but the outcome will depend chiefly on the effort put forth and the competence of the people in the less-developed countries in dealing with their resource problems and potentials.

For the United States, historical data do not point to increasing scarcity in any general sense. Indications as to future technology and supply possibilities, when matched against projected demands to the year 2000, likewise do not indicate a general tendency toward increase in scarcity. This does not mean there will not be supply problems for particular resources at particular times and places; rather it means that in this country technological and economic progress, building upon an ample and diversified resource and industrial base, gives assurance that supply problems can be met. If this rather favorable prognosis is to be guaranteed in fact, scientific and technological advance will have to continue unabated and the results will have to be translated into economic reality. In addition, it will be essential to extend, or at least maintain to the present degree, a world trading and investing system in which raw material deficits can be met through imports from other countries with a surplus of these materials.

The historical data for most of the world, particularly the less developed areas, are not extensive or reliable enough to support more than tentative conclusions regarding long-range future adequacy of natural resources and raw materials. For the more-developed countries, particularly in Western Europe, where the data are reasonably good, the trend is not unlike that for the United States. The importance of a viable world trading system is, if anything, greater for most of the other more-developed countries than for the United States since they tend to rely more heavily on raw material imports and upon exports of processed goods, services, and other raw materials to pay for them. The success of the European Common Market and the European Coal and Steel Community over recent years is an indication of the importance of widening the area of freer trade.

In the less-developed areas of the world, the data are extremely thin;

projections are hazardous. One simply does not know enough about historical trends to gauge the rapidity with which technical advances already made in the more-developed countries will be applied in the less-developed ones. Nor can population projections be relied upon as coming very close to what will actually happen.

Nevertheless, the record, such as it is, indicates that living levels in most countries can increase over the coming years, with diets improving slowly and energy and mineral use more rapidly. The process depends heavily on education, motivation, favorable government policies, and social adaptations. We do not believe that shortages and inadequacies of natural resources and raw materials are likely to be the limiting factor.

It is nevertheless likely that a slower rate of population increase, due to a decline in the birth rate, would be associated with a faster increase in per capita levels of living. This is largely because the population would contain a smaller percentage of children and a larger percentage of persons in the working ages; there would be fewer mouths to feed compared with hands to work; and it would be easier to increase the proportion of invested capital to labor.

We must reiterate here that we have examined the future only as far as the year 2000. Projecting population growth beyond that at, say, 2 per cent per year soon leads to very high figures—12 to 15 billion by 2040, 25 to 30 billion by 2080, and so on. That the resource base of the world could accommodate such growth for more than a century is open to serious question. Of course, technology would not stand still either, and one must not underestimate the capacity of individuals and social institutions to respond intelligently and constructively to emerging problems, even though one cannot see exactly when or how such adaptations will be made.

There are certain escape hatches from any tendency toward increasing scarcity, and it is important that these be kept open. In fact, the challenge of public policy and private management of resource enterprises is to keep them open, both in developed and less developed countries. These escape hatches include: substitution of more plentiful, convenient, and cheap materials for those becoming scarcer; multiple-purpose development and use of land and water areas; importation of raw materials from other countries where supplies are more ample, and the increase in world commodity trade generally; and intensification of research, conservation, development, and management of resources.

Much of the answer to the central question of whether resources are becoming scarcer lies outside the resource industries and activities themselves. General programs of education and more specialized programs for training scientists, technical personnel, and managers are important. The capacity of people in less-developed countries to make use of technological improvements already successfully demonstrated in more-developed areas will be of particular significance. Social organization and willingness to experiment with new policies frequently will determine whether or not a country will be successful in its development and use of natural resources. For example, land tenure arrangements, laws and customs regarding the ownership and use of water, and willingness to try out new agricultural and forest management techniques are of great significance. Institutions which make possible rapid transfer of knowledge and techniques from more to less developed areas should be given special attention. Extension service activities will be of critical importance.

Further investigation of past resource development and use trends will make it possible to project future situations more accurately. As more work is done along these lines, it should be possible to specify more clearly the emerging problems of scarcity so that farsighted corrective policies can be installed in advance of the onset of tight situations. As time goes on we should be able to answer with less and less indecision the central question as to whether resources are becoming scarcer over the world.

Frank W. Notestein, Dudley Kirk
and Sheldon Segal

7

The Problem of Population Control

The previous chapters have posed the problems of population growth. Here we shall examine the prospects for checking rapid

FRANK W. NOTESTEIN *is President emeritus of the Population Council. He was formerly Professor of Demography and Director of the Office of Population Research, Princeton University, and also served as the first Director (Consultant-Director) of the Population Division of the Bureau of Social Affairs of the United Nations. He is a past President of the Population Association of America, a Fellow of the American Statistical Association and of the American Association for the Advancement of Science, and a member of the International Union for the Scientific Study of Population.*

DUDLEY KIRK *is Professor of Demography, Stanford University. He was formerly Director of the Demographic Division of the Population Council. He served on the faculty and as a research associate at the Office of Population Research at Princeton; and also as demographer and in various other posts in the State Department. He is a past President of the Population Association of America, current President of the American Eugenics Society, a Fellow of the American Statistical Association, of the American Sociological Association, and of the American Association for the Advancement of Science, and a member of the International Union for the Scientific Study of Population.*

SHELDON J. SEGAL *is Director of the Bio-Medical Division and Vice President of the Population Council. He served formerly on the Faculty of the State University of Iowa and is presently on the Faculty of Rockefeller University. He is President of the International Society for Research in Reproduction and has held offices in several other scientific societies. He is a member of the International Institute of Embryology, the Endocrine Society, the American Fertility Society, the American Eugenics Society, and the American Association for the Advancement of Science.*

population growth through reduction of the birth rate, particularly in the less-developed areas. We can best approach this problem of population control by considering first the reduction in fertility that has taken place in the West. What were the forces that brought about that reduction, and are these applicable in other parts of the world?

The Background

FERTILITY AND MORALITY IN NINETEENTH CENTURY EUROPE

Western Europe in the nineteenth century was the scene of increasing political order, agricultural innovations, the commercial and industrial revolution, and the growth of medical science. Together these produced a gradual but persistent decline in the death rate. At the same time, birth rates fluctuated in the middle and high 30s (expressed as the number of annual births per 1000 population). These rates are lower than the birth rates in most of the underdeveloped areas in the twentieth century because marriage was generally rather late and a substantial number of women remained unmarried. The century was a period of sustained but slow population growth in Europe, rarely exceeding one and one-half per cent a year in any country.

Beginning about 1875, fertility rates in Western Europe began a decline that continued through the late 1930s, by which time they produced a very slow growth. (It should be noted that the decline of the birth rate in France and in certain other areas began much earlier—probably in the eighteenth century. The causes are not clear, but the trend probably reflects the early rise of rationality in these populations.) In many countries there was a rebound in the birth rate after World War II, but this has largely subsided. Birth rates in Europe today exceed death rates, but only enough to perpetuate a rather slow rate of population increase.

An explanation of the decline in Europe's birth rates has been attempted along three different lines, related to changes in reproductive capacity, to the development of improved contraceptives, and to social and economic changes that encourage the small-family idea—the last representing part of the complex process often referred to as "the demographic transition."

CHANGES IN REPRODUCTIVE CAPACITY

J. deCastro is perhaps the most popular exponent of the view that a change in reproductive capacity is responsible for the transition from high to low fertility. In *The Geography of Hunger,* he sets up the hypothesis that improved diet may impair the ability to reproduce, since laboratory animals on high-protein diets have been shown to have litters of reduced size. He then correlates crude birth rates with caloric intake for nations around the world, and finds that the nations with the poorest diets have the highest birth rates. Hunger, he suggests, is the cause rather than the consequence of population pressure.

There are some obvious weaknesses in this reasoning. First, the litter size of laboratory animals has no demonstrated relation to human reproductive performance. Secondly, correlation is a measure of association, not of causation. Finally, and most damaging of all, deCastro neglects the pertinent evidence that negates his hypothesis. Many studies of middle-class well-fed American, British, and Scandinavian wives have shown conclusively that, unless they practice contraception, they conceive at rates that would yield a marital fertility quite as high as any in the poorest underdeveloped countries. If anything, well-nourished and healthy women are better, not poorer, reproducers than impoverished and disease-ridden women.

There may or may not be differences in reproductive capacity from country to country. If such differences exist their effect on birth rates is obscured by the large effects of differing social customs, and especially by the prevalance and effectiveness of voluntary restriction of births.

THE DEVELOPMENT OF IMPROVED CONTRACEPTIVES

The second theory attempts to explain the decline of fertility in Western Europe as a result of the invention of effective contraceptive methods, particularly the condom and the diaphragm. The theory has been supported by Henry Pratt Fairchild and William F. Ogburn, among others, and was suggested by the decline in the British birth rate that followed the Bradlaugh-Besant trial in 1877—an event that gave great publicity to newer birth control methods.

The theory fits many of the known facts. Birth rates began to decline first in the upper classes and in the urban centers, where information about the new inventions would spread most rapidly. It seeped gradually down through the social strata and spread from industrialized northwestern Europe to the agricultural southeast. A good case can, therefore, be made for the view that the invention of better birth control methods was a critical factor in the onset of the fertility decline.

There is at least one outstanding exception. In Ireland the crude birth rate declined in much the same way as in other parts of the modern world, but the fertility of married women remained as high as one would expect in the absence of contraceptive practice. The decline in Ireland was the result of the growing proportion of spinsters and the advancing age of marriage. Such postponement of marriage, or not marrying at all, are also ways of reducing the birth rate. Late and less frequent marriage has contributed to reductions in the birth rate historically in Europe and more recently in such countries as Japan, Korea, Singapore and Ceylon.

Nevertheless it is quite clear from numerous studies that the major factor in the reduction of birth rates was the rapid spread and growing effectiveness of contraceptive practice, together with some increase in abortion.

Although the importance of contraceptive practice cannot be denied, there is one serious obstacle to an explanation of the modern reduction of fertility in terms of the invention of improved contraceptive methods. A wide range of studies during the last 35 years have shown that large sectors of the population control their fertility without recourse to modern contraceptives. Millions of couples are successfully practicing *coitus interruptus* to control fertility. This method has been known for thousands of years, and used to some extent by all the major peoples of the world. There is substantial evidence that *coitus interruptus* began to be widely practiced in Europe when birth rates began to fall. The failure of birth rates to fall in other parts of the world clearly turns less on lack of effective means than on the absence of strong motivation.

THE DEMOGRAPHIC TRANSITION IN EUROPE

An appreciation of the motivational problem is easily gained if we consider the situation of mankind up to a moment ago in history. The problem has always been survival, not rapid population growth. We have no reason to suppose that any child born more than two centuries ago had an even chance of living as long as 30 years. In the face of heavy depletion by death, high fertility was a requirement for survival. The populations that have survived to inhabit the world's major regions all entered the modern era with the physiological capacity to reproduce abundantly, and with social institutions that fostered high birth rates.

There is great variety in the detailed forms in which the world's societies evolved to meet the challenge of survival, but the goal of high fertility is universally evident in the forms of economic organization, marital and familial institutions, educational systems, religious beliefs, means of gaining status, and even the informal sanctions of gossip and slander. There were few alternatives to early marriage and continuous childbearing as a means of livelihood or a sense of fulfillment for women. In the static self-sufficient peasant societies there was little social mobility. Parents generally aspired to have their children "become their stations in life" rather than rise in the world. Individuals found their social position largely in terms of their parentage. Parents desired large families both as a labor force and as a guarantee, in days of uncontrolled mortality, that there would be surviving children to care for them in their old age. In short, the prevalent ideals emphasized the perpetuation of the family and the importance of large numbers of children.

The technological revolution brought changes that made the old ideals obsolete. In the burgeoning cities, neighbors knew little of each other's antecedents. What a man could do and what he possessed became more important for his status in life than his familial origin. Education became common. New occupations developed, offering new channels for advancement. Mortality came under progressive control, so that many children were no longer necessary to assure a few survivors who could care for the aged parents. Under such conditions a new set of standards gradually began to emerge. People began to want fewer children, to whom they could give better opportunities for health, education, and advancement. The practice of birth control became more widespread and more effective, and birth rates gradually began to fall.

On the other hand, people have always sought to avoid illness and postpone death by any means. Witchcraft, incantation, prayer, and pre-modern medicine all had very limited success, but the end was highly desired and all available means continued to be used, regardless of their efficacy. As soon as effective means of controlling disease became available, death rates declined.

The decline of the birth rate came more slowly, pending the obsolescence of ancient values centered on the perpetuation of the extended family group, and the emergence in the modern setting of new values centering on the welfare and opportunities of the nuclear family. As the new ideals began to emerge, the population began the extensive practice of birth control. It is the lagging decline of the birth rate behind the death rate that accounts for the major part of the modern epoch of population growth.

This account of the "demographic transition" in the West is oversimplified, but it is essentially correct. Technological modernization almost inevitably entails transitional population growth, because the reduction of mortality requires only effective means, whereas the reduction of fertility involves questions of both means and ends.

DEMOGRAPHIC PROSPECTS IN DEVELOPING COUNTRIES

It should be noted that Europe was fortunate in the circumstances of its demographic transition. There was room for increase in numbers—Europe itself was rather lightly populated at the beginning of the modern era, and there was more than enough room for expansion in the New World. The control of mortality was being learned only gradually, and the decline of death rates was slow. In historical terms population growth was rapid, but in the light of trends in the underdeveloped countries today the growth of Europe's population was relatively slow. Still the transition from a system that had maintained the population on the basis of high birth rates balanced by high death rates, to the modern system that maintains it on the basis of low birth and death rates, involved a three-fold increase in Europe, and a five- to seven-fold increase of European populations throughout the world.

The nations undergoing modernization in the twentieth century face an entirely different situation. Thanks to the efficiency of the pre-modern rice culture, many of the Asian nations enter the period of modernization with relatively dense populations. We have become marvelously efficient in the control of disease—at the comparable stage of development in nineteenth century Europe, death rates were dropping only one-third to one-fifth as fast. Today some of the lowest death rates in the world are to be found in the underdeveloped areas where public health protection is relatively advanced, as in Ceylon, Singapore, and Taiwan. In its period of modernization Europe faced annual rates of growth of 1 per cent or less. Today 2 per cent is general, and many countries are growing at from 3 to 3½ per cent annually. Some appreciation of the difficulties that these rates impose in terms of economic drain may be obtained from the fact that 1 per cent doubles a population in 69 years, whereas an annual increase of 3½ per cent doubles it in about 20 years. Moreover, many of the newly modernizing countries have no space for expansion such as the New World afforded Europe during its epoch of modernization.

Such a description of the difficulties now faced occasionally elicits the response that it represents a purely arithmetical prediction. Demographers have been wrong before and doubtless they will be wrong again. But our fallibility offers no reassurance. We cannot be certain the population will grow, but we are certain that, if birth rates remain unchanged, only a catastrophic rise in death rates will prevent growth. Such a rise in mortality would demonstrate the bankruptcy of all our efforts. No one, least of all the people involved, can look forward to a rising death rate as a desirable mode of escape from the problems of population growth. Those who advocate letting the birth rate take its natural course may indeed be implicitly fostering a resurgent death rate and the failure of our efforts at modernization.

The Problem

THE NECESSITY OF POPULATION CONTROL

If we value life and health, education, and relief from poverty, the need for an early reduction of the birth rate is acute. Birth rates in the past have fallen most rapidly in the context of modernization and social-economic change. But there is nothing in the European experience to suggest that we must rely solely on gradual and automatic changes in society. One often meets the glib generalizations, particularly in the underdeveloped countries, that it is only necessary to concentrate on social and economic modernization since it is well known that we can rely on these processes to bring the birth rate down automatically. The argument neglects the time-span required for such an adjustment, and the tragic consequences that may follow to the entire society if the trend does not come rapidly enough. Even if we could be assured of rapid social and economic development the lag in transition between reduction of death rates and reduction of birth rates poses enormous problems of population growth. At worst such growth may completely consume economic growth and undermine the progress necessary to induce lower fertility. It is a sad anomaly that often the countries most in need of relief from the pressure of high birth rates are also the ones that have the poorest prospects for rapid economic and social progress.

There is every reason to believe that the process of reducing the birth rate can be greatly accelerated. We shall return to the question of ways and means when we come to an appraisal of future prospects. But first it may be useful to consider what influence the world's various religions may have on the possibilities of spreading the practice of family planning.

RELIGION AND BIRTH CONTROL

As a matter of doctrine, Moslems, Hindus, Buddhists, and Confucianists have no generally accepted or firmly administered opposition to birth control. Distinguished representatives of each can be found with all shades of opinion, but none is in a position to carry dominant sections of the laity with him. Moreover, recent governmental pronouncements favorable to the control of fertility have helped to give weight to the leaders who favor birth control.

The Roman Catholic position presents the only major theological obstacle to population control, as reaffirmed in Pope Paul's Encyclical of July 1968. The Catholic position does not concern population growth, but individual obligations for procreation and parental responsibility. Within that framework, constraints relate entirely to means by which fertility is regulated. From an exterior point of view the Roman position embodies certain advantages for the future regulation of fertility. It is so tightly drawn and carefully elaborated that, as an obstacle to the limitation of fertility, it is vulnerable to circumvention by advances in scientific knowledge. If we should learn how to forecast ovulation within 48 hours, fertility could be "licitly" controlled by abstention for only two days a month. Needless to say, such knowledge would have importance in the solution of the problems of population growth far beyond the confines of the Catholic group.

The major difficulty with the Catholic position, from the point of view of fostering the spread of family planning, lies less in the substantial impact of that position on its own adherents than on the Church's political influence. Fear that a soft position will foster the use of methods it opposes has led the Church's adherents to be very cautious about supporting both national family planning programs and international programs of technical aid for countries seeking help for their birth control programs, and to advocate legal constraints to such practices by Catholics and non-Catholics alike. There is, however, some indication that efforts of this kind are being reduced.

The major influence of religion on reproductive behavior often lies outside the strictly theological field. It lies in the changes of the way of life which the religious tend to impede—for example, the rising status of women, aspirations for social mobility, the values attaching to secular education, and the like. In Europe such matters have not greatly differentiated Catholic and non-Catholic. Today it is noteworthy that birth rates are lower in several Catholic countries than they are in the United States. The methods used to attain such regulation are not well known. Undoubtedly they are partly "licit" but partly "illicit" from the Catholic point of view. By contrast the highest rate of population growth for any major region of the world is found in "Catholic" Latin America. Thus the behavior of Catholic populations runs the gamut of world-wide experience and reflects chiefly the varying cultural background and socioeconomic development of its adherents.

The same can be said of the other major religions. To the extent that all religions tend to perpetuate traditional modes of behavior, they are of course obstacles to change. In this they are not essentially different from other institutionalized aspects of the value system—for example, the political and economic structure, and the familial organization. In all aspects of social life the detailed arrangements that foster fundamental goals have developed in the historical setting. This fact is not to be regretted, for it is doubtful that man could survive without the binding cement of non-rational loyalty to traditional goals, of which those relating to religion represent only a part. The difficulty is that means of attaining fundamental goals, which were effective in the past, may become obstacles to their attainment in new and radically different settings. The problem of education, whether in the political, economic, social, or religious field, is not so much a problem of shifting fundamental and universal human values as of fostering the growth of appropriate means for their attainment in a new setting. It requires delicacy of timing and the wisdom that avoids loss of orientation, while permitting sufficiently rapid change to meet the requirements of accelerating technological development. These two-fold needs have many manifestations, but in the field of birth control they imply the necessity for educational efforts stressing such fundamental values—the welfare of the nuclear family, the protection of motherhood, the responsibility of parenthood, the health and educational opportunities of children, and the dignity of individual life.

FAMILY PLANNING PROGRAMS

Social inertia is undoubtedly an obstacle to the rapid spread of family planning. But it is not an insuperable obstacle, as is sometimes hastily inferred from the fact that relatively few governmental programs have thus far measurably reduced birth rates. The inference is false. Full-scale programs are of recent origin and most of them could scarcely have been expected to bring about major reductions in the birth rate in so short a time.

The more remarkable fact is that population policies have so rapidly become an established part of government in the less-developed regions. Ten years ago only India had an official policy for promoting family planning and the program has been enlarged to a major national effort only in the last five years. Today at least 70 per cent of the population of the less-developed regions live in countries with definite policies promoting family planning. These include Communist China, South Korea, Nationalist China (Taiwan), Hong Kong, Malaysia, Singapore, India, Pakistan, Nepal, Ceylon, Iran, Turkey, Egypt, Tunisia, Morocco, Kenya, Mauritius, Trinidad and Tobago, Barbados, Jamaica, Costa Rica, and El Salvador. Efforts to promote birth control are being assisted by governmental and quasi-governmental institutions in a growing number of other countries, including Indonesia, the Philippines, Thailand, Venezuela, Colombia, Peru, and Chile.

Critics of these policies are prone to write them off as failures without recognizing the problems they must overcome and the time required to establish an effective family planning program in an underdeveloped country. As in every other endeavor, a policy is not necessarily a program. The word is often taken for the deed. Great progress is being made, but many ambiguities in policy and many administrative problems exist.

Government commitment to family planning programs is often initially weak and even timid. There are political and sometimes religious reservations about government intrusion into this sensitive area of private behavior. There are also ambiguities about the goals of slowing the rate of population growth. Thus there may be recognition that reduction in the present rates of population growth would be economically advantageous. But there is also the contrary feeling, often ambiguously combined in the same individuals, that growth is in some way automatically good and that national prestige and power will be enhanced by rapid population growth. In many countries of the less developed world, notably in Latin America and Africa, there are large empty lands. There is hope, often quixotic, that rapidly expanding populations can be turned to national advantage in settling these areas. Unfortunately, most such empty areas are thinly settled for compelling economic and climatic reasons. Furthermore, it is the *rate* of population growth, as much as the absolute number, that inhibits economic progress in the less-developed countries. Arguments in favor of strong family planning programs are gaining ground, but governmental commitment understandably lags behind policy pronouncements.

Even when a firm commitment to a family planning program has been made it is not easy to put into effect. Almost by definition less-developed countries lack the institutional structure and the substantive know-how to mount such a national program quickly and successfully. To spread family planning rapidly a substantial and well-organized program is required. The effort must be consolidated with the newly developing health, communication, and community development services of the nation. It requires large cadres of paramedical personnel to reach the villages, and a well-trained supervisory force to administer the programs. It requires national institutions to set standards and maintain them, to train personnel, and to develop such educational materials as film strips, posters, leaflets, and the like. In short, national family planning programs must draw on all the instrumentalities of adult education. At present there are still far too few institutions in either the underdeveloped or the advanced countries able to supply the necessary development work and training. They must be built. Fortunately both here and abroad public health institutions are moving in this direction.

The case of birth control is more difficult than, for example, public health. Efforts in public health have drawn on a large fund of experience with problems that are similar throughout the world. Programs introducing birth control do not have such a fund of experience to draw upon. In this the West is not a leader; the less-developed countries must find their own solutions.

This fact has dictated the necessity for research. While the major institutions and programs are being built there has been a wide range of field trials to test the suitability and efficiency of alternative approaches and of different methods of birth control. Outside agencies, private and public, have an especially important role in such activities through funding and technical assistance. Such research is not an alternative to action but a necessary complement to it. Organizational and instructional work can go ahead while such research is in progress. We can all learn while we are doing, and quickly incorporate new knowledge into the general programs. The most successful programs, such as those in Korea and Taiwan, have had the closest integration of research and action.

If most governmental programs to promote birth control have not been operating long enough or on a sufficiently large scale to demonstrate their effectiveness, why then our confidence that they can become effective? It rests on two grounds, the first general, the second specific. In the first place, educational programs have clearly been effective in modifying individual behavior. This is demonstrably true in agriculture and health. The same principles are involved in birth control.

And each year educational advances and rapidly growing communication facilities enlarge the means for such influence. Field surveys in country after country show attitudes favorable to family planning in large segments of the population.

What is even more to the point, several family planning programs have already achieved notable success. In South Korea and Taiwan over a fourth of the women of childbearing age are using modern and effective methods of contraception, to a large extent through the family planning programs. In these countries, and in Hong Kong and Singapore, there are rapid declines in the birth rate clearly related in part to the private and government birth control programs.

Family planning programs of course cannot claim all of the credit. In these countries birth rates had begun to fall anyway and surely would have continued to do so in the absence of government-sponsored programs. Other factors, such as rising age at marriage, changes in the age and sex composition of the population, and the spread of abortion and birth control through private channels, were reducing birth rates. The impact of the family planning programs is difficult to disentangle from other influences on the birth rates, and this is the subject of much technical debate. However, the debate is not whether there was an impact but rather how much. Surely birth rates would not have fallen so fast in the last few years "in the normal course of events" without organized birth control programs. In three of these areas (Korea does not have reliable records) the reduction of the birth rate has recently been at a pace scarcely ever reached in the Western world. In the decade 1957–1967 the reported birth rate in Taiwan dropped from 41.4 to 28.5; in Hong Kong from 35.8 to 23.0; and in Singapore from 43.4 to 27.1.

It would be foolhardy to suggest that the experience of these small and relatively prosperous areas will quickly be duplicated in the larger Asian countries and in other less developed regions. But this experience shows that birth rates in less developed areas can fall very rapidly and that birth control programs *can* make a difference.

At the opposite extreme of size and poverty is India. The government nominally adopted a population control policy in 1952 but in the first two five-year plans (i.e., 1951–1961) the actual expenditures in the family planning program were much too small to have an impact in a country as large as India. Even by the fiscal year 1960–1961 the program expenditures were only 9.8 million rupees (i.e., some two million dollars) or about ½ cent *per caput*. Important beginnings were made in public education, in training of workers, in provision of clinical services (chiefly in the towns) and in sterilization camps, but only beginnings.

The program was stepped up markedly in the Third Five Year Plan (1961–1966) but only at the end of this period was the program large enough to be regarded as a truly national effort, with expenditures of 120 million rupees in 1965–1966. Throughout the program heavy emphasis has been placed on sterilization, and by July 1968 some five million men and women had voluntarily been sterilized through vasectomies and tubectomies provided by the program. In 1966 intra-uterine devices were introduced and by mid-1968 had been accepted by a total of 2.5 million women. Attention has been turned more recently to promotion of "conventional" contraceptives, notably the condom. The Indian government has been cautious in introducing oral contraceptives and has done so only on an experimental basis.

Nevertheless, India has been innovative in many ways. It was, of course, the first country to adopt a national family planning policy. It was the first country to establish a full-fledged Department of Family Planning (in April 1966). It has experimented with many uses of mass media, utilizing such diverse approaches as television, radio, newspapers, films, mailings, folk songs, puppets, exhibitions, wall paintings, bus boards, rickshaw boards, notices on railway engines and in coaches, matchbox labels, postage stamps, and even elephants garlanded with family planning messages. The symbol of family planning—four faces on an inverted vermillion triangle with the slogan "Two or three children—that's enough" is becoming ubiquitous in India. India is also a leader in the non-clinical distribution of information and of contraceptives through such organizations as railways, the military, post offices, industries and plantations, as well as in subsidizing the normal marketing channels (e.g., for condoms).

The goal of the present program is to reduce the birth rate from an estimated 41 per thousand to 23 per thousand in 1978–79. The achievements so far are promising, but there is obviously a long way to go. The impact of the program is rapidly accelerating—an estimated total of .2 million births were averted by the program in 1965–66, .5 million in 1966–67, and .9 million in 1967–68. The last figure is still small in relation to some 20 million births occurring in India each year. But any reasonable extrapolation of present progress of the program will mean a significant reduction of the Indian birth rate in the next few years.

Great importance attaches to the Indian program because of India's poverty and because of its vast population, which is larger than those of Africa and Latin America combined. India is perhaps the most difficult test. Other larger countries, Pakistan excepted, do not yet have so highly developed a program as India nor such successful ones as South Korea and Taiwan. Most rely on rather limited, though expanding, clinical services to women without the extensive use of communication media and non-clinical approaches recently developed in India and Pakistan. As in India only two or three years ago, most countries are far short of having full-fledged national programs. But more and more are moving in this direction. Family planning programs are gaining momentum. There is no evidence that they have yet reached or remotely approximated a plateau of achievement except in those few oriental countries where the programs have already reached a large segment of the population and the birth rate is declining very rapidly.

Sometimes there is a disposition to delay major effort until scientific advances give more effective, cheaper, and more acceptable methods. The suggestion is dangerous. The work of training, organization, and pilot testing takes time. It can be undertaken effectively now with methods that are already available. If the educational and organizational work is not done, any new discovery will make small difference in the immediate future, since without the preliminary work it cannot be brought to the people.

Heavy and repeated emphasis has been laid on the problems of motivation and education because they are too often neglected. It is clear, however, that means are also important. The difficulties of the motivational situation only underscore the need for a wide range of effective, cheap, and esthetically and morally acceptable methods to meet requirements in different parts of the world. Little research was formerly devoted to either the scientific or the technological aspects of fertility control. Fortunately, this situation has changed and the prospects for future developments are excellent.

Physiologic Fertility Control

The physiologic control of fertility includes enhancement as well as suppression of fertility. For many years the major incentive for research in reproduction was the problem of infertility. More recently the emphasis has shifted, and there has been increased awareness by scientists of the importance of providing new means to restrict fertility.

For centuries mankind has attempted to prevent pregnancy by the direct procedure of preventing sperm from making their way to the arena of fertilization in the fallopian tube. Ingenious means have been contrived to thwart the ascent of spermatozoa. They have been confronted with various forms of vulcanized roadblocks, or plunged into lethal pools of jelly, cream, foam, or effervescent fluids. For all of these so-called conventional methods, the scientific basis has been the realization that the ejaculate contains the male factor responsible for fertilization—a fact that had been written thousands of years ago at the dawn of the historical era of mankind.

The modern era of contraception began within the last decade with the development of effective oral contraceptives and intra-uterine contraceptive devices. It is estimated that by the end of 1968 eighteen million women were using oral contraceptives and six million women had initiated the use of intra-uterine devices. Although these procedures have a high level of effectiveness, both have disadvantages and limitations. The use of either method is not without some level of medical anxiety. Oral contraceptives have been linked causally with an increased rate of thrombo-embolic disease, and a number of other metabolic disorders associated with their use are still under investigation. Intra-uterine contraception involves a known risk of uterine perforation and a possible increased incidence of pelvic infection. But these adverse effects, which represent minimal risks when compared to the hazards of pregnancy itself, do not constitute the major disadvantage of these methods. Rather, it is the fact that a high percentage of women who initiate the use of either method discontinue after a brief period. Continuation-of-use rates with intra-uterine devices are higher than with oral contraception use, when measured in comparable populations under similar circumstances. Nevertheless, there is considerable room for improvement and this realization provides continuing impetus for research on new means to regulate fertility.

No single method of fertility limitation may be expected to satisfy the diverse needs of the world's expanding populations. An effective method may be perfectly acceptable in one society and completely useless in another part of the world, for reasons of culture, religion, environmental conditions, or because of physiologic differences. Even a single country's contraceptive needs are varied. It becomes essential, therefore, to consider research in contraception not as a search for "the pill" or the "inoculation" but as an effort to find several acceptable means based on a variety of action mechanisms.

Research has shown that there are several steps in the reproductive process which may be vulnerable to controlled interference and could thus provide means for the voluntary regulation of fertility. Most experimental efforts to regulate fertility are aimed at interference with a key link in the chain of hormonal processes that control the reproductive process in the female or male.

INHIBITION OF OVULATION

Although the original hormonal contraceptives (progestin plus estrogen) probably have other biological effects that contribute to their contraceptive effectiveness, they are basically ovulation inhibitors. The effect on ovulation is subsequent to suppression of the release of gonad-stimulating hormones from the pituitary gland. This effect is the result of an action by the administered steroids on the floor of the midbrain (hypothalamus) or higher brain center. Ovulation suppression by means of a primary action at the level of the central nervous system (CNS) can be achieved experimentally by a number of other pharmacologic agents, including tranquilizers, narcotics, and some cardiovascular drugs. Morphine, for example, has been shown to inhibit ovulation in women. A practical application of these observations for the purpose of controlling ovulation seems unlikely, however, since there is no evidence that the anti-ovulatory effect can be isolated from the general pharmacologic effect of these compounds.

Another possibility for the interference with ovulation through an effect at the central nervous system stems from our growing understanding of how the CNS-pituitary link operates. Chemical substances from the brain which regulate the release by the pituitary of gonad-stimulating hormones (gonadotropins) have been identified. They appear to be relatively simple molecules, but the precise chemistry remains to be established. Until then, the possibility of using these releasing factors or analogues that may act as competitive antagonists as a basis for fertility control must remain conjectural. Of greater potential applicability perhaps is the recent finding that the hypothalamus may produce, in addition to gonadotropin-releasing factors, inhibitory substances which provide a physiologically normal means to suppress gonadotropin production. The inhibitor has been found in the brain of infants and prepubertal children, suggesting that it may play a role in holding the pituitary-gonadal circuit in check until puberty.

Direct suppression of gonadotropin production at the pituitary level, or interference with action of circulating gonadotropins, can be achieved by immunologic means. Antibodies to gonadotropins can be induced in experimental animals by immunization. In the male, sperm production (spermatogenesis) is impaired; in the female ovum maturation or ovulation is prevented. There remain, however, several important issues to be resolved so that a practical application of these experimental findings in human subjects is not imminent. We cannot, for example, envisage now a means for imparting controlled reversibility to a method of fertility inhibition based on active immunization with gonadotropins.

Another approach to the inactivation of circulating gonadotropins has been the study of natural plant products. At least two plants, one a North American prairie grass, have been reported to have this activity but years of study have failed to reveal an active and stable constituent that is devoid of undesirable side effects. In general, the evaluation of plant extracts for antifertility action by means of gonadotropin inactivation or any other route of activity has been discouraging and unrewarding. From time to time, a plant product is described that has a clear antifertility effect in laboratory rodents. Almost invariably these results can be ascribed to a mild estrogenic activity common in many legumes and other plants, an activity that has no practical significance for contraceptive purposes.

It appears, therefore, that control of fertility based on ovulation suppression will in the foreseeable future continue to depend on the action of synthetic hormones similar to those now in use as constituents of the widely used oral contraceptive agents.

TUBAL TRANSPORT OF OVA

The zygote or newly fertilized egg normally spends several days passing through the female reproductive tract before it begins the process of implantation in the uterus. This is a carefully timed sequence which must proceed in phase with preparatory changes occurring in the lining of the uterus (endometrium). If the zygote arrives too early from the fallopian tube, the uterus is inadequately developed and the zygote will degenerate.

Ovarian steroid hormones have a major regulatory influence on the tubal transport of ova. Estrogens increase the rate of secretion of tubal fluid and increase the peristaltic activity of the tubal musculature. Progesterone generally has the opposite effect on each parameter. Upsetting the proper sequence of hormonal influences, therefore, can disturb the normal passage of cleaving ova in the fallopian tubes. Indeed, this has been demonstrated by many experiments, but no simple unifying concept can be synthesized from the reported observations.

Nevertheless, the apparent lability of the regulatory mechanism for normal tubal transport of ova provides an attractive basis for controlled interference with fertility.

An influence on tubal transport of ova or zygotes may be involved in the effectiveness of post-coitally administered hormonal agents in the prevention of nidation in subhuman primates. Pregnancy in the rhesus monkey can be prevented by the administration of an estrogen during the four-day period after mating when the fertilized egg is traversing the fallopian tube. Accelerated tubal transport is a possible explanation because, in other species, the relationship has been established between post-coital estrogen treatment and acceleration of tubal transport of ova. Estrogen induces premature expulsion of the ova from the fallopian tubes of rats, rabbits, and guinea pigs. The effect has now been reported with a variety of compounds, both steroidal and non-steroidal, but it becomes evident that the common feature of all is their estrogenicity. The data available on the application of this principle to human subjects are too few to permit an evaluation, although it has been reported that no pregnancies occurred in a limited number of rape cases and volunteer subjects treated with estrogen four to six days after mid-cycle insemination. A systematic analysis of the potential antifertility action of post-coital estrogen treatment in the human female is required. Assuming that the activity in animals would carry over to the human, an interesting method of fertility control is suggested. Pills taken orally for a day or two after intercourse would prevent pregnancy even if fertilization had occurred. There would be no disruption of the natural menstrual cycle and no manifestation whatever of the pregnant state.

CORPUS LUTEUM FUNCTION

The uterine environment is not essential for survival, implantation and early development of the fertilized egg. In some species ova can be fertilized and cultured *in vitro,* and a human ectopic pregnancy is quite independent of the uterine environment. Nevertheless, in all species studied, a successful intra-uterine pregnancy requires progestational preparation and maintenance of the endometrium. It seems likely that the same situation prevails in the human female.

On this assumption, several investigators have sought steroid inhibitors of implantation by examining a variety of compounds for their antiprogestational effect, and a few compounds have emerged that appear to have implantation-inhibiting activity. At least one compound with an excellent record in biological assays has been carried to preliminary clinical trial and evidence for antiprogestational activity obtained. Extensive trials in subhuman primates will be required before the antifertility potential of this and related compounds can be established.

In addition, several laboratories have reported antiprogestational or anti-implantation activity for a number of synthetic hydrocarbons which have been available for a number of years and several of which are used clinically as synthetic estrogens. One, which has excellent antifertility activity in laboratory rats, proved to be remarkably effective for the induction of ovulation in cases of human infertility and is now prescribed for that purpose (clomiphene). Another was, in fact, tested as an antifertility agent in women, but without success (MER-25). Still others, in spite of interesting laboratory findings, have not been evaluated in the human subject. These compounds have been variously described as antizygotic, blastotoxic, antinidational, weak estrogens, anti-estrogens or antiprogestational, depending on the assay system used. A systematic analysis of the potential usefulness and safety of this type of compound for human contraception should be undertaken.

Another approach to the elimination of the progesterone needed for nidation has been to interfere with the function of the corpus luteum by pharmacologic means. Several pharmacologic agents, when studied in the rat, appear to have this effect either directly or through a depressing effect on the pituitary production of luteotrophin. This type of activity could have significant applicability for fertility regulation.

A similar luteolytic effect by inhibition of luteotrophic hormone release is believed to account for the antifertility activity of ergocornine, an antihistamine of the ergot series, which prevents implantation in the rat or mouse when administered during a limited period of tubal transport of fertilized ova. Future development of this particular compound for contraception is not likely in view of apparent toxicity in clinical trials.

The present disappointment notwithstanding, antifertility action through a luteolytic effect is one of the more intriguing prospects on the research horizon. In theory, an oral preparation active in such a manner could be taken by a woman either monthly, at the time of the expected menses, or only on the occasion of a suspected fertile cycle as evidenced by delay in the onset of menstruation. Efforts along these lines will be stimulated by the growing evidence for the existence, in many species, of a luteolytic substance produced by the uterus and transmitted by tissue diffusion and common blood supply to the ovary. Partial purification of the luteolytic factor from sheep uterus has revealed the material to be a small protein molecule that has adequate stability for further purification and testing.

There are three likely loci for interfering with male reproduction; sperm formation, sperm maturation, and the constitution of the seminal fluid.

SUPPRESSION OF SPERM PRODUCTION

The testis, like the ovary, depends upon stimulation by pituitary gonadotropic hormones in order to perform its normal function of producing sex hormones and sperm. Like the ovary, the testis can be secondarily suppressed by a procedure that stops the production of gonadotropins. The oral progestins, for example, could be effective agents for the inhibition of sperm production. Doses required, however, have the unwelcome effect of inhibiting the secretion of sex hormones by the testis; as a consequence, potency and libido are reduced. There are, however, long-acting androgen esters now available that may provide long-term suppression of spermatogenesis while maintaining libido and general well-being. At the moment, this approach seems more encouraging than the search for compounds with minimal toxicity that act directly on the testis.

There are other orally active chemical compounds that stop sperm production without interfering with testicular hormone secretion. Several classes of chemical substances have been found to have this effect, but all have accompanying side effects that render them unsatisfactory for contraceptive purposes. One group of such compounds is the nitrofurans, which have had wide use as inhibitors of bacterial growth. They are very effective in stopping sperm production in man, but the doses required cause nausea and headache.

Another promising compound, a dinitropyrrole, impairs spermatogenesis in the rat for as long as four weeks after a single oral dose. An infertile state can be maintained indefinitely by administering single doses at intervals of four weeks. Sperm production recovers fully when treatment is stopped. Toxicologic findings resulted in the withdrawal of this compound from investigation, but it is possible that a related compound may be discovered which retains the antispermatogenic activity while being devoid of toxicity.

Testicular antigens that can be used for specific immunization to prevent spermatogenesis have been isolated. Indeed, even non-purified, crude testicular extracts can cause the arrest of spermatogenesis in the guinea pig and in the rat. An attempt has been made to immunize human males with testicular extract believed to be purified for the spermatogenesis-inhibiting factor, but the results have not been notable. Immunization with tissue extracts for the purpose of inducing sterility in either the male or female organism seems distant at this juncture. The basic problems of cross-tissue reactions, specificity of antigens, controlled reversibility of the immune reaction, development of acceptable adjuvants, still impede progress in this field.

FERTILIZING CAPACITY OF SPERMATOZOA

Mammalian spermatozoa may appear completely normal and have normal motility without possessing the capacity to fertilize ova. This vital function is achieved through a final maturation stage of sperm that has been termed "capacitation." Evidence for capacitation has been obtained in a number of mammalian species, including rabbit, rat, hamster, sheep and ferret. From the viewpoint of fertility control research, the intriguing extension of the capacitation concept is an understanding of the manner in which it can be inhibited. Sperm do not capacitate in the uterus of a rabbit injected with progesterone or in the uterus of a rabbit in the pseudo-pregnant state (progestational condition).

Although the process of capacitation has not been demonstrated as an essential element of sperm maturation in primates, the assumption that it does occur seems reasonable. With the greater availability of subhuman primates for reproductive research, this issue should be clarified before long. In any event, the evidence from other mammals suggests that interference with sperm capacitation may account for the contraceptive action of continuous low-dose progestin therapy that imparts an antifertility effect without the benefit of added estrogen and without inhibiting ovulation.

The role of progestin in influencing the ability of sperm to capacitate in the female tract raises the question of a possible influence of this hormone while sperm still reside in the male storage system. The effect of progestins in the male at doses below the threshold for inhibition of spermatogenesis has not been systematically analyzed in any species. Changes on the surface coat of the sperm could perhaps control the ability of the sperm to fulfill its role in fertilization. Whether such changes could be brought about, by hormonal or other means, while the differentiated spermatozoa are stored in the epididymis, warrants careful study.

HUMAN SEMINAL FLUID

A primary function of the ejaculate in all species is to act as a carrier of the spermatozoa from the male to the female reproductive tract. However, the great chemical complexity of the seminal plasma suggests other and more subtle relationships to the function of spermatozoa. The chemical composition of the seminal fluid in man has been analyzed in considerable detail. It is known, for example, that the seminal fluid contains several trace metals, e.g., iron, copper, zinc, and magnesium. Fructose is formed in the seminal vesicles and its formation is dependent upon the secretion of testosterone by the testis. It remains to be explored if mild anti-androgenic substances can influence seminal fluid chemistry at doses below the threshold for other, undesirable, anti-androgenic effects. Adverse conditions of the fluid medium could influence the spermatozoal surface in a manner that would impair its ability to reach the fallopian tube or to penetrate an ovum. It is possible, also, for exogenous substances to enter the seminal fluid by way of the bloodstream. Following the administration of estrogen to the male rat or rabbit, for example, estrogen can be found in the ejaculate. Ethanol and sulfonamides from exogenous sources have also been found in seminal fluid. A pertinent question, therefore, is whether spermicidal substances might be found which could reach seminal fluid after ingestion or injection.

The areas of research cited here are among those topics most likely to give rise to new means to regulate fertility. Yet, all studies in the biology of reproduction create the information base which will precipitate future advances in the field.

Practical Prospects

As the foregoing suggests, given the necessary research effort, the prospects for the development of new and more appropriate methods of limiting fertility are excellent. It is only essential that the work be pushed while the organizational, educational, and training programs with existing methods go forward.

THE GROWING WORLD CONSENSUS

A few years ago international agencies were precluded from actively promoting family planning by political opposition. Today there is little disagreement about the existence of a grave threat implicit in the present demographic situation. The facts and the danger are now generally accepted. Ideological and religious controversies on these issues have receded. The Soviet Union and other communist countries no longer present monolithic opposition to birth control on ideological grounds, and in Communist China birth control is actively promoted. The opposition of Catholics to birth control has rapidly diminished in the past few years. The papal encyclical of July 1968, reaffirming the ban on artificial means, has scarcely checked the tide of support for family planning. Indeed, the encyclical has perhaps done more damage to the Church than to the cause of family planning.

The United Nations and the other international agencies are moving to support of family planning. In the last few years the United Nations itself has moved from research to the provision of technical assistance and of population program officers posted in various countries. It has sent advisory missions on family planning programs to both India and Pakistan at their request. It has established a special trust fund to promote its work in this field.

There is growing political support for such work by member governments. In December 1967, in a dramatic observance of Human Rights Day, U Thant presented a declaration on population signed by the heads of 30 states calling attention to the world problem of population and the need for cooperative efforts to cope with it. In different ways the World Health Organization, the World Food and Agriculture Organization, UNESCO, the World Bank, UNICEF, and the regional commissions of the United Nations have gone on record favoring action in the field of population. Such reiteration is valuable, not only because of policy implications for each agency, but because each of such pronouncements appeals to a different constituency, such as physicians, agriculturalists, educators, bankers, welfare personnel and regional leaders. Even in the Americas, where the role of the Catholic Church is most important, the Organization of American States held a conference in Caracas in September 1967 which for the first time recommended national action on the problems created by very rapid rates of population growth in the region.

These pronouncements are very likely more important than actual or potential technical assistance, important as these may be. The repeated declarations on the seriousness of the world population problem are creating a sense of international approval and urgency for national action in family planning. A national family planning program has become highly respectable in the community of nations.

THE SITUATION IN DEVELOPING COUNTRIES

Where do we stand? On the one hand there are many discouraging elements. Some of the underdeveloped countries are extremely heavily populated for economies that depend on agriculture. The levels of income are low. The birth rates are higher than those of pre-modern Western Europe, although they are not higher than those of the United States about 1800, or of Russia in the early twentieth century. Population growth has been speeded by the efficiency with which contagions and infections are now controlled. Death rates have been dropping in the underdeveloped countries at a faster rate than seemed possible even twenty years ago. The rates of growth are now much higher than those of Europe while it was undergoing modernization and its demographic transition. The risks of failure in the efforts of development are very great unless today's underdeveloped countries can reduce their birth rates much more rapidly than Europe did. The problem could scarcely be more urgent, and it must be faced now and for at least the next two or three decades.

There are also hopeful factors. Europeans reduced their birth rates in the face of opposition by their governments and their religious and civic leaders. They did so because in the new setting of a modernized society the individual citizen took action in spite of the public position taken by his leaders.

Today we have a radically different situation in the developing countries. Government after government is coming to understand the urgency of the problem and is beginning to do something about it. This changed official posture adds a wholly new element to the situation. Just as the Western world had to do the innovating in the field of public health, India and other countries are learning by experience how to tackle the problem of reducing fertility. This will be facilitated by two favorable forces—improvements in contraceptive technology (discussed above) and changes in attitudes and motivations accompanying modernization.

There is not a country in the world today that, aside from war and acute civil disorder, is not moving in the direction of modernization as measured by such indices as more education, lower mortality, some degree of urbanization, better communication facilities, and at least the beginnings of industrialization. In the majority of countries there is also a rising trend in *per caput* income. These are forces that in the past have created the setting for reductions in natality. A growing number of less developed countries are moving into the "threshold" area in which such forces have generated fertility reduction. In quite a few, birth rates are already falling rapidly, as in Ceylon, in Malaya, in Chile, in Puerto Rico, and in the former British West Indies. Thus family planning programs are going with, rather than against, the tide of socio-economic influences. Given the continuation of present trends, family planning programs will be operating in an increasingly favorable socio-economic environment for fertility control.

Paradoxically the very rapidity with which death rates are being reduced should contribute to more rapid reduction in birth rates than occurred in Western Europe. This is true for two reasons. First, the decline of mortality, and especially infant mortality, is leading to larger families of *living* children. There is more economic pressure to control family size, especially when ways of life are changing and aspirations for children are rising. On the land peasants must be concerned about greater fractionalization of their holdings; in the towns couples must deal with acute problems of feeding, housing, and clothing larger families. Second, it is no longer necessary to have so many children to be assured of survivors, especially of sons, to carry on the family name and responsibilities. From awareness of these facts comes stronger motivation to restrict family size.

The evidence for general changes in public interest and attitudes does not have to rest on theory. In many countries field surveys have been taken of knowledge, attitudes and practices concerning family planning. These show that in many and diverse countries a substantial majority have favorable attitudes toward family planning and that there is a large reservoir of couples who would like to limit their childbearing. Where repetitive studies have been made these show an increase in these proportions over time. Some of these studies have methodological weaknesses and, of course, verbal response is not a sure guide to action. But the overwhelming evidence is that peoples in the less developed world are moving toward more favorable attitudes concerning family planning, gaining greater knowledge of methods, and feeling more motivation to practice birth control.

Despite these favorable factors there are some who feel that the situation is so desperate that many countries cannot wait for gradual measures based on voluntary participation. This concern is characteristic of the widely prevalent crisis psychology with its apocalyptic visions of "inevitable" mass famines in the next decade. Much of this derives from the very grave food shortages in India in 1965–66, since recouped by better weather and, increasingly, by greater use of fertilizer and by the rapid spread of the new high-yielding grains.

Happily it is fair to say that the great majority of persons directly concerned in problems of development—economic planners, agricultural economists, agronomists, demographers—do not see an immediate threat of mass starvation or total economic collapse (American Assembly, *Overcoming World Hunger*, 1969). They give more emphasis to the need for longer range building of infrastructure in agriculture, for example, to make the increased food production promised by the current "green revolution" effective and most widely distributed. They do not see a simple problem or simplistic solutions. The problem is much more accurately seen as the arousal of world conscience and effort to meet long-standing problems of undernourishment and malnutrition greatly intensified by the pressure of growing numbers. Very few doubt the need for checking population growth. There is general agreement that it is of the greatest importance to speed the reduction of birth rates.

What are the alternatives to intensification of present family planning programs? Alarmists call for crash programs of population control. Among the suggestions are coercive measures by the government such as mass use of antifertility agents (not yet invented) in the water supply or in staple foods; temporary sterilization of all girls at puberty and of women after each delivery by means of a time-capsule contraceptive, with reversibility only on government approval; compulsory sterilization of males with three or more living children; compulsory abortions of illegitimate pregnancies. Less drastic proposals include economic incentives such as bonuses for sterilization, child-spacing and non-pregnancy; and economic disincentives such as withdrawal of tax, educational, medical, and welfare benefits after the Nth child. Economic incentives may prove important in the future but those suggested entail obvious administrative difficulties. Small payments in India are indeed made both to men receiving vasectomies and to persons making the referrals. Disincentives have the serious drawback that they tend to punish living children for the action of their parents. In any case most underdeveloped countries have relatively few such benefits for *any* children. Aside from proposals to intensify existing research and educational campaigns, few such suggestions are technologically or politically feasible at the present time, quite apart from the moral issues involved. In our view, radical measures involving coercion or "punishments" for having children are more likely to bring down governments than birth rates. No innovation so radical as birth control will be accepted en masse overnight; nor does any reasonable person expect family planning programs or any measures of population control to solve the problems of the less developed countries by themselves. As perceived by governments in most countries, family planning programs are integral parts of much larger plans for socioeconomic development, including education, health, agriculture, industrialization, communications and much else. Reduction of runaway population growth is a necessary but certainly not a sufficient condition for achievement of development goals.

It is the view of the authors that family planning programs are making real headway; that the gains being made are at a pace very few would have dreamed of as recently as ten years ago; and that the pace of present progress, if maintained, promises to have a major impact on birth rates of the less developed world in the 1970s.

A second major doubt is that, *even if successful,* voluntary family planning programs cannot be expected to resolve the world population dilemma. Even in the more developed countries, and notably in the United States, surveys show couples desiring more children than are necessary for replacement. According to this reasoning, even if *all* births were planned there would still be continuing and substantial world population growth. Thus we cannot rely on the self-interested choices of individual couples to meet society's needs. The only acceptable goal is zero rate of growth because any rate of growth continued long enough leads to astronomical figures. Given existing preferences in family size, governments must go beyond voluntary family planning. To achieve zero rate of population growth governments will have to do more than cajole; they will have to coerce. In the long run they may have to change basic institutions. The logical target for legal and institutional pressures is the family: pressures to postpone marriages; economic pressures and inducements for married women to work outside the home; provision of free abortions for all women requesting them; downgrading of familial roles in comparison with extrafamilial roles; and restriction of housing and consumer goods. It may be noted that in communist countries, including mainland China, these institutional pressures actually exist; though they were created for a different purpose (e.g., to maximize the labor force), they doubtless are a major factor in the low birth rates now existing in Eastern Europe and the Soviet Union. Such institutional changes supply motivation for family limitation and the provision of free abortion affords a means.

The implications of such major institutional changes go far beyond population control. The family is the basic social unit of society and its major institution for the socialization of children. Evolutionary changes accompanying modernization are indeed promoting later marriage, a changed status of women and growing importance of extra-familial roles. A number of countries (for example, India) are considering legislation for permissive abortion as an extension of voluntary family planning. But to impose more drastic changes on a large scale implies many risks, not least to the regime that undertakes them. The price for this type of population control may well be the institution of a totalitarian regime.

The goal of zero rate of growth has a rational appeal but little validity or meaning for the immediate future. No government in the less developed regions, communist or non-communist, has declared a target of achieving zero rate of population growth nor is this a realizable goal for most countries in the next decade, and for many even in this century. As explained in an earlier chapter, the inertia of present age structures precludes quick achievement of a stationary population short of a catastrophic increase in the death rate or a reduction of fertility far below the level of replacement. The acute problem is correctly seen as the containment of runaway rates of population growth now existing in most of the less developed countries. It is much more vital to reduce population growth from 3 to 2 per cent, and from 2 to 1 per cent, than from 1 per cent to zero. In any case the first two are necessary antecedents to the last. Thus far the term "population control" is generally used in the sense of checking runaway growth, not in the sense of manipulating population to some ultimate quantitative objective. In the long run this may be necessary, but the countries concerned are in most cases still very recently converted or still in the process of conversion to the idea that *any* curtailment of population growth is desirable through government action.

It is our view that governments in the less developed countries at this time have neither the will nor the ability to apply radical and coercive measures in the interests of population control, and in their judgment, as well as ours, efforts at governmental coercion would do more harm than good. Quite aside from their probable inefficacy, coercive measures in control of family size intrude government prerogative into very private areas of life. One has only to recall the Nazi era in Europe to view with the greatest misgiving the adoption of any legislation giving government the authority for compulsory sterilization or mandatory control of family size.

In any case, family planning programs based on voluntary participation and democratic procedures have not yet had a fair trial. No one knows how rapidly and how far birth rates can be induced to decline if governments commit themselves to major family planning programs over a sustained period. Where this has happened the initial results are promising.

To the new driving force of governmental leadership we must add the fact that the prospects are excellent for obtaining much more suitable methods of birth control than were formerly available. There are substantial reasons for optimism and there is no basis for the view that only tragic developments are possible. The answers will surely depend on the energy and resources with which the governments themselves approach the problem, and the vigor of technical support provided from the developed countries.

It should not be supposed that the foregoing optimistic view suggests that populations can be quickly stopped from growing, much less reduced in absolute numbers in any near future. The control of mortality is much too efficient and the age distributions are so heavily loaded with young people progressively moving into the reproductive years that substantial growth is inevitable. We can, however, hope for a very considerable curtailment of the rates of increase. On such a curtailment in a few decades depends much of the chances for modernization and escape from elemental poverty.

This chapter has dealt primarily with the problems in reducing birth rates and the prospects for containing runaway population growth in the less developed areas. It has not dealt with the question of reduction of population growth in more advanced countries, which is very different. This is discussed in the next chapter along with more general consideration of policy issues.

Frank Lorimer

8

Issues of Population Policy

Population as a World Problem

Questions of policy relative to population trends are, in large part, regional and specific. An attempt to treat the problems of the United States, Africa, France and Pakistan in the same terms is likely to promote confusion rather than enlightenment.

Yet the accelerated increase of mankind is having and will have (see Chapter 2) far-reaching consequences which can not be easily formulated but which profoundly affect the whole basis of human life and the structure of society.

"The present era is unique in that a predominance of man in the earthly environment is being established such as has never before existed" (United Nations, *The Future Growth of Population*, p. 21). We

FRANK LORIMER *is professor emeritus of Sociology in the Graduate School of American University. He has had such important demographic assignments as: Technical Secretary to the Committee on Population Problems of the National Resources Committee; Consultant to the National Resources Planning Board; Consultant to the Office of Strategic Services; Chief, Economics Function section in the Foreign Economic Administration; Chief of the Population and Employment Branch of the Supreme Command, Allied Powers, Tokyo; and Research Associate of the Office of Population Research, Princeton University. He has served as administrative Director of the International Population Union. He is a past President of the International Union for the Scientific Study of Population and of the Population Association of America.*

are in the midst of an *ecological revolution*. This revolution is as irre-
versible as the leveling of mountains by rain and wind. It is due in
part, though only in part, to the rapid proliferation of the human
species. It affects the springs of water in the woods—with which many
of our older citizens have been, but fewer of our younger citizens will
be, familiar. It must also affect the springs of human experience and
its expression in art, music, and poetry.

The ecological revolution is changing the natural basis of human
existence, society, and experience. It will bring good and evil of unforeseeable kinds and magnitudes. Is mankind spiritually prepared to
deal appropriately with these revolutionary changes? Would it not be
wise, if this were possible, to modify these trends so that our passage
from the natural ecology in which human societies were formed into
the uncharted, more "artificial" world of mass societies in constricted
space may be less precipitous?

In a more immediate sense, trends which threaten the national
aspirations of more than half the world's population present a problem
to all nations. Frustration breeds envy, suspicion and violence. The
security of the lucky nations with large natural resources, accumulated
wealth and advanced techniques may be critically affected by the progress or reverses experienced in less fortunate nations during the next
few decades.

The development of American policies relating to population trends
must, therefore, be framed in a world context.

Obstacles to Objective Analysis

Much of the discussion of population questions during the previous century was channeled through well-worn grooves to a false
dichotomy. In spite of the movement today toward more objective
analysis of the complex issues which involve population, reverberations
of the controversy between the proponents and opponents of the
Malthusian thesis, along with other predilections, hamper a realistic
approach to policy formation in some circles.

Malthus' original essay was polemical. His exposition of population
increase as the cause of poverty was developed as a refutation of Con-
dorcet's call for the "perfectioning" of mankind by restructuring social
institutions. It was, nevertheless, developed with acute observations
and elaborated in subsequent studies. Though an over-simplification,
it had a larger measure of validity for societies with relatively static
technology and culture. He observed that population trends prior to

his time were determined mainly by the interaction between two primordial forces: the trend toward increase resulting from "the attraction between the sexes" and the "positive checks" of death and sterility due to hunger, disease, and vice. He assumed that production of the means of subsistence in any country, at a given stage of the slowly emerging arts, is largely determined by its natural resources. An advance of the arts releases a wave of population which soon absorbs the gains and reactivates the forces of misery. He held that the only way in which a nation can escape from perpetual poverty, due to the pressure of population on resources, is to restrict population growth by the exercise of prudential restraint. He did not comprehend the potentialities of science and technology, and his followers have persisted in minimizing their importance. They also minimize the importance of changes in social structure, culture and economic institutions. And, incidentally, they fix attention on absolute ratios of population to resources, as contrasted with the dynamic interrelation between demographic and economic changes, which may be more important over a considerable period than the absolute ratios.

Reactions to Malthusian dogma by proponents of changes in social institutions and by those concerned with the advancement of agriculture, the control of disease, etc., often lead them to an equally dogmatic denial of the economic and social effects of population trends.

A classic anti-Malthusian dogma was formulated by Karl Marx. The phenomenon described by Malthus as "over-population" is interpreted by Marxists as a "relative surplus" of labor. This is said to be an essential characteristic of capitalism, but nonexistent in other types of society. The relation was stated as follows by T. V. Ryabushkin in "Social Aspects of Population Structure and Movement," United Nations: *World Population Conference,* 1954 (Volume 5, meeting 28):

> Every social system has its own concrete laws of population. . . . In conditions of capitalistic mode of production a certain part of the population systematically becomes relatively superfluous. . . . In socialistic society . . . the problem of excessive population no longer arises (pp. 1032–33). Thus the Malthusian theory is completely wrong and fruitless to explain historical facts. But maybe it has some sense for population policy in the future? Maybe it makes some sense to reduce rate of increase of population in any economically backward country in order to increase to some extent the level of well-being of population in the nearest future? To these questions we also give a sharp negative answer. *The Malthusian theory is harmful because it distracts attention from really scientific ways of increase of the working people's well-being.* (p. 1038, italics added.)

These dogmas present a false antithesis. They imply that the control of population and advances in economic productivity, health and education are *alternative* solutions to the problem of mass poverty. Most modern scientists, on the contrary, agree that they are essentially *complementary* and, in fact, mutually dependent.

Opposition to human intervention in the physiological processes initiated by coitus and terminating in birth is prevalent in many religious traditions. This stems in part from the view of natural processes as sacred and the fear of manipulating them in any untraditional way. Contraceptive devices a century ago were commonly dubbed "unnaturals." In Christian tradition (as in Gandhi's thought) this motif was reinforced by asceticism and emphasis on the assumed antagonism between "the flesh" and "the spirit." The taint of sexual relations, even within marriage, was justified only as a creative act to engender new life. The practice of contraception was, therefore, condemned officially in all branches of Christianity prior to the Lambeth Conference of the Church of England in 1930, which hesitantly reversed its previous teaching on this subject. This action was followed by positive endorsements in all Protestant communities, except in some Fundamentalist sects.

The great scholastic theologian, Thomas Aquinas, had given Catholic doctrine in this field a firm theoretical structure on the basis of Aristotelian metaphysics. This rests on the theory of natural law and the distinction between the "primary" end of marriage, interpreted as procreation, and its "secondary" personalistic aspects. This position was vigorously reaffirmed by Pope Pius XI in the encyclical, *Casti Connubii*, in 1920. The distinction between the primary and secondary ends of marriage was relinquished in the Second Vatican Council, and the inference from the principle of natural law in this field is now questioned by many eminent Catholic theologians. Recognizing the gravity of problems concerning population and the regulation of procreation, the great humanist, Pope John XXIII, established a special Papal advisory commission on this subject, including social scientists, physicians and moralists. This was formalized by his successor, Paul VI, and later enlarged to include 15 bishops and cardinals. This commission approved by a large majority (70 of the 84 members) the assignment of final responsibility for decisions in this matter to the conscience of individuals in consultation with their spiritual and medical advisors. Meanwhile a popular movement toward relaxation of the traditional position progressed rapidly and was voiced in the Third World Conference of Catholic Laity, Rome, 1967. Nevertheless, the traditional doctrine was reaffirmed by Pope Paul VI in the encyclical *De Humanae Vitae*, July, 1968, without substantial modification (except omission of the traditional distinction between the primary and secondary ends of marriage). Since the promulgation of this encyclical, widespread dissent has been voiced by many Catholic laymen (including a majority of all Catholics in the United States, according to a Gallup Poll), many of the leading Catholic theologians, and by the major Catholic episcopates in European countries north of the Alps and east of the Pyrenees. The Council of Bishops in the United States supported the Papal edict, but urged those who disobeyed its injunction to continue to seek the benefits of the sacraments. It may be that, as in the case of the conflict between the doctrine of usury and the expanding credit system in the modern world, official ecclesiastical endorsement may be withheld until the conflicting practice has become practically universal. There is, nevertheless, at this time a severe tension within the Catholic Church concerning the respective roles of the Roman magisterium and other institutions and persons within the Catholic community whereof the outcome is unpredictable. It is difficult to evaluate precisely the probable influence at present of official Catholic dogma on the analysis of demographic problems and the formulation of population policies. According to present indications its effect in the more advanced European nations, in North America, and in most Asian and African countries is likely to be fairly negligible. It may, however, exert considerable restraint on public policy in Latin America and other countries of Iberian culture.

Ideological considerations may influence ostensibly objective judgments, as well as policy judgments, in several ways. They may lead to the adoption of one of the extreme antithetical positions defined above. For example, the statement by Paul VI to the General Assembly of the United Nations that increase in production rather than reduction in population increase is the true answer to hunger in the less developed countries seems to imply rejection of the informed judgment of the staff of the Food and Agriculture Organization that *both* increased production and diminished population increase are required to meet this need. Similarly, in reply to a proposal by the President of the International Bank for Research and Development that the Bank encourage recognition by the less developed nations of "the extent to which rapid population growth slows down their potential development" and give assistance both to research in this field and to facilities needed to carry out family planning programs, the Spanish Minister of Finance expressed his "surprise and concern" as a member of the

Bank's Council at its meeting in December, 1968, at this endorsement of "artificial birth control." He said, "In order to re-establish the balance between our needs and resources, I believe that the world's effort should concentrate on increasing our resources, instead of the supposedly easier and quicker method of reducing our requirements." He added, "At the time of making decisions, the opinions of the highest spiritual and moral authorities should be very much borne in mind." (Quotations cited by *Population Bulletin*, November, 1968.) Repugnance to contraception may also lead its opponents to exaggerate the potentialities of international migration as a means of alleviating the consequences of rapid natural increase.

Finally, ideological opposition to all physical or chemical means of regulating fertility may lead to excessive optimism about the possible role of periodic continence, ignoring the strong association between the efficacy of this method and social status, so that it is least effective where it is most needed. For example, according to the results of an intensive, large-scale survey in the United States in 1965, among Catholic wives at ages 18–39 years, 90 per cent of the college graduates had tried to regulate their conceptions and 57 per cent had relied wholly on church-approved methods, but among those who had not gone through high school only 10 per cent had relied solely on abstinence or rhythm though about half of them had used physical or chemical means. The evidence now at hand suggests that the rhythm method of regulating fertility is acceptable and may be quite efficacious for a sophisticated clientele, but offers little promise to those who are poor and ignorant. This aspect of the problem presents social and ethical problems that demand more serious attention than they have usually received.

There are other more subtle difficulties in an objective appraisal of population trends. Many of the words commonly used in demography are loaded with implicit values. An increase of population is the composite result of elements that are generally good in personal experience. In all societies, a birth is normally a "blessed event" whereas death is tragic. Positive evaluation of procreation and population growth is deeply rooted in the traditions of most societies. The very idea of "growth" has happy connotations; "bigger" has semantic associations with "better." Increases in crops, revenue, or population (though usually *not* increases in mental disease or in crime) are reported in official statistics as "gains"; decreases are reported as "losses" or "declines." Similarly, when a demographer writes about the number of births "needed" for the maintenance of a population, his readers and in some cases the demographer may unconsciously assume that this mathematical relation implies some sort of moral or social obligation.

There is no sound basis for an *a priori* assumption that the increase or decrease of a population in any particular situation is either good or bad. The evaluation of actual or possible population trends is properly based on examination of their determinants and consequences in relation to accepted goals or values. Presumably no one would view with equanimity a trend toward the extinction of the human species, or of the nation of which he is a part. But any such fears today, with respect to mankind or to the United States, would be fantastic. The trend of the American people, which is now determined mainly by the preferences of potential parents, demonstrates that under normal conditions the spontaneous interests of individuals in marriage and parenthood assures the perpetuation of the human stock.

Under some conditions a temporary, or even a long-term, decrease of the population of an area or nation may be salutory. The sudden decrease of population in Ireland from about 8 million in 1841 to 4.4 million in 1861, due to excess deaths and flight to other countries caused by the blight of the potato crop on which its economy depended, was the symptom rather than the cause of a catastrophe. Rapid increase of the Irish population during the previous century had intensified the crisis. Its subsequent gradual decrease through successive decades to about 2.8 million persons in 1960, due to delayed marriage, moderate fertility, and continued out-migration was a salutary adjustment to limited resources. Similarly, decreases of population in many rural countries and in the central cities of some metropolitan areas in the United States are normal accommodations to changing conditions.

It is our responsibility as citizens of this nation, and in a moral sense citizens of the world, to analyze population trends objectively and to study their determinants and consequences in relation to accepted social goals and human values. This task requires freedom from traditional dogmas, including academic dogmas, and from the tyranny of words. None of us can achieve complete freedom from prejudices, but we can put ourselves on guard against some of the latent pitfalls in current dicussions on this subject.

The Complexity of Developmental Processes

The "Development Decade" began with high expectations of rapid progress in the impoverished nations that comprise a majority of mankind, optimistically referred to in international parlance as "the developing nations." It is ending in disillusionment and a rising sense of frustration among those in need. In most of the low-income countries, with a few notable exceptions, the rise in production has barely exceeded the growth of population and it has lagged behind in some, whereas "development" has gone forward rapidly in countries with more advanced technology, greater wealth and power. The disillusionment must be attributed largely to an over-simplified conception of development in classic economic terms, to the neglect of its critical political, social, and demographic aspects. Among other errors, excessive reliance was placed on in-puts of foreign capital—though it is true that international transfers of capital on a much larger scale than at present are one of the essential requirements for realizing innovations in technique and enlarging the infra-structure of new economic activities.

The complexity of developmental processes is evidenced by considering the variety of underlying conditions affecting technical progress in different regions and at different stages in recent world history. It is also indicated by a critical examination of diverse conditions affecting economic and social life in different countries today. Recognition of the complexity of the conditions of progressive economic and social change implies the necessity of concomitant action along several lines of critical importance—including measures conducive to the regulation of population growth. Although the most important conditions of rapid and sustained development are at least partially interdependent, each merits specific attention. Thus, needed action in the demographic sphere, though insufficient in itself to assure economic progress, will contribute directly to economic and social development and, incidentally, tend to facilitate rather than to impede constructive action along other lines.

In the early stages of industrialization in Western Europe and Northern America, technological progress was a gradual "spontaneous" process in which governments played a minor role in the formation and allocation of capital resources—though they did support the advance of industry by imperialistic ventures, the protection of merchant marines, and other measures to insure favorable terms of international trade. The lead role was then played by strong entrepreneurial classes with large resources drawn from prior advances in agriculture and commerce, and habituated to ventures subject to risks but holding the promise of large profits if successful. They operated in expanding markets created by improvements in agriculture, the exploitation of previously untapped resources, and/or favorable terms of international trade. (The "generosity" of donor nations today in granting capital credits is generally vitiated by their close-fisted refusal to assure favorable terms of trade in exchange for the products that the less-developed countries are able to offer.) Moreover, the gradual industrial revolution in Europe was carried through in countries with relatively low rates of population growth (usually in the vicinity of one per cent per year), due to moderate fertility (with birth rates in the low thirties per thousand), quite high mortality, and wide opportunities for migration to new lands or to new industrial centers at home or in other countries. In North America the open frontiers offset its rapid population growth. Those who could no longer find satisfactory activities in established rural villages could, therefore, be effectively absorbed in new situations—as contrasted with the swollen "surplus" populations today on the farms and in the city slums of most low-income nations.

From the last decades of the nineteenth century on, governments have necessarily played an increasingly important role in economic and social development in the nations that have achieved a "breakthrough" and sustained advance. In fact, the prime condition of such progress today seems to be the existence of a firmly established government with the determination and capacity to perform certain critical functions. Available resources and a considerable share of current energies must be channeled into key developmental activities in agriculture, power and mechanical industries, transportation, education and health. Corruption and nepotism on such a scale and at such points as to hamper progress must be rigorously suppressed. Both the entrenched interests of reactionary, privileged classes and excessive demands by rising new classes must be restrained. A new spirit of enterprising energy and civic and industrial discipline must be generated. It is also interesting to note that the governments of the less developed countries that most clearly exhibit such qualities generally recognize the importance of programs designed to check excessive fertility.

The problems presented by the gross disparity in levels and opportunities of life in different regions and nations will plague the world for many decades, and are becoming increasingly urgent. They are being constantly aggravated by the disparity in population trends and the association of high rates of increase with poverty and related cultural conditions. They demand, first of all, deep objective analysis—and, taking the results of such analysis into account, coordinated action along many lines, some of which depend on the initiative of the people and governments of the particular nations in need, whereas others require effective international cooperation.

An enlightened approach to the demographic aspects of this situation and the promotion and facilitation of rationally planned parenthood will not solve all the ills of the world, but it does offer one of the clearest and simplest lines of constructive action.

Demographic Aspects of Economic and Social Development

Some of the important relations between demographic trends and economic and social conditions can be briefly summarized.

POPULATION DENSITY AND POPULATION GROWTH

Current rates of population growth are, in general, much more important in their influence on economic and social affairs than absolute man-land ratios or other aspects of population density. High population density is not necessarily a barrier to effective economic development—as illustrated by the examples of England, Japan, and, more recently, Taiwan, Hong Kong, and Singapore. A relatively small, densely populated nation is, nevertheless, critically dependent on favorable relations in external trade. Moreover, even a large densely populated nation must rely in its agricultural activity on intensive methods of cultivation whereas any extension of cultivated area is likely to run into marginal lands and to require expensive reclamation projects. In some parts of the world the densities to be expected if present trends are continued may present formidable, and perhaps insuperable, obstacles to progress.

FERTILITY AND AGE DISTRIBUTION

An important demographic principle, which was not clearly recognized until quite recently, is that the age structure of a population is largely a function of levels of fertility. The influence of mortality is much smaller, and its direction varies under different conditions. The plausibility of this principle becomes apparent by reflection on the simple fact that the ratio of infants to persons in the central parental ages is determined purely by the levels of fertility and infant mortality; so a decline in infant mortality, comparable in this respect to a rise in fertility, *raises* the ratio of children to adults. The numbers at later ages are strongly influenced by the numbers of births in previous periods. Consequently, high fertility and rapid population growth generate a population with a high ratio of dependent persons, heavily weighted with children at preschool and school ages, to persons in the economically productive ages. (See chapter 4.) This ratio is now nearly twice as high in some South Asian and Latin American countries as in most European countries or Japan.

This situation aggravates the relation between consumption requirements and potential production. Perhaps its most serious effect is that it retards advances in the scope and quality of education. A given effort and expenditure per productive adult on provisions for education in a nation with a relatively large child population must be limited to a smaller proportion of its children, or spread out with inferior resources per child, than can be provided with the same effort per adult in a population with moderate fertility and slow population growth.

ECONOMIC ASPECTS OF RAPID POPULATION GROWTH

Rapid population growth tends to reduce the proportion of current production that can be allocated to investment in new capital equipment and other facilities, due both to the larger volume of goods required for immediate consumption by individuals and to the larger public expenditures needed for transportation, communication, social services, etc. At the same time, in a population with a rapidly increasing labor force a larger proportion of current investment must be used *extensively*, to provide new workers with resources at the standards already in effect, than in a population with relatively fewer new workers each year, so that less of the current investment is available for *intensive* use in raising levels of productivity per worker. What actually happens in many low-income countries is a dualistic trend toward a significant intensive development in a small segment of the economy, where conspicuous advances are made in productivity and incomes, while the major part of the labor force remains trapped in activities with low productivity and a rising number of totally or partially unemployed persons. In this respect, however, we must recognize the unfortunate circumstance that there is an inevitable lag of some 15 years or more between a reduction in the birth rate and its effect on the trend of the labor force. Those who will be desperately in need of new employment opportunities during the next 15 years are already on the scene. (See Chapter 4.)

Rapid population growth complicates developmental planning and increases the burden of governmental operations in a transitional period when provision must be made both for new types of industrial production (which are often capital-intensive, or "labor saving") *and* their essential infra-structure *and* for labor-intensive economic activities to sustain the welfare and cultural advances of the large segment of the labor force that can not readily be absorbed in modern modes of production but tends to sink into the category of "surplus population." Failure to meet needs spells the perpetuation of poverty. Unfortunately, investments by outside corporations (which the business communities of wealthy nations sometimes view as an alternative to inter-governmental operations) are unlikely to make much contribution to meeting the need for the development of a sound infra-structure or the need to develop the receiving nation's "human resources." These vital needs, which must be met through the action of the nations immediately concerned and through inter-governmental cooperation, are aggravated by rapid population growth and its corollary age structure that has a high ratio of children to adults.

Relation Between the Control of Fertility and Other Developmental Processes

In general, the voluntary control of fertility and other developmental processes are complementary and mutually supportive. The rational regulation of fertility depends on personal motives. Under favorable conditions, governmental programs may influence the formation of popular attitudes in this field—in part merely by bringing the idea of controlling fertility without undue cost or personal strain into the consciousness of persons who have not previously thought of this as a real possibility. Governments may also influence behavior by providing more efficacious and acceptable methods of controlling fertility. Officials, publicists, doctors and teachers may influence attitudes and behavior in other ways. Nevertheless, the question of personal motivation is always fundamental. (See chapter 7.) The effective control of fertility requires individual initiative and sustained effort. People who do not really believe that it is possible for them to improve conditions of life for themselves or their children will not undertake a radically new venture or put forth the sustained effort required for success in this undertaking. Where hope is weak, contraception will be absent or ineffective.

In any case, so long as children are, in an economic sense, capital assets that require relatively small investment and soon yield appreciable returns from their labor—as well as being objects of affection and a source of personal satisfaction and prestige—parents have no strong reason to limit the number of their offspring. The situation is changed radically by the introduction of new standards of child care and protection and, in particular, new educational opportunities and aspirations.

Furthermore, at a time when two-thirds of the infants born alive were likely to die before reaching maturity, only a moderately large family gave assurance against childlessness in old age—especially in societies where parental ambitions are focused exclusively on males. The reduction of infant mortality removes one of the strong motivations for unlimited procreation. Associated practices and values, such as attendance at clinics, the use of scientific medicine, and interest in hygiene and nutrition, are also conducive to the formation of rational attitudes favorable to effective family limitation.

It is important to recognize that motivation for family planning is not a simple "Yes" or "No" proposition, but varies in intensity through a wide scale. The decision of any particular person in this matter is also likely to be strongly influenced by his neighbors' behavior and the climate of neighborhood attitudes. A movement toward family planning in one class or neighborhood tends to spread with a "snowball effect" through other classes and neighborhoods, so that the delayed results of an experimental program may far outweigh its initial effects. In situations where the motivation for family planning is weak, perhaps little more than a mere wish, and cherished traditions reinforce inertia and people are not accustomed to disciplined, rigorously timed behavior, the types of method at their disposal may strongly affect decisions about family planning and the efficacy of any attempts to do so. New scientific contributions to the battery of birth-prevention methods, notably oral contraceptives and intra-uterine contraceptive devices, and in some societies new surgical techniques for sterilization or abortion, are radically changing the prospects for population control through the voluntary action of individuals depressed by poverty and handicapped by ignorance. (See chapter 7.) For example, in Pakistan there were 1.6 million IUCD insertions and 0.3 million vasectomies from July, 1965, through June, 1968, and in India 2.5 million IUCD insertions and 3.6 million vasectomies from January 1965, through July, 1965. Insertion rates for IUCDs are rising in both countries. Although the cumulative IUCD totals are in one sense deceptive, because there is progressive loss through fallout or removal for reasons other than planning pregnancy, experimentation with this method also stimulates interest in other methods. In some other countries there is a strong preference for oral contraceptives rather than intra-uterine devices. The new contraceptive methods are having wide acceptance in South Korea and in the non-mainland Chinese populations in Asia. There is now a vigorous population control program in mainland China, but we lack definite information on the results. In the Soviet Union, Eastern Europe and Japan new contraceptive methods are only gradually replacing the initial primary reliance on clinical abortions. Meanwhile, rapid advances are being made in the experimental development of effective methods of communication in this field, and in the provision and dissemination of supplies. The rational regulation of fertility is still in its initial stages in most of the less developed world, but stark pessimism about the possible effects of public programs for the promotion of planned parenthood is no longer tenable.

The situation in this aspect of social and economic development is somewhat comparable to that with respect to food production. Until very recently the outlook for the effective application of scientific techniques on the farms of low-income countries was rather dismal, due in this case with the regulation of human reproduction to ineffective communication, cultural inertia, and fear. A critical factor in the recent breakthrough of new methods in agriculture in these countries was the development and dissemination of new techniques, notably new plant strains, of such demonstrable superiority as to stimulate popular response among farmers who had previously clung to traditional operations. (See chapter 6.)

It is always difficult to appraise casual interactions among correlated changes. A lowering of fertility rates has generally appeared in association with advances in technology and education. One can not usually define precisely the extent to which the demographic change has reflected other lines of progress or has, in itself, been a primary determinant. The interaction has undoubtedly differed widely in different situations. Perhaps the simple recognition that the control of fertility is one of the essential aspects of complex developmental processes and that advances in this or any other critical factor facilitates progress along various lines is all that can be, or need be, confidently asserted.

The Trend Toward a Secular Consensus on the Central Issue of Population Policy

During the first half of the twentieth century relatively few persons were much concerned about relations between population growth rates and human welfare, except for the flurry of fears about supposed trends toward declining national populations during the inter-war period, especially in Europe. There were wide differences of opinion on population questions among competent demographers and economists. General concern about the adverse effects of rapid population growth in the world was largely centered in countries with Anglo-Saxon traditions. The provision in the Charter of the United Nations for an inter-governmental Population Commission and a corresponding Division of the Secretariat to study questions in this field was greeted as a surprising innovation.

The movement of ideas throughout the world on this subject during the last two decades has converged toward a universal consensus which, though still incomplete, has now received sufficiently wide and clear expression to reveal a cultural force as irresistible as the expansion of electronic communication or the monetary credit system in the modern world.

This secular movement is the result of the confluence of two basic forces. The *primary force* has been the actual acceleration of population increase in the world as a whole, and especially in the less developed regions—due to the phenomenal reduction of mortality, while fertility in many countries has remained near the levels determined by sexual impulses and ancient traditions. The major *complementary force* has been a rapid advance in the social and biological sciences during these years. The progress in demography and related social sciences has promoted the objective analysis of population trends and their interrelations with social and economic conditions. The scientific work sponsored by the United Nations and allied agencies, not only in their central offices but also in various regional centers, has made important contributions in this respect. The membership of the International Union for the Scientific Study of Population has increased ten-fold during these two decades, reflecting the expansion and intensification of research in this field in private and governmental institutions. The Population Council, established by John D. Rockefeller 3rd, has sponsored the advanced education of promising young scientists from many countries and supported demographic studies throughout the world. It has also played an important role in sponsoring and stimulating research on the biology of human reproduction which has already led to significant advances in knowledge about possible means of controlling fertility. (See chapter 7.) Meanwhile, knowledge in these fields has been disseminated and ideas clarified through the exchange of information and experience in publications and conferences, including numerous academic assemblies and two World Population Conferences sponsored by the United Nations (Rome, 1954; Belgrade, 1965) and in the official deliberations and acts of the United Nations General Assembly, Councils and Commissions and those of its allied agencies. In short, factual changes have made new policies imperative, and knowledge about the facts has made this need apparent to governments and people across the world.

We need mention only briefly a few of the milestones in the formation and expansion of this emergent consensus. The two World Population Conferences were wisely restricted to the exchange of ideas and experience among individuals, excluding the proposal or action on any resolutions. Discussion at the 1965 World Population Conference in Yugoslavia was still clouded by a good deal of confusion, particularly in exchanges between eastern and western scientists (though, as noted below, there was a significant movement toward rapprochement in this sphere almost immediately after the conference); nevertheless, the dialogue at this time was freer and more enlightening than it had been in 1954.

The first serious consideration of population policy in the General Assembly of the United Nations came in its Seventeenth Session in 1962 on a resolution concerning "Population Growth and Economic Development" sponsored by four African, four Asian and four European countries. Action on this resolution revealed sharp differences of opinion among the member states. During the preliminary action in Committee II, one operative section (Article 6) which explicitly authorized the organization to give "technical assistance, as requested by Governments, for national projects and programmes dealing with problems of population" was retained by a narrow margin. The resolution as a whole then received 43 affirmative votes and 14 votes in opposition (Argentina, Austria, Belgium, Colombia, France, Ireland, Italy, Lebanon, Liberia, Luxembourg, Peru, Portugal, Spain, Uruguay), with 44 abstentions (including the Communist bloc, 11 African and 8 Latin American countries). The United States abstained from the vote on Article 6, but in doing so affirmed that the Secretary General already had such power; it voted affirmatively on the resolution. After the deletion of Article 6 in the General Assembly, the resolution was approved by 69 votes but with 27 abstentions. A proposal was approved at this time to invite statements by all member governments on their needs and interests in this field.

During the half-decade after this first discussion of population questions in the General Assembly of the United Nations, there was a remarkable set of congruent intellectual movements in different cultural spheres. Immediately after the World Population Conference, there was a lively, constructive dialogue among the leading Soviet economists, demographers and statisticians on the economic implications of population trends—carried out mainly through a series of articles in *Literatura Gazeta* in late 1965 through 1966, and reflected in an article by Urlanis in the UNESCO *Courier*, February, 1967. It may be suspected that the previous vigorous opposition by communist leaders to public concern about the depressing economic and social effects of rapid population growth, which had originated in the old Malthusian-Marxist controversy, was maintained chiefly as an aspect of the "Cold War" propaganda, directed against the emphasis on population questions by exponents of public policy in western countries and the tendency of some scholars to ignore the critical importance of institutional changes in their approach to economic and social development. This suspicion is supported by the liberal provision of abortion services and the encouragement of contraception in communist countries (including a recent plan for the large-scale manufacture of IUCDs in the Soviet Union). If this hypothesis is correct, it is obvious that the recent lively interest in population questions in Asian and North African nations rendered the continuation of this line of propaganda futile and injurious to communist interests. Moreover, in recent years the scientific community in the Soviet Union has been allowed greater freedom in thought and activity than is tolerated in the public-at-large or among artists. In any case, leading Soviet spokesmen no longer insist that the policies directed toward lowering fertility in many situations are necessarily futile, or oppose the extension of assistance by the United Nations to national programs in this field.

Meanwhile, there has been an equally important shift in secular thinking on this subject within the Roman Catholic community. This was expressed in 1967 both in the majority report of the Papal Commission of Population and in a conference of lay Catholic leaders in Rome in the same year. Although Pope Paul VI eventually decided on theological grounds to reffirm the condemnation of contraceptive practices by Catholic communicants, there has been an important modification of official Catholic policy in this field which does not violate accepted theological positions and is, in fact, quite in line with a position developed by Thomas Aquinas—namely, that the Church is not obligated to attempt to enforce moral principles by legal action in situations where such action can not be expected to receive broad public support. The Church has, therefore, relaxed its opposition to public policies in this field. The thirty "World Leaders' Declaration on

Population," presented at the United Nations on Human Rights Day in December, 1967, included the signatures of the heads of state of the Philippines and of three Latin American countries, including Colombia whose ambassador accepted the honor of presenting the declaration. The movement of thought toward approval of contraceptive practices and public programs in this field among Catholic laymen, priests and bishops which gathered force during the long interval while this issue was studied by the Roman Magesterium is apparently still rising.

Thus, action in this field by most governments and by international agencies no longer encounters strong ideological opposition either from communist or from Catholic centers—though some governments, notably Ireland, Spain, Portugal, Argentina and Uruguay still offer objections. The movement toward world consensus during the 1960s was also furthered by inter-governmental assemblies in Asia, Africa, Europe, and Latin America.

A World Leaders' Declaration on Population Growth and Human Dignity and Welfare had first been presented at the United Nations over the signatures of 12 heads of state in December, 1966, prior to the Twenty-first meeting of the General Assembly. The Secretary-General in transmitting this text added an endorsement of its principles. This included the following sentences:

> Accordingly, I take this occasion to emphasize that population growth is not only an important factor in the rate at which nations can attain their economic goals, but that the size of family is a fundamental human problem which must be based on the decisions of responsible parents concerned with the dignity and well-being of their children.
>
> In my view, we must accord the right of parents to determine the numbers of their children a place of importance at this moment in man's history.

On December 17, 1966, the General Assembly *unanimously* adopted a resolution on Population Growth and Economic Development. This called attention to prior actions in this field by the United Nations and specialized agencies, with particular note of positive actions by WHO in 1965 and 1966 and of UNESCO in 1966. It recognized "the sovereignty of nations in formulating and promoting their own population polices, with due regard to the principle that the size of the family should be the free choice of each individual family." It emphasized the role of international agencies in developing knowledge and extending scientific and technical assistance to nations. It called on these agencies:

. . . to assist, when requested, in further developing and strengthening national and regional facilities for training, research, information and advisory services in the field of population, bearing in mind the different character of population problems in each country and region and the needs arising therefrom.

In view of the emergent consensus on the central issues of population policy as it affects a majority of the world's population, debate on the ideological aspects of this question gives way to innumerable pragmatic questions, such as the possibilities of effective employment of the still growing masses now occupied in low-productivity farming in order to enhance their dignity and direct their energies into productive activities, the problems created by swollen, impoverished city populations, the acceleration of research on human reproductivity and the discovery of new techniques of controlling fertility, experimentation with the relative acceptability and efficacy of available techniques, methods of communication and stimulation of rational responses to present needs, the marshalling of resources now dissipated in unproductive investment or conspicuous expenditure, the wise allocation of limited governmental resources to key aspects of economic and social development, and so on.

The importance for world peace and human well-being of aiding handicapped nations (at their request) in meeting urgent population problems is now recognized by both the Executive and the Legislative branches of the American government and by our leading foundations, along with concern about actions that may enable our own people to cope more effectively with our domestic problems. These activities merit continued emphasis and expansion. One must, nevertheless, insist that assistance to other nations in implementing their population policies does not relieve this affluent and powerful nation of its other responsibilities to the more impoverished segment of humanity, such as creation of terms of foreign exchange that will make it possible for struggling nations to earn through their own efforts a substantial part of the funds needed for their economic and social development.

Domestic Population Policy

CONCERNING THE TOTAL POPULATION TREND

Some issues of population policy are so complex that there is room for wide differences of opinion among sincere and intelligent persons on many points. This is conspicuously the case with respect to the relation between the general trend of population in the United States today and the trend of production. This relation is in net effect ambiguous—as indicated by the series of papers presented to a Conference on Demographic and Economic Change in Developed Countries, sponsored by the National Bureau of Economic Research (Princeton University Press, 1960). On the other hand, present tendencies affecting the distribution of population in this country and differences in reproductviity among various segments of the nation give rise to issues that need urgent attention. We shall return to this topic at a later point.

The most serious concern about the trend of our nation's population as a whole may be its effects on the quality of American life rather than its purely economic aspects. This point of view has been vigorously affirmed by Dudley Kirk, formerly Demographic Director of the Population Council: "Finally the answer posed by our title [Our Growing Population: Threat or Boon?]. Our growing population a threat? No, not yet to our affluence; but to our quality of life, *Yes*." Economists by tradition and econometricians by necessity leave out of account such intangible values as beauty, personal identity, security, and joy in life, but some philosophical economists do turn their attention to these vital affairs. Thus Joseph Spengler in his Presidential Address to the Population Association of America in 1957 chose as his title, "The Aesthetics of Population." He said, ". . . satisfaction of the demands of the stork absorbs resources which might otherwise have been devoted to satisfying the criteria of beauty and to meeting the requirements of excellence. Population growth also accelerates the dissipation of resources and intensifies many kinds of insecurity. . . . We have given so much rein to the stork because we do not prize the beautiful. Ethical and aesthetic values play but a small part in ordering the behavior of many of those upon whom largely depends the aggregate growth, demographic as well as economic, of the American Leviathan."

Though it is true that the destruction and pollution of natural resources and the congestion of urban aggregates must be attributed mainly to technological and commercial forces, these trends, as noted in the preceding quotation, are intensified by population growth. Again, though America is still more "beautiful for spacious skies and amber waves of grain" and "for purple mountain majesties" than many other nations, there is no reason for recklessly dissipating these resources. Aesthetic considerations are brushed aside by some persons as matters of interest only to those rich enough to own large estates, adorn their homes with precious *objets d'art* or travel far and frequently. On the contrary, the most serious aspects of squalor and congestion are their depressing effects in the lives of the poor and underprivileged members of our society. This is recognized by John Galbraith in his insistence that we must ". . . have the social planning that erases grime and squalor and which preserves and enhances beauty. A price in industrial efficiency may be necessary. Indeed, it should be assumed. Economic development enables us to pay the price; it is why we have development. We do not have development in order to make our lives more hideous, our culture more meretricious or our lives less complete." (Quotations from the article by Kirk in *Transactions of the Thirty-Second North American Wildlife and Natural Resources Conference*, 1967.)

These and similar considerations about the ecology and quality of American life have led some social philosophers to propose "a zero rate of population growth"—at least apart from the increase due to net immigration which at present is relatively small (adding about two-tenths of one per cent per year)—as an American goal. A rational approach to this proposal, as contrasted with a hasty commitment to this thesis at all costs or its hasty rejection as contrary to our traditional goals, must take carefully into account the gains and costs of the conditions and programs that might be conducive to this effect. In this, as in other matters, a wise evaluation of *ends* involves an intelligent evaluation of *means*. The American people would certainly, with good reason, reject any programs in this field that involved compulsion or institutional pressure on the free decisions of individuals in their personal and family lives. On the other hand, public opinion in this country would strongly support every possible means of enabling all individuals to regulate procreation effectively in accordance with their own aspirations and values. The relation of other social changes that might indirectly affect the trend of the nation's population to this hypothetical goal may require more intensive examination and more extensive consideration.

The trend of fertility is now the major variable in the growth of the American population, and this is largely determined by social and psychological factors affecting marriage and parental aspirations —though inflated by unwanted births and deflated with somewhat similar force by sterility and sub-fecundity. The generally prevalent values affecting marriage and parenthood in any society are obviously subject to variation with changing social and cultural conditions, but they seem on the whole to have remained fairly constant in this country during the postwar period, though there may have been some downward trend in parental aspirations in recent years. The relative importance of various factors (including changes in age composition, ages at marriage and the spacing of births, as well as the diffusion of new contraceptive techniques) in the recent lowering of the crude birth rate is still problematic. (See chapter 5.) Nevertheless, it must be recognized that in a society with the high survival rates made possible by modern science and health services and a high frequency of marriage, the force of death in a stable population is balanced by a low average frequency of births—about 2.11 births per married woman. So if most couples want at least two children and many want three or four or more, completely planned parenthood would still give a positive intrinsic rate of natural increase, unless offset by rather high abstention from marriage or a relatively high frequency of childless or one-child families.

The series of population projections by the Bureau of the Census, published in March, 1968, but projected from mid-year 1966 as base, assumes a constant net immigration of 400 thousand persons per year and one set of age-specific death rates but four alternative sets of age-specific female fertility rates. The fertility rates are held constant but, due to changing age structures, the implied crude birth rates change in time. They range at the start from 17.9 (Series D) to 20.7 (Series A) per 1,000 population. The implied peak rates of annual increase in the late 1970s or early 1980s range from 1.2 to 1.9 per cent and decline to the range 1.1 to 1.8 by 1990. The subsequently observed increase from July 1967 through June 1968 fits the lowest hypothesis on fertility (Series D), but even on this hypothesis the expected population in the year 2000 will be 283 million persons; in Series A the expected population would then be 361 million. Assuming that the continued multiplication of the human species, or of any nation, even at a moderate rate would eventually destroy the ecological basis of human existence, our present reproductive buoyancy can not safely be projected indefinitely. This poses a long-range dilemma to which there is no obvious solution—apart from the possibility of a cultural milieu in which the expectation of parenthood is viewed as merely one possible aspect of a satisfying and creative life rather than as an essential requisite or as a moral obligation.

In any case, the most critical issues in American population policy in the immediate future are, at least in this writer's opinion, not those concerning our national population as a whole but rather the social implications of its distribution, diverse reproductive trends, and in-

ternal migration. We shall turn to these issues after brief comments
on the present situation, prospects and problems with respect to immigration.

IMMIGRATION

Reasons for abandoning the national origins quota system in the
regulation of immigration to the United States were set forth in the
first edition of *The Population Dilemma*, published in 1963. Legislation to this effect was recommended by President Kennedy and passed
by Congress in 1965. After a transition period, the new regulations
became finally effective July 1, 1968. The total number of immigrants
from outside the Western hemisphere is limited to 170,000 persons,
apart from parents, spouses or children of United States citizens.
Preferential categories are established with respect to familial relations,
special skills or refugee status, and the total number from any country in any year is limited to 20,000 persons. Otherwise, all applications,
regardless of national origin, will be treated on a "first come, first
served" basis. Congress also imposed an annual limit of 120,000 on
the volume of immigration from other independent nations in the
Western hemisphere—though this section had been opposed by the
Administration. Although the new policy eliminates the discriminatory
aspects of the former system, it limits the total force of immigration
to this country to a small fraction of its potential magnitude if the
open door policy of the previous century were still in effect. It is
unlikely that there will be any radical change in the American policy
now established in this field for a long time—apart from some hypothetical change in the whole structure of international relations.

Official estimates of "net-immigration" as a component in the population growth of the United States (now 50 states and the District of
Columbia) take account so far as possible of all changes in residence
across the national boundaries of the area as thus defined—including
movements from and to Puerto Rico and other "outlying areas." In
this statistical sense, "immigration" and "emigration" include the
movements of persons who are not "immigrants" or "emigrants" in
legal terms and who, in fact, are part of the national "demographic
pool." In this sense the population of the United States in 1960 was
nearly four million greater than that of its 50 states and the District of
Columbia. The two principal items in the external segment of the
pool were 1,374,000 Americans abroad (chiefly armed forces and

civilian employees of the Federal government and their dependents) and 2,350,000 residents of Puerto Rico. The Puerto Rican segment of our demographic pool also includes, of course, the 888,000 persons of Puerto Rican birth or parentage who were residents of the United States at that time.

The attention of the nation is now focused mainly on our own domestic problems, including the role of ethnic minorities in the nation's affairs. It is also deeply concerned with urgent issues related to the need for a peaceful world order. It can afford to enlarge its financial contribution to the advancement of people in other regions, but it can not afford at this time to complicate its domestic problems by the introduction of new demographic strains on a scale that would have an appreciable effect on the development of large impoverished nations.

Eventually, an enlightened humanity may demand that all nations, especially those with vast resources relative to their numbers, such as the United States and the Soviet Union, pay serious attention to the persistent inequality between world regions in income and levels of living which, though largely institutional in nature, is also affected by differing relations between population and resources. Even so, the most promising approaches to the relief of this inequality may be found through transfers of capital, terms of trade, and a more rational ordering of economic functions. As the present excessive rates of natural increase in the less-developed countries are brought under control, this great long-range issue will not evaporate but it will be mitigated and clarified. New conditions may lead to earnest reconsideration of American policies affecting international migration, but at the present time it would be unreasonable to expect any radical change of the newly established policies in this field.

Demographic Aspects of Domestic Social Problems

All responsible citizens are now aware that our nation is confronted with acute social problems that threaten its integrity and vitality. We are aided in meeting these problems by recent advances in the social sciences as well as by much vigorous and deep-searching inquiry. Yet firm knowledge on many critical issues is still severely limited, tentative and beset by elusive issues on which there is no clear consensus. Here we must concentrate our attention on certain demographic aspects of these problems, though these can not be wholly abstracted from their larger context.

ASPECTS OF THE DISTRIBUTION OF OUR NATIONAL POPULATION

There are valid reasons for a strong emphasis today on the diffusion of power and responsibility and on more active participation at local levels in the formation and administration of policies by those most immediately concerned.

On the other hand, present population trends have implications that point in the opposite direction. One can not clear a pool merely by skimming out its debris if water keeps trickling in from muddy sources; one must treat the whole ecological complex in which it is set. If the children born and nurtured in Skowhegan, Hazard, Natchez, and San Juan stayed in these localities through their lives and reared their descendants there, one could plausibly argue that their affairs, including for example their schools, are solely their responsibility—though even this would need qualification in view of their participation in the nation's political and cultural life. But obviously this is not the actual situation. People constantly stream into our urban centers from rural northern New England, the Southern Appalachians, the old cotton and tobacco belts and other disadvantaged areas. About half of the young Negroes aged 20–24 years and 69 per cent of those aged 40–44 years living in the whole northeastern region of the United States in 1960 were born in the South (as defined in the census to include its border states). Yet in spite of the massive out-migration of Negroes to other regions, slightly over half were still living in the South in 1968—though mainly in non-farm locations—where they were still more disadvantaged in many respects than those in other parts of the country. Even in the cities of the South the median income of non-white families in 1960 was only 51 per cent of the white median, whereas the corresponding ratios in the urban areas of the three northern and western regions were all in the vicinity of 70 per cent. Using 1968 data, the Negro-white median income ratios were as follows: the South, 54 per cent; Northeast, 66 per cent; North Central, 78 per cent; and West, 74 per cent. The South also includes more than its share of poverty stricken native whites.

Various other minority elements in our national demographic pool still have strong roots in particular areas where they are subject to severe disadvantages. Data on median years of schooling completed by persons over 14 years of age in 1960 afford a rough but significant index of these inequalities. The medians for several of these minorities were roughly similar to those for Negroes (males 8.3, females 8.9), which were then far below the national average, though the gap between Negroes and whites in this respect was significantly narrowed during the 1960s (due in part to continued inter-regional migration). For the 888,000 persons of Puerto Rican origin resident on the mainland in 1960 (who are about one-fifth of all Puerto Ricans in the hemisphere), the medians were males, 8.4; females, 8.2. Obviously, conditions of life in Puerto Rico are, in long range, a subject of almost as much vital interest to American citizens, especially in the Northeast, as the conditions immediately affecting those already resident there. For the large, heterogeneous class of persons with Spanish surnames in five southwestern states (about 3.5 million persons), the medians were 8.8 and 9.1, respectively, for the two sexes, but for those born in Mexico they were only 4.5 and 5.0. Although Mexicans do not have unlimited access to the United States, the number already here approaches a million and will be undoubtedly augmented in the future. The medians for the half-million persons recognized as Indians were 8.4 and 8.5. Even lower medians were reported for some of the more isolated old native white communities in the Southern Appalachians. (The Japanese and Chinese in the United States are now well integrated in the economic and social life of the nation; the schooling medians were over 12.0 for both sexes in both of these ethnic classes.)

The contrast between the policies of (1) dispersing power and responsibility, and (2) the recognition of federal responsibility for national support and the maintenance of national standards throughout the country presents a dilemma only if either is pressed to the exclusion of the other. The design and administration of programs serving the essential values of both these approaches is a key issue in American political life today.

THE SOCIAL STRUCTURE OF METROPOLITAN AGGREGATIONS

About two-thirds of all Americans now live in population clusters centered in cities of 50,000 or more inhabitants. These aggregations have no political structure corresponding to the realities of their present existence, but rather a confusing set of discrete systems in different spheres of activity. One of the well-recognized aspects of this situation is the erosion of the financial resources of the core cities for meeting their increasingly urgent needs.

The population of the nation's metropolitan areas as a whole increased a little more rapidly during the 1950s than in the 1940s, and the economic, social and ethnic differentiation between inner cities and outer localities was intensified during the 1950s and again during the first half of the 1960s. The centrifugal trend of population within metropolitan areas has recently been complemented by a centrifugal movement of industrial and commercial plants into the suburban areas. This aggravates the difficulties of poor people in the central cities in seeking appropriate and promising employment.

The total number of white persons living in all the central cities was only slightly greater in 1960 than in 1950, and actually declined between 1960 and 1968. Meanwhile, the number of Negroes in these cities rose from 6.5 million in 1950 to 9.7 million in 1960 and 12.1 million in 1966; and Negroes came to outnumber whites in several large cities. In striking contrast, the white population of the suburban areas increased by 17 per cent from 1950 to 1960 and at about the same rate during the next eight years, whereas their total Negro population was only about 1 per cent larger in 1966 than in 1950. There was then a change in the net effect of Negro movements within the nation's metropolitan regions as a whole. Between 1966 and 1968, the Negro population of the inner cities as a whole remained constant or declined slightly, and the number in suburban areas definitely increased— though only by a small percentage (0.4), well below that of the white suburban population (2.2 per cent). If this proves to be the beginning of a new trend it could prove highly significant. It is possible that the proportion of non-whites in the outer segments of metropolitan areas will rise well above its present low level (5 per cent).

Policy proposals now being advanced by thoughtful persons for dealing with problems created by the present social structure of metropolitan areas emphasize three different ecological approaches: (1) Attention is generally directed mainly to upgrading conditions of life in the core cities. (2) Another approach, advocated by Senator Eugene McCarthy among others, focuses attention to the planning and promotion of balanced residential and industrial "new towns" in the outer rim beyond the "white suburban noose" around the core cities. This approach is sometimes supported by reference to developments of this sort in England and by references to its possible facilitation by radical innovations in rapid transit. (3) Still another approach is directed toward the residential establishment of employees, without respect to race, in the vicinity of the new industrial and commercial plants now existing or coming into existence in many suburban communities. This approach is sponsored among others by Jeanne R. Lowe, consultant on urban affairs to the *Saturday Review*, who emphasized the crucial role that could be played by enlightened business leaders in furthering this development. These three approaches can reasonably be viewed as complementary rather than as competitive, but they do present problems with respect to priority and emphasis in policy and programs. We leave them as open questions, but some points developed in the following section may be relevant to this subject.

The central issues related to the social structure of metropolitan aggregations raise questions about the dispersion of power and responsibility among units or segments of the population and the proper role of larger political structures and social agencies, questions similar to the contrasting policies of local versus Federal programs considered in the previous section. Local community action contributes in many ways to the enrichment of our national life, and can be important in resolving elusive issues in inter-personal and inter-group relations. On the other hand, there are serious grounds for defining and limiting more strictly the power of local units in matters affecting the more complex social structures in which they are involved and on which they are dependent—as, for example, zoning provisions that may be in effect exclusive and injurious to the interests of other communities.

THE DIVERSE EFFECTS OF RAPID MASS MIGRATION

The rapid, large-scale movement of people from disadvantaged areas to places that appear to offer larger opportunities may improve the lives of some migrants and bring greater misery to those who are less able to cope effectively with the possibilities and difficulties of the new situations in which they find themselves. This general observation seems particularly pertinent to the city-ward and interregional movement of Negroes from Southern rural communities—where, a generation ago, their families were sustained, though at a low economic level, through traditional agricultural and related activities, and where their cultural life was supported and constrained by kinship and neighborhood ties and cherished local institutions. Their relocation in large northern and western cities has notably advanced the economic and social status of some, opened new avenues of intellectual development, and stimulated the acceptance of larger responsibilities and more vigorous initiative. Others have found themselves trapped in depressing situations, beset by new anxieties, and disheartened by thwarted aspirations and insuperable obstacles.

The particular problems of this ethnic group are complicated by the persistence of stereotyped patterns of behavior, mythology and attitudes originally formed to maintain and justify the slave system and then enforced by local social and legal sanctions to perpetuate the basic economic and social relations of the slave system after it was in theory abolished. These stereotypic patterns were to some extent diffused through the whole nation, affecting the inner consciousness of both "blacks" and "whites." The situation has now been complicated, as the result of mass migrations, by sudden new confrontations that have generated new animosities, suspicions and fears. The new responses tend to be cast in old stereotypic molds, so that people of different color are often treated primarily not as *persons* but as *members of a set*. This type of response is common in all inter-tribal, inter-national and inter-ethnic contacts, but it operates with peculiar virulence in the relations today between the descendants of slaves and those whose ancestors were free persons. One damaging aspect of the old stereotypic pattern is that descendants of slaves were not expected or allowed, much less encouraged, to exercise responsibility and initiative, but were constantly subjected to detailed supervision or, at best, benevolent patronage. They, in turn, learned to ease their burdens by accommodation to these expectations. These attitudes and counter-reactions complicate the status and roles of Negroes within the institutional frames of a technologically advanced society. Opportunity for employment in positions that afford a basis for self-respect and offer promise of further advance may be as important, especially for young Negro men, as increases in levels of family income.

Information on the occupational distribution and economic status of persons classified by color or race and on changes in these characteristics, provide a substantive basis for treating objectively some aspects of the present situation and current trends. Some of the most pertinent data, drawn from sampling surveys by the Bureau of the Census, are available only on a two-fold classification by "white" and "non-white." Though generally reflecting Negro-white differences reasonably well, they may be biased in this respect at some points by the inclusion of other ethnic groups in the non-white category. Some data on occupational distribution and trends are summarized in the following columns:

	Percentage distribution of employed persons by broad occupation classes, 1968*		Percentage change in numbers within each class, 1960 to 1968	
	Non-white	White	Non-white	White
Total (in thousands)	*8,011*	*66,561*	*14%*	*11%*
Professional and technical	7%	14%	80	30
Managers, officials, etc.	2.6	11	17	6
Clerical	11	17	77	23
Sales	1.7	7	22	2
Craftsmen and firemen	8	14	49	13
Operatives	23	18	33	14
Service workers, except household	19	9	23	23
Household workers	10	1.4	−17	−23
Non-farm laborers	11	4.0	−7	−2
Total non-farm	95	95	23	15
Farmers and farm workers	5.3	4.7	−52	−31

* The rounded percentages shown here and the summary census figures on which they are based are subject to small computing errors. In view of the still larger possible sampling and other real errors, only rounded percentages are used except for proportions of 5 per cent or less.

The sharp decrease of non-white workers in agriculture tended to inflate all the positive percentage increases for other occupational classes, and the very low proportions of non-whites in the more prestigious classes in 1960 made possible very high percentage gains with relatively modest numerical increases during the next seven years. Moreover, the increases within these broad classes were not distributed equally among specific occupations. Nevertheless, the information presented here shows that many non-white workers are now achieving a significant advance in occupational position, though non-white workers are still a long way from equality with white workers in their present distribution. The small increase in the percentage of white workers classed as "managers, officials, etc.," is at first surprising, until one remembers that this class includes a large number of petty entrepreneurs, many of whom tended to be displaced by the growth of larger concerns. The small percentages of non-white workers in this group and in sales personnel reflect their relatively weak position in commercial fields. Inclusive of those engaged in farming, as operators or laborers, household servants and non-farm laborers still made up

23 per cent of all other non-white workers in 1967, as contrasted with only 6 per cent of all other whites.

The statistics just cited refer only to workers with jobs at the time of the inquiry. The disadvantage of a large part of the non-white labor force in its present situation is revealed more forcibly by information on employment and unemployment. In 1967, 7.4 per cent of the nation's non-white labor force was unemployed, as contrasted with only 3.4 of the white labor force. The former percentage was 83 per cent of that in 1949 (when the proportion of non-whites in agriculture was much higher), whereas unemployment for whites in 1967 was then only 60 per cent of its level at the earlier date. The lagging decline of unemployment among non-whites can be attributed in part to the shift of some workers from under-employment in rural communities to unemployment in cities. An especially serious aspect of the recent situation is that in the 20 largest central cities 32 per cent of the non-white youth aged 16 to 19 years who were out of school and able to work had no jobs. (The corresponding figure for white youth was 12 per cent, also showing a serious, though less appalling, situation.)

The proportions of persons below the "poverty line" (as officially estimated, taking into account changes in purchasing power of the dollar and the relation of income to needs as affected by size and composition of families and by the distinction between farm and non-farm residence) declined significantly during the 1960s both for non-whites and for whites, but 35 per cent of the non-whites fell in the poverty class in 1967. These then formed a little more than one-fourth of all the nation's poor people on this index.

Nevertheless, the ratio of the median income of non-white families to white families rose during the 1960s—notably between 1963 and 1967. Separate estimates for Negroes are available for the last four years; these show a rise in the Negro-white median income ratio from 54 per cent in 1964 to 59 per cent in 1967. The change in the proportion of non-white families receiving $8,000 or more (with purchasing power as in 1967) is even more striking; it rose from 11 per cent in 1959 (one-third the proportion of white families at this level) to 27 per cent in 1967 (one-half the corresponding proportion of white families). Some allowance, however, must be made here for the inclusion of Japanese and Chinese families at high income levels. Though their inclusion also influences, it is not mainly responsible for the marked difference between regions in the proportions of non-white families in this high income bracket: 15 per cent in the South as compared with 37 per cent in all other regions combined.

The economic information cited above shows a widening distribution—one might say a bifurcation—by economic and social status within the non-white population. A rising proportion is able to take advantage of new opportunities opening to them, but a large number remain trapped in depressing conditions. This is undoubtedly also true with respect to the quality of education now being received by different elements within this ethnic category—ranging from the best for some to the worst for others—though data on this subject are more complex and less easily summarized. Moreover, the sudden massive transfer of Negroes from rural communities in the South to metropolitan areas in all parts of the country may be largely responsible for apparent increases in conjugal instability, illegitimacy (rising from 17 per cent of all registered non-white births in 1940 to 28 per cent in 1966) and crime. We must, however, add that this cannot be the whole story, because somewhat similar trends seem also to be characteristic of more prosperous white elements long assimilated to urban environments. This must have a deeper cause in our whole social structure and culture. The lower frequency of illegitimacy in the white population (even with due allowance for more frequent concealment on registration certificates) must be attributed, at least in large part, to the more effective contraception among whites in extramarital sexual relations.

It may be that the redistribution of Negroes within the nation has passed or is approaching its peak, and this may also be true with respect to their concentration in the inner cities of metropolitan areas. Future trends in these distributions will depend on changing circumstances, and can be significantly effected by public policies. The Japanese and Chinese are already fairly well distributed geographically in relation to opportunities, but this is certainly not true of Indians or of some ethnic minorities classified as white, notably Puerto Ricans as well as Mexicans and persons of Mexican tradition who are still concentrated in certain areas in the Southeast. And there are still regional poverty pockets of old European stock.

The adverse effects of migration could be reduced by checking the "push" of poverty and other depressing conditions in areas that still hold a large share of the nation's children. Truly effective Federal programs for increasing employment opportunities, assuring higher incomes, improving conditions of living and equalizing the level and quality of education in the component areas of the nation and among the ethnic elements of its "demographic pool" would have three important effects:

1. It would enable those who migrate to other localities to be more adequately prepared to participate in the opportunities and to cope with the demands of the new situations in which they find themselves.
2. It would moderate the flight of migrants from areas that are now underprivileged. This now tends to draw off many of the energetic young from poor rural areas and, simultaneously, to nullify the effect of efforts to improve conditions in large industrial areas due to the continued influx of ill-equipped migrants.
3. It would dampen the excessively rapid natural increase of the economically and socially most handicapped elements within the nation—because poverty and ignorance, especially in rural communities, lessen the motivation for family planning and reduce the efficacy of attempts to regulate reproduction.

The agricultural adjustment program initiated during the depression was designed primarily to reduce surplus agricultural production and secondarily to promote soil conservation. As continued, in conformity with the interests of politically dominant groups, it has accelerated technological advances in commercial agriculture and reduced the percentage of the nation's labor force dependent on farming. All this was sound from a narrowly economic viewpoint, but it involved a heavy cost in terms of human welfare. A broad program aimed at the economic and social development of what are now impoverished rural areas might include provisions for promoting economically viable, locally controlled, predominantly Negro agricultural-industrial community clusters. This would contribute in a limited but quite feasible way toward realizing the aspirations of many Negroes for greater autonomy in their economic and cultural life.

An effective program for the equalization of opportunity in America might cost more than the war in Vietnam or the plans of the "military-industrial complex" for the expansion of our military apparatus, but it could make a greater contribution to our immediate welfare and perhaps, if complemented by imaginative policies in international relations, a greater contribution to our future national security.

DIFFERENTIAL REPRODUCTION WITHIN THE DEMOGRAPHIC POOL

Turning attention first to reproductive trends within the white majority of the nation's population, we must dispel the illusion that the negative relation between income or education and fertility has already vanished or has been reversed by the spread of family planning —although the differentials have, in fact, been narrowed. At least, such equalization or reversal was not already in effect according to the data on fertility supplied by the 1960 census. Taking the average number of children ever born to all white women in a given age class as a base (100), the indices of fertility for white women aged 35–39 years by years of schooling completed ran as follows:

College, 4 years or more	83
College, 1–3 years	93
High school, 4 years	93
High school, 1–3 years	101
Grade school only or none	111

The non-white population as a whole is now increasing more rapidly than the white population. According to the latest population projections by the Census Bureau (cited in a previous section), the non-white population as a proportion of the national total is expected to rise from 11 per cent in 1965 to somewhere between 13.4 (Series D) and 14.2 per cent (Series A) in 1985. This is a prospect that many of us would welcome if it implied a trend toward a multi-ethnic society with such harmonious social relations as now prevail in Hawaii. Moreover, it is a prospect that might be especially welcomed by members of minority racial groups if it could be expected to enhance their social status. Unfortunately, both of these conditions are subject to serious qualifications because the increase is coming disproportionately from the most disadvantaged elements in non-white population.

Differential fertility in relation to income, occupational class or education is much wider within our ethnic minorities than in the white population. Among non-white women aged 35–39 years in 1960 the indices of fertility comparable to those given for white women, but in this case, taking the average for all non-white women at these ages as the base (100), ran as follows:

College, 4 years or more	55
College, 1–3 years	74
High school, 4 years	82
High school, 1–3 years	100
Grade school only or none	106

In this case, fertility at the lowest of these educational levels is 93 per cent above that of the college graduate, whereas among whites the ratio was only 34 per cent. In fact, among all high school graduates as a whole, the fertility of non-white women was somewhat less than among white women of similar educational status. The greater prolificacy of the non-white population was wholly a function of the

relatively less restrained reproductivity of those with meager schooling. This trend hampers the advance of the nation as a whole, and
it particularly tends to retard the economic and social advance of
non-white communities. Similar differences, with similar consequences,
are also present in disadvantaged regional and ethnic groups classified as white in the United States and also in Puerto Rico. Data on
births in Puerto Rico in 1962 show a cumulative total fertility of
4.6 to 4.8 births per women with less than 8 years of schooling, 3.7
births per women with 9–11 years, 3.4 for those who completed secondary school, and 2.3 per women with education beyond the secondary
school level.

Home background and childhood associations in neighborhoods and
schools are key conditions in the intellectual and personal development of children. This is a matter of common observation. Moreover,
in spite of much confusion about the results of the "Coleman Report," [1]
especially with respect to some of its apparently negative implications,
(due in part to limitations in methodology and in still larger part to
misinterpretation of its results), this study incontrovertibly establishes
the basic principle here maintained. The value of the "Head Start"
program and of more imaginative methods of elementary and secondary education warrant increased attention to, and stronger public
support for, these approaches. They can mitigate and partially offset,
and in some cases may overcome the adverse effects of limited home
background and prejudicial cultural forces. It is, nevertheless, naive
to assume that the influence of such conditions as the education of
parents, their degree of economic security, their living conditions and
their inter-personal relations within the family can be wholly offset
by any public institutions or programs. The level of formal education
is, of course, only one of the complex variables in home background
and perhaps not the most important, but it is a factor of some importance, especially in new or changing situations, and it tends on
the whole to be associated with other favorable factors—in part just
because it is highly prized in our society. It can, therefore, be taken
as a useful, though imperfect, index of differences in home background
affecting intellectual, social and economic prospects. Moreover, if home
background is a major determinant of individual development and
prospects, it follows that *the distribution of births* in relation to
variations in home background and the conditions of early life is an

[1] James S. Coleman et al., *Equality of Educational Opportunity* (Washington:
U.S. Department of Health, Education and Welfare; U.S. Office of Education, 1966).

important force in the social life of the nation, and within its component sectors.

The most extensive and, at the same time, intensive investigation of factors affecting the distribution of births in the United States was carried through in 1960 on a nationwide scientific sample of white and Negro couples with wives aged 18–39 years (reported by Whelpton, Campbell and Patterson in a publication by the Princeton University Press in 1966). The study was limited to couples in unbroken first marriages by both husbands and wives. The number of Negro couples interviewed in this study was relatively small, but it produced some statistically significant and enlightening information on this, as well as on other topics. Couples were classified on an index of "expected fertility" obtained by combining the number of births to date with the number of additional births which the wife thought most likely. Variations on this index agree quite well with observed variations among couples with completed fertility. One important finding is that the expected levels of fertility among families with low educational achievement differ significantly from the *desired* levels, especially among Negroes. Both white and Negro women with only elementary schooling expressed on the average a preference for 3.5 children. This was higher in both cases than the average numbers of children wanted by those with secondary or more schooling, but the average number of *expected* births by white wives at this education level was only 3.7, whereas the Negro wives in this educational category expected an average of 4.7 births. The expected number of births was also well above the number wanted by Negro wives who had attended but not completed high school, though this was not so in the case of white wives at this educational level. At higher educational levels the numbers expected conformed closely to the numbers wanted among both whites and Negroes—and both the desired and the expected numbers were lower among Negroes than among whites. In 17 per cent of all white families and 31 per cent of all Negro families one or more of the children born to them was unwanted by the wife or the husband or both at the time of the conception. Among those with only elementary schooling the proportions of families with unwanted children rose to 32 per cent among whites and to 43 per cent among Negroes. At this educational level 28 per cent of the white wives and 43 per cent of Negro wives stated that they had never practiced any method of regulating reproduction and had no present intention of ever doing so —as contrasted with less than 10 per cent of those of either ethnic group

at the highest education level. Among all the couples that had practiced any form of birth control, two-thirds of the Negroes but only
40 per cent of the whites had relied entirely on douching or vaginal
suppositories. It is, therefore, evident that families with limited educational advantages lack the needed enlightenment and facilities for
the effective control of procreation. The high fertility of the less ad-
vantaged is largely due to this deficiency.

One encouraging aspect of this situation is that the continued expansion of educational opportunities in all segments of the American
population is tending to reduce the present force of uncontrolled fertility among the families that now suffer the most severe handicaps.
In the case of the Negro population it was shown in this study that
the high fertility among non-white families is strongly associated with
residence on farms and, also, though in lesser degree, with previous
residence in farming communities. There is little difference in marital
fertility between white and non-white persons who have always lived
in urban localities. As the percentage of city-born persons rises in the
non-white sector of our population, both the inter-racial differential
and the social class differential in fertility within the non-white sector
will, one may expect, tend to narrow and perhaps to disappear. This
trend can, in any case, be accelerated by more vigorous and well-
designed programs for the diffusion of information concerning methods
of controlling contraception and the provision of contraceptive facilities and services to all people in all parts of the country.

The persistent Negro-white differential in *mortality* is one of the
most impressive indices of racial inequality in economic and social
conditions. According to a searching examination of this subject by
Demeny and Gingrich at the University of Michigan, the differential
may be even wider than indicated by the official life tables, due to
defects in the basic registration data. Using an ingenious technique
that gives plausible though inconclusive results, they obtain estimated
expectations of life at birth for the decade 1950–59 of 56.4 years for
Negro males and 62.3 years for Negro females, as compared with the
official values of 60.3 and 73.3, respectively—even on the assumption
that the official values at ages over 5 years are correct. The results obtained by this technique differ more from the official values for Negroes
than for whites. Their study does indicate a rise in ratios of the expectation of life at birth for Negroes relative to the expectation for whites
from 63 to 86 per cent for males and from 65 to 85 per cent for females between the first and middle decades of this century, but the
difference is still large. The high infant and child mortality of the non-

white population reduces the demographic effect of its high fertility on the actual size of its families and on its natural increase, but only by a small margin, in the vicinity of 6 per cent, as contrasted with a comparable reduction of about 3 per cent in the white population. High infant mortality is associated with the frequency of large families and of extra-marital maternity in the disadvantaged sectors of our population, and these conditions are associated with depressed economic and social status, as well as with inadequate health services. The major policy implication of these conditions is the need for action along all possible lines to reduce inequalities in conditions of living among the nation's families. Its more specific implication is the need for more adequate health services compatible with personal self-respect and dignity. Our affluent nation is one of the few technically advanced countries that has no comprehensive social program of health services, even for mothers and children.

The United States is now firmly committed to the policy of making contraceptive information and facilities available to all families—and this principle is generally extended in practice, though sometimes with hesitation and reservations, to all persons. The decisive turn in this direction came under President Kennedy's leadership. It was explicitly affirmed by President Johnson in a message to Congress that included the following sentence: "It is essential that all families have access to information and services that will allow freedom to choose the number and spacing of their children within the dictates of individual conscience." The principle is carried forward under President Nixon. The failure as yet to meet this need fully is due in part to the inadequacy of our public provisions for serving the health needs of all people, mentioned in the previous paragraph.

A sense of concern is now rising among thoughtful persons throughout the nation about the social costs, both to the individuals immediately concerned and to the communities in which they live, of the unplanned procreation of unwanted children by persons who neglect or are unable to exercise effective precaution against unwanted pregnancies, especially in the case of disadvantaged young girls. No responsible persons have proposed any compulsory public action to reduce the frequency of such events—except provisions in some states for the sterilization of persons afflicted by major physical or mental disabilities (with their consent if competent or otherwise with the consent of their guardians). Some women who discover that they are accidentally pregnant want to keep and nurture the children thus engendered, or at least to bear them even if they must transfer the responsibility for their nurture to others. It is generally agreed that in such cases the mothers must be assisted in every possible way to carry out their decisions. Other women would, if possible, terminate such unwanted pregnancies at an early stage. This is now technically possible at relatively small risk to health under competent medical auspices. However, most Americans refuse to sanction such action on moral grounds or for psychological or cultural reasons—differing in this respect from most people in Japan, eastern Europe and, in varying degrees, many other countries. On the other hand, the Governing Council of the American Public Health Association adopted the following resolution in January, 1968:

> It is generally accepted that individual women and couples should have the means to decide without compulsion the number and spacing of their children. This personal right has been supported and enhanced through governmental action at all levels. The APHA and many other groups have joined with public agencies to secure this right and to make widely available those services that will provide a range of choice of contraceptive methods consistent with personal beliefs and desires. However, contraceptive methods vary among users in effectiveness and suitability. Pregnancies sometimes occur due to rape, incest, and difficulties in obtaining contraceptives and sometimes because of contraceptive failures.
>
> In order to assure the accepted right to determine freely the number and spacing of their children, safe legal abortion should be available to all women. Further, the provision of abortion within the usual channels of medical care will reduce the well-known adverse effects of illegal abortion.
>
> The APHA urges that access to abortion be accepted as an important means of assuring the right to spacing and choosing the number of children wanted. To this end, restrictive laws should be repealed so that pregnant women may have abortions performed by qualified practitioners of medicine and osteopathy.

The present writer lacks the wealth of social, medical and psychological experience that those who framed this resolution were able to bring to bear on its consideration. Any comment by him on its social aspects would be an act of supererogation, but he must add that in his judgment the proposed course of action would have a salutary effect on our nation's constantly changing "demographic pool."

Index

About the American Assembly

The American Assembly holds meetings of national leaders and publishes books to illuminate issues of United States policy. The Assembly is a national, non-partisan educational institution, incorporated in the State of New York.

The Trustees of the Assembly approve a topic for presentation in a background book, authoritatively designed and written to aid deliberations at national Assembly sessions at Arden House, the Harriman (New York) Campus of Columbia University. These books are also used to support discussion at regional Assembly sessions and to evoke considerations by the general public.

All sessions of the Assembly, whether international, national, or local, issue and publicize independent reports of conclusions and recommendations on the topic at hand.

American Assembly books are purchased and put to use by thousands of individuals, libraries, businesses, public agencies, nongovernmental organizations, educational institutions, discussion meetings, and service groups.

The subjects of Assembly studies to date are:

1951 — United States–Western Europe Relationships
1952 — Inflation
1953 — Economic Security for Americans
1954 — The United States Stake in the United Nations
— The Federal Government Service
1955 — United States Agriculture
— The Forty-Eight States
1956 — The Representation of the United States Abroad
— The United States and the Far East
1957 — International Stability and Progress
— Atoms for Power
1958 — The United States and Africa
— United States Monetary Policy
1959 — Wages, Prices, Profits, and Productivity
— The United States and Latin America
1960 — The Federal Government and Higher Education
— The Secretary of State
— Goals for Americans
1961 — Arms Control: Issues for the Public
— Outer Space: Prospects for Man and Society

Second Editions: